The President's
New Clothes

By G. A. J. Coleman

ISBN: 1515264912
ISBN 13: 9781515264910
Library of Congress Control Number: **XXXXX (If
applicable)**
LCCN Imprint Name: **City and State (If applicable)**

Introduction

Most Americans never contemplate losing their country. The piece of land will remain but the home of the brave and land of the free is fast becoming the home of the corrupt and the land of the exploited. Wars cause tremendous damage and hardship but infrastructure can be rebuilt and invaders vanquished. Recovery from loss of culture is far more difficult, if not impossible. It is culture that dictates a county's success or failure. The USA and European nations are facing a unique situation which, if not addressed, is likely to escalate into serious erosion of their historical ways of life. The primary threat is not from any other nation but from their own electorates. Whereas they are theoretically democracies in which citizens vote to elect representatives who will follow policies which will benefit the country, in reality significant proportions of the electorates have been thoroughly brainwashed into supporting agendas guaranteed to irreversibly destroy the centuries old original cultures and the prosperity that previous generations worked so hard to achieve.

I wrote the original version of this book in 2013 after five years of the Obama administration. It was clear that those who called the shots in his policy decisions had a very different agenda than the majority of the electorate were led to believe. During the eight years of this administration the country was pushed into the realm of socialism, race divisions were stirred up and the very organs of government were subverted. This agenda, by design, created a division not seen since the Civil War. The age-old strategy of divide and conquer was the objective. This also caused a loss of confidence in our justice and intelligence departments. The Trump administration sought to reverse all this damage and had considerable success despite multiple plots to tarnish and discredit it, enthusiastically supported by the media and the Democrat leaders. Sadly the Corona virus provided an opportunity to damage the economy and manipulate the voting system and we are asked to believe that the Biden/Harris ticket, the weakest in history, garnered five million more votes than Trump. Considering all this recent controversial series of events I have updated the book.

There have always been political divisions between conservatives and liberals but the current liberal doctrines go far beyond the bounds of reality and practicality. Many are simply absurd. Unless this trend is reversed soon, sheer demographics and population increase will result in the civilized democracies descending to third-world status. There are four primary culprits in the brainwashing scheme in the USA. The media, the Democrat party, billionaire activists and university faculty. Whereas the first three have ulterior motives, the faculty is simply naive and also a victim of the brainwashing. However, they are complicit in extending the brainwashing to entire generations of students. The tools employed are the human emotions of jealousy and self pity, the most destructive of all human emotions. Naive citizens are taught that they are victims of something and they should be offended by many things. All their troubles are caused by someone else and others must solve their problems. Many have embraced this self-destructive philosophy. They believe in "globalism", that every human instinctively loves his brother and everyone will live happily in paradise. The "government" will take care of everybody.

What is the objective of those who seek to mislead and indoctrinate the electorate? It is clear from history that this agenda can only lead to disaster. The primary proponents want a compliant and ignorant population that can be easily manipulated. Once in this state, domination of the entire world can be accomplished by a small group of people and the theory is that this will ensure perpetual peace. Prosperity will be limited to those in power and their families and friends. It is possible to observe the effectiveness of this strategy by examining the various "religious" cults which exist throughout the world, led by unscrupulous gurus and phony evangelists who have no compunction in exploiting their followers for personal gain. The adherents to these cults obey every instruction willingly no matter how absurd, including donating their entire fortunes to the leader. In November 1978 the 900 followers of evangelist Jim Jones first poisoned their children and then poisoned themselves voluntarily upon his instructions. The United States is the primary obstacle to completing this plan for world domination. Once weakened financially and militarily it will be powerless to prevent the submission of other countries and eventually itself .

The federal government of the USA was never intended to be a democracy which governed individual citizens, except for certain safeguards stipulated in the Bill of Rights. It was set up as a republic of independent democratic states with the federal government only empowered to involve itself in issues affecting all the states. These were clearly enumerated in the Constitution. This was much like a military alliance but with other areas of co-operation included. Whereas democracy with a universal franchise in the best of circumstances is a very imperfect means of government, the world is now confronted with an unprecedented deluge of information which has no boundaries. Until the beginning of the twentieth century citizens could get information from books, newspapers, flyers, radio and conversation with other citizens. Lies, half-truths and distortions were more difficult to propagate. Many were not interested in or incapable of informing themselves and simply remained in ignorance. Today even the poorest in the world have cell phones, televisions and access to the internet. Whether they are interested or not, inevitably they are exposed to propaganda from multiple sources and consciously or subconsciously many are brainwashed. With this tremendous amount of unverified information flooding the airwaves, internet and print media even the most persistent researcher has difficulty in determining the truth. Big corporations have the means to block any views they consider contrary to their agendas. The purveyors of subversive and deceptive information have an open field. The indoctrinated person seeks out information which reinforces his or her predetermined philosophy. There is an ample supply of this to suit every taste. No opposing views are sought and the result is a fanatical and uncompromising belief in what one wants to believe. This is a dangerous phenomenon in a democracy.

We can already see the effect of changing demographics and brainwashing in the elections of members of Congress. Never before have so many naive, inexperienced and unaccomplished persons been included in this formerly august body. Anyone listening to debates in the house or senate must be appalled at the dialogue of predominantly absolute drivel. Many members of Congress are simply obedient puppets put in office by groups with their own agendas. The public naively believe that the candidates they vote for are patriotic independents who only seek to improve the lives of their constituents. Most are simply there to improve their own lives. The election of president Donald Trump was a repudiation of the lifelong politicians. He was the first president since Theodore Roosevelt to have the courage of his convictions and to declare that the Emperor has no clothes. Half the electorate supported his realistic agenda. The other half and the media were determined to destroy him. We have seen extremely powerful forces and billions of dollars devoted to destroying Trump. Since before the

2016 election this has been the only objective of the Democrat party and some Republican members of Congress. The Trump doctrine threatened to put an end to politics as usual and get back to reality.

It will probably never be possible to ascertain the role of the Chinese government in propagating the Corona virus around the world. What is certain is that this epidemic has devastated western economies and played a major role in Trump's defeat. Trump was China's worst nightmare, having exposed China's predatory trade practices and theft of intellectual property and instituted harsh measures to curtail these. Weakened western economies are to China's advantage in the military sense as well. The Democrats have seized upon this situation to prolong the shut-downs and the millions of people currently unemployed have been willing participants in demonstrations, burning and looting throughout the country. The failure to stop these, the mob attacks on statues and the insane call to eliminate police were all part of a strategy to beat Trump. The election itself was unlike any other. Using the virus as an excuse, massive mail in voting was authorized and polls opened weeks before election day. The result was an unorthodox election with ample opportunity for ballot-harvesting and manipulation, giving Joe Biden, the weakest candidate in history, a decisive win. Trump did a great job as president, campaigned hard and won over unprecedented numbers of blacks and Hispanics. He understandably got 12 million more votes than in 2016. Biden has done nothing of consequence in his 44 years in public office, did no campaigning and yet amazingly got 15 million more votes than Hillary Clinton. It would appear that he knew the fix was in.

Americans should think carefully about the impact of the loss of their culture. Whereas Russia, China, Vietnam, Cuba and others have all suffered the deprivations of communism and socialism, they have retained their cultures and demographics. This means when they abandon their destructive behaviors they can recover. In the case of the US, once the demographics have irreversibly changed there can be no recovery. Since legal immigration laws were changed in 1965 and the more recent onset of uncontrolled influx of illegal aliens across the southern border and via visa overstays and chain migration, the demographics of the country have changed dramatically. The vast invasion of generally poor, unskilled and poorly educated people who do not think or behave like the average American is unlikely to add to the safety and prosperity of the nation. These people will have children who under current law, will automatically be entitled to US citizenship and the vote. There is even talk of allowing anyone who happens to be in the country to vote. This will guarantee a Democratic majority for the foreseeable future, which no doubt is one of the party's objectives.

A country's culture is related to its crime rate. This also applies in microcosm to cities. Smart and decent citizens do not rob and kill one another. In looking at the world, the least successful countries also have the highest crime rates. The same with cities. The migration of populations from high-crime countries to the USA inevitably brings more crime with it. It can be argued that crime is a result of poverty and this is true to some extent. However, this is a chicken and egg situation. Successful countries have lower poverty rates because they manage their affairs better, work harder and do not rob and murder one another.

The US taxpayer already supports almost half the voting public via some form of welfare program and has no business welcoming more poverty, ignorance, disease and crime from other nations. The national debt stands at a record twenty eight trillion dollars and is increasing exponentially. The conundrum is the long-term objectives of the powerful forces driving the open-border policy and socialism. It is difficult to imagine anything but financial and social ruin can result from this agenda. The Globalists of the world see it as a path to world government. The reality is a path to misery.

For centuries sovereign countries have defended their cultures and treasures by military means. In the second world war for example, England risked everything to repel invasion and occupation by Germans. This was not because of any antipathy against Germans in general. The British royal family had a heavy German component and the cultures of each country were very similar. It was because they wanted to keep their own way of life and maintain control of their affairs. More recently the Brexit referendum in Britain demonstrated the public's desire to regain control of their own affairs and belatedly end uncontrolled immigration. Encouraging uncontrolled immigration from vastly different cultures is indeed comparable to a military invasion in the context of the end result. Whereas it may be charitable to share good fortune with those less privileged, in the end everyone will suffer

For those who might wonder why a person of English heritage, born and raised in the English colony of Southern Rhodesia, might presume to write about the American Constitution and American politics, the answer is quite simple. I have personally experienced what happens when "democracy" runs amok. My ancestors arrived in what is now South Africa in the early 19th century. Everyone worked hard to build southern Africa into a first-world powerhouse. It is now being rapidly destroyed. The beautiful country of my birth has descended into anarchy and ruin. It need not have happened. There can be no recovery short of military conquest. I chose to immigrate to the USA in 1972 because it was clear that my own delightful and well governed country was going to fall prey to the misguided politics of other nations. In 1980 fifteen years of strangling United Nations sanctions forced the abdication of an honest and responsible government in favor of a corrupt and incompetent one which quite predictably rapidly degenerated into a vicious dictatorship. Zimbabwe is now a failed, chaotic, bankrupt state after 38 years of dictatorial rule by Robert Mugabe. His successor, Mangagwa, is no better. Elections still occur but the outcomes are predetermined. Africa is a good example of the disastrous effects of one man one vote applied in countries where the average citizen has no concept of the likely consequences of his vote and intimidation and indoctrination are the norms. The Chinese and Russians have moved in. They are there to loot the continent of its treasures and have absolutely no regard for the welfare of its inhabitants. I have personally observed the rapid descent into chaos and anarchy when the citizens elect the wrong representatives to run their government.

I chose the USA as being best suited for the pursuit of my own profession of engineering and because I believed its citizens would never inflict the same destruction upon themselves. Having lived and worked in the USA for forty eight years I have concluded that the departure from reality has not abated in the western world and the USA faces the prospect of decline and regression. From city mayors to presidents and Congress, authorities have completely lost touch with the principles set out in the US Constitution. Many naïve citizens support them. Like the family that is the envy of the neighborhood with a lavish lifestyle, ostentatious house and fine cars, this all comes tumbling down when the creditors repossess everything for failure to service the huge loan which enabled this lifestyle. The USA is living on borrowed money: a lot of it, with a debt that is growing exponentially. At current interest rates of almost zero, nobody seems to be very concerned. The time will come when creditors lose confidence in the dollar and interest rates will rise. At 5% the $28T loan will require interest payments of $1.4T per year which is 38% of the predicted 2019 federal revenues. In fact the $3.7T revenues need to be understood. Of this, $1.3T, or 36%, is derived from special payroll taxes which must be used to pay for Social Security and Medicare and is not available for general budget items.

The more alarming problem is the loss of American culture caused by the complete departure from reality fostered by the mainstream media, academia, Hollywood and many politicians and enthusiastically supported by naïve citizens. Information from these sources is routinely manipulated and distorted so that no-one can be sure what the truth and facts are. The social media add more confusion. The public has access to an unprecedented amount of information but without taking the trouble to do the necessary research it is difficult to distinguish fact from fiction. People tend to believe what they want to believe and the media accommodate them. The American public have simply been thoroughly brainwashed by "political correctness". The freedom of speech guaranteed by the First Amendment has been forgotten by most. They are prepared to say only what is deemed to be "correct". Social media decide what can be posted on their sites.

The mainstream media have become blatant arms of the left.

The USA is committing cultural suicide. The Judeo-Christian culture upon which the country was founded and prospered has now been eroded by naive and misguided policies on immigration, religion and social behavior. Standards and values have been abandoned in the names of "freedom", "equality" and "equal opportunity". Many have abandoned religion. The predictable result has been a burgeoning public debt to finance lavish social programs and a generation with a large segment of poorly-educated, dependent adults who expect others to take care of them. These people are voters who, not surprisingly, continue to vote for candidates who perpetuate the cycle of dependency. They do not realize that their votes result in far less freedom, equality and equal opportunity. This did not happen by accident. Politicians do not want well-educated, smart and informed voters who will hold them accountable. For this reason schools and universities have been dumbed down and freedom of speech in these institutions limited to the ultra-liberal secular agenda. As John Adams, the nation's second president, wisely observed " Our Constitution was made only for a moral and religious people. It is wholly inadequate to the government of any other".

Engineers deal in fact and logic. They do their best to make things work. A good engineer will always ask himself why a mechanism or process was designed a certain way before he attempts to change and improve it. If possible, he consults with the person or team responsible for its design. The very good reason for this is that he may not be aware of certain factors affecting the operation which its original designers discovered and which are essential to its function. The same rationale needs to applied before changing time-proven customs and laws. There were reasons for their adoption and before changing, these reasons must be examined and understood. Change for the sake of change is naive and dangerous.

To some, the following may simply sound cynical and critical. It is. To others, hopefully, it will clarify the current predicament the country finds itself in, how the country arrived at this point and what can be done to improve the situation. Cynicism denotes a distrust of the sincerity of human motives and where politics is concerned, this is well justified. By definition, a politician is a seeker or holder of public office who is more concerned about winning favor or retaining power than about maintaining principles. If the choice is between being cynical or naive, in politics it is safer to be cynical. When a system does not function as well as it should, criticism is necessary to identify the causes and suggest solutions. Hindsight requires no talent and it is easy to look back through history and point out errors others have made. The important thing is to correct the errors where possible and devise a system which will preclude making the same errors in the future. This book is about the gradual and almost imperceptible degradation of the American Constitution and why it is essential that the country returns to the original terms and constraints set out by the Founding Fathers.

This is not to say that government should not involve itself in the affairs of individuals. It is a question of the level of government which regulates the daily lives of citizens. The Federal government was set up by design as a body to co-ordinate the common interests of the states and to provide certain basic safeguards to the citizens of all the states. State governments were to be free to set up systems of their own choosing as dictated by the residents of each state. The country has now reached the point where the Federal government regulates almost everything and state governments are powerless to resist.

The book is simply my candid appraisal of events in history which, in my opinion, have played a part in getting the USA into the predicament it now finds itself. I have applied my own logic and arrived at my own conclusions and many will disagree with these. I bring these views after having lived and worked in sixteen different countries in North and South America, Europe, Africa and the Far East. I have been involved from the boardroom to the factory floor and the fields. I started my adult life at the bottom, four thousand feet below the surface of the Earth in a Zambian copper mine. The last 20 career years I served as an officer of a large multinational corporation. I have dealt with the smartest to the simplest and the most honest and sincere to the most corrupt and devious. The human being is indeed a most complicated animal and designing a system of government which is not subject to distortion and abuse to bring out the best and discourage the worst is no simple task.

History is only as accurate as the person or persons recording it perceive it. Most of us assume that when we read an account of something that we did not personally witness that it is reasonably close to the truth. What is true is that accounts of discoveries, voyages, conquests etc. are often embellished to favor the philosophy or attributes of the person responsible for creating the account. Politicians and journalists collude in reporting according to their own agendas. Whereas there may not be direct untruths involved, selective omissions and inclusions can portray a version very different from the true facts. We read about the most popular presidents but does this mean they were the best in terms of having done what was best for the country? Not necessarily. Could Lincoln have negotiated a phase-out of slavery without dissolution of the Union and war? Was Franklin Roosevelt's New Deal really good for the country or was it the beginning of our escalating national debt, entitlement culture and abdication of personal responsibility? Did Lyndon Johnson's Great Society create the culture of dependency we see today? To get as close to the truth as possible it is necessary to research all accounts of the period from all points of view.

At the heart of the problem is the gradual hijacking of the Constitution by special interests unconcerned with its original intent. The distorted system is now so entrenched it will be almost impossible to correct without making the electorate aware of the facts and educating them to understand the perils and solutions. Whereas it makes sense to follow the changes and distortions of the Constitution chronologically, on certain topics I have departed from this in order to adequately address these topics.

CHAPTER 1: THE GRAND DELUSION

The Emperor's New Clothes is a short children's tale by Hans Christian Andersen about two crooked weavers who promise their emperor a new suit of clothes that is invisible to fools and incompetents. When the emperor parades before his subjects in his new clothes, eliciting effusive applause, an innocent child cries out, "But he isn't wearing anything at all!" This story was first published in Denmark in 1837 but the moral applies to the politics of the civilized world today. It is the fable that demonstrates the power of propaganda when applied to the vanities of the human being. It is the grand delusion. It is the public acceptance of the absurd, outrageous and ridiculous because it is unfashionable to disagree. The modern weavers are those who control the media and the big money and seek their own rewards and have their own agendas, unrelated to the good of the country. It is time that we realized that the presidents and congress's of the United States of America have not been at all what the modern "weavers" and their naïve accomplices in the electorate would like us to believe. Their policies over the years have slowly eroded the original American values and duped a large percentage of the public into believing the unbelievable. In the last twenty years the pace of erosion has increased exponentially largely due to the proliferation of social media and the unabashed partisanship of the mainstream media. A large part of the damage is irreversible. A country's material success is dictated by its cultural success. Since the 1965 change in immigration law and failure to enforce the laws the culture of the USA has changed significantly.

On June 1st 1980 CNN launched the first 24-hour cable news network in Atlanta, Georgia. Before this, radio and TV stations had periodic short news clips at specific times of day giving the public useful and generally factual reports of significant events throughout the world. CNN began as a bona fide news station but it soon became clear that there was insufficient interesting news to fill 24 hours per day. Gradually the station began airing opinions as well as news and today it and other cable stations have evolved into partisan propaganda machines promoting the political agendas of their CEO's. On top of this, newspapers have become large conglomerates also reflecting the views of their managements. Contributing even more to the misinformation propaganda, the vast array of social media on the internet have created a situation where nobody can determine the actual facts.

To most reasonable adults certain things should be obvious.
Open borders is a bad idea
Visa overstays is a bad idea.
Chain legal immigration is a bad idea.
Constant massive deficit spending is a bad idea.
Giving our technology to our potential adversaries is a bad idea.
Giving special privileges to specific groups of citizens is a bad idea.

Moving critical manufacturing to other countries is a bad idea.

Undermining law-enforcement is a bad idea.

The current tort system is a bad idea.

Having schools and universities indoctrinate students is a bad idea.

Appointing personnel based on any criterion other than competency is a bad idea.

Mail-in and early voting is a bad idea.

And so-on. And yet the US government is continuing to do all these things and the electorate seems not to care or notice. It is the certain path to disaster.

To add to the insidious indoctrination of many of the public, the very institutions charged with protecting the country, upholding citizen's rights and ensuring the fair and just application of the laws have been subverted and undermined. The CIA, NIH, FBI, IRS, Justice Department and even the Supreme Court have been guilty of partisanship and/or dereliction of duty. The public has lost trust in all these bodies with good reason and they are now tarnished with the partisan brush. It will be extremely difficult for them to recover. Every day we see two standards applied when enforcing the laws of the land and investigating American citizens.

In science and engineering, the only fields in which humans have made lasting progress, each new idea builds upon the lessons learned from many previous ideas and experiences. Engineers and scientists know from this history what works and what does not work, what is true and what is false. Sometimes they discover what was considered to be true is not in fact, but this is rare. In politics however, humans keep repeating the same mistakes, believing to be true what their predecessors found to be false and implementing policies which prior generations found to be harmful to society. The human being has changed little in the last 10,000 years so it would seem prudent to deduce that failed policies of the past will fail in the future.

Donald Trump was elected president in 2016 because a large segment of the population saw him as a patriotic man with a solid record of accomplishment who very clearly saw that the Emperor had no clothes and was not reticent in publicizing this. Like many Americans, he was appalled at the partisan and corrupt politicians going down the road to disaster. In the US system of government with three co-equal branches it is almost impossible for any one person to make radical changes. This is by design but there is a high price to pay if the legislature is incapable of correcting course. It seems the majority of Congress likes the current cozy system of unlimited terms, generous perks, lobbyist contributions and zero responsibility. Members of both parties did everything in their power to avoid a Trump victory. Sadly, they were prepared for the next election and used unprecedented voting tactics created by the Corona virus to defeat Trump.

A country's culture should not be taken lightly. In the politically correct jargon put out by the media, multiculturism and globalism are promoted as being desirable and beneficial. This is true in small doses but when other cultures overwhelm the base culture the country will change radically. It can be argued that bringing the European cultures to the Americas, Africa and parts of the Far East benefited the indigenous inhabitants. Conversely, in areas where this culture was driven out, the countries regressed. The city of Berlin gave a stark comparison between two cultures during the period it was divided. On the western side of the wall everything was neat and tidy, the people smiled and dressed in bright colors, the architecture was attractive and the average citizen prospered. On the Russian side the streets were shabby, the people seldom smiled and dressed in depressing blacks and grays and the architecture was bland and unpainted, giving an atmosphere of gloom. Nobody except a few oligarchs and politicians prospered in the east.

Different groups of people from different parts of the world behave differently and require forms of government to accommodate their natural behaviors. There is no "one size fits all" solution. The Constitution of the USA was drafted based on Judeo-Christian principles and Anglo-Saxon behavior. It made sense for this group and has served well in general. Democracy means the majority of voters decide who gets elected to Congress and the laws that are made by this body should reflect the wills of the majority as long as they serve the country well. Minorities must accept these laws. Whereas decent people should not wish to mistreat or disadvantage any group of citizens, the majority preferences must prevail. No small group should have the means to thwart the will of all other citizens. No group should be accorded special privileges or deprivations.

Whereas constitutions are usually written by lawyers and politicians because they are skilled at drafting language that covers all possible circumstances in human behavior, engineers and scientists deal in truth and reason. Very few engineers and scientists enter politics. In the 117th Congress there are only 12, the vast majority are professional politicians. Those who have the moral fortitude to state the hard facts and truths to the public are unlikely to get elected when competing with those who have little regard for the truth. Politicians are adept at creating problems where engineers are skilled at solving problems. The major problems facing the country are not difficult to define and each has a logical solution. The reason none has been solved is that the logical and correct solutions are often in conflict with large business interests and unpopular with the electorate in the short term and those in Congress who support them are at risk of losing their seats at the next election. In the following descriptions and analysis I have tried to state the facts and apply logic.

Governments do not produce or supply anything that is not funded by taxpayer money or borrowing. They are necessary only to provide security, basic infrastructure and the rule of law so that citizens can go about their business efficiently. The USA, since its inception, has prospered due largely to a constitution which limited the role of government and a core population of adventurous and industrious people. It is probably the most logical country in the world, where the best ideas are embraced and innovation thrives. By and large, the citizens are hard-working, honest and generous. Individual Americans give more to charities than any other country and never hesitate to respond to world catastrophes. The average American is a decent human being. However, because of this basic decency and as a result of living in a country which is reasonably civilized, the average citizen is naive when it comes to judging people from other cultures. This has led to innumerable scams and gross misconceptions regarding the corruption in US politics and the behavior of citizens of other countries.

It should be understood that whereas the average human is capable of many different tasks and can be trained to perform certain tasks well, the execution of large projects requires more. Firstly the vision. To build a great cathedral for instance, someone has to promote the idea. Next he or she must assemble a small group to decide upon the design and scope of the project. From here architects and engineers must develop detailed plans and submit a budget. The project leaders then must arrange financing, which is the most challenging part. Only after this point can artisans begin to actually start construction. So for politicians to claim that entrepreneurs and CEO's "did not build this" is ignoring the fact that without these instigators little of any significance would be built. Artisans are in plentiful supply and follow instructions. Entrepreneurs and visionaries are rare. The USA has an illustrious history of visionaries who think big, investors who are prepared to take risk and a workforce which is diligent and efficient. Other countries are not so fortunate. This is the heart of American culture and it must be preserved.

Many American politicians and much of the public believe that everyone else in the world thinks like they do, aspires to the same goals and adheres to the same principles. The US foreign policy and much of the philanthropic work overseas is distorted by these illusions. Other cultures think, believe and behave very differently from one another. Until this is accepted and understood, meddling in the affairs of other nations and admitting all and sundry to immigrate to the USA will continue to the detriment of all Americans.

For a country to prosper and for its citizens to live in reasonable comfort without suffering starvation, attack or disease, certain basic requirements must be met. Most importantly, good leadership: no enterprise is successful for long without a good leader and the task of leader falls squarely on the President. However, for him to effective he must have a good Congress which puts country before party. The people themselves are also important. They must, in general, be willing to work hard and to make good decisions. Many people do not appreciate the fact that good work is a privilege. The busy person is more inclined to be a happy person. All humans need a sense of accomplishment to feel good about themselves and enjoy the free time that they do have. Idleness spawns discontent and mischief. The demise of the great civilizations of history can all be attributed to poor leadership, abuse of power, corruption and declines in the productivity of the general population. In order for the leader, his subordinates and the population to function well, a good system of government is vital.

Successful countries where some form of democracy is practiced require two important conditions: the electorate must be reasonably well informed with the truth and the culture must embrace personal responsibility and integrity. Once the majority of the electorate is ignorant and apathetic and the culture expects the government to address the basics needs of individuals the country will decline, the rule of law will be subverted and eventually anarchy will prevail as can be seen in Africa today. As Winston Churchill correctly observed, a five minute conversation with the average citizen is the most persuasive argument against democracy.

In a democracy with a universal franchise it can be argued that the citizens deserve the government they have. This is quite true. The citizens have the means to elect candidates for the offices of president and members of congress. The pitfalls are that many competent people do not want to run for office because of the outrageous cost,   unrelenting attention and scrutiny they will be subjected to and that the general voting public does not take the trouble to properly examine the candidates or the important issues. Many do not vote at all. Many voters do not know what they want nor which candidate is best for the long-term success of the country.

It is very evident that all governments are corrupt and inefficient and it is naïve to believe they will use public funds wisely. For this reason the Founding Fathers wanted to be sure that the Federal government would be small, have strictly defined responsibilities and powers and would not have the authority to tax the income of individuals or businesses. Alas, their worst fears have come true.

The country has drifted very far from the governing principles set out by the Founders in the Constitution. The concept of government of the people, for the people by the people is now a complete illusion. The country is controlled by money, not principle. Politicians are elected by auction, not democracy. They are beholden to their donors and not the electorate. Once in office, they must repay their contributors with litigation favorable to their interests or lucrative government positions with prestige and power. The media by and large spew forth misinformation tailored to the agendas of its owners. The rule of law is subverted by presidential decrees and outrageous litigation costs.

The country is in a mess. The prior Presidents and Congress have interfered in other countries and involved the US in foolish wars which have benefited no-one except producers of arms and war materials.

The concept of democracy is based on the assumption that civic minded citizens will elect honest and intelligent representatives to govern them in a way that allows them the maximum freedom and creates a prosperous country with the rule of law fairly enforced. Each representative including the President acts according to his or her personal analysis and conscience. In reality this is not the way the US government functions. The party system puts party before country. Before every important vote in both houses of Congress, the party "whip" circulates and persuades or cajoles each member to vote along the party line. If necessary the party leader and even the President get involved. Resistant members are threatened with dire consequences or enticed with favors or rewards. If a president wishes to advance his agenda he goes to great lengths to persuade Congress to support it. The result is that most members submit, and their own ideas and opinions are irrelevant. The leaders of the parties in power in the House and Senate run the show. In recent years many important bills have been voted upon strictly on party lines. This means that the individual legislators really play no part and the leader of the party with the majority in each chamber decides the outcome. This is equivalent to having just two people in each house of Congress, and it might as well forego the expensive and time consuming charade of 535 votes.

The country has reached the point where logic, common sense and the lessons of history have all been abandoned in favor of a bogus culture rooted in fantasy. Left is right, up is down and dark is light. The majority must dance to the tunes of minorities. The problems the country faces are obvious and the solutions are attainable and yet nothing is done. The USA is undergoing a total failure of government at the federal level. This situation cannot be corrected by the simple electoral process because it has reached the point of distortion which makes it self-sustaining. The only chance for reform is the tool of last resort in Article V of the Constitution, a Convention of States, which, with a 75% majority, has the power to amend the Constitution without going through Congress. This is, by design, a very difficult process and a long shot at best.

Article V states the following:

*The Congress, whenever two thirds of both houses shall deem it necessary, shall propose amendments to this Constitution**, or, on the application of the legislatures of two thirds of the several states,** shall call a convention for proposing amendments, which, in either case, shall be valid to all intents and purposes, as part of this Constitution, when ratified by the legislatures of three fourths of the several states, **or by conventions in*** *three fourths thereof*, *as the one or the other mode of ratification may be proposed by the Congress; provided that no amendment which may be made prior to the year one thousand eight hundred and eight shall in any manner affect the first and fourth clauses in the ninth section of the first article; and that no state, without its consent, shall be deprived of its equal suffrage in the Senate.*

This tool has never been used, but the threat of its use several times has probably led to forcing Congress to act to address concerns identified by the states. The clause was inserted in Article V to expressly protect the states and the people from a rogue Federal government which sought to erode their rights. This point has now been reached. Unfortunately there is no defining endpoint in the failure of civilizations. The decline is slow and therefore not readily apparent to the citizens until the point of no-return has been passed.

All humans need to understand that life on Earth is hard. As the actor John Wayne correctly observed "Life is tough. It's even tougher when you're stupid". Regardless of what circumstances a person is born into and what happens during his/her life, except for a very small number, life is hard. People dream of wonderful lives and some suspect that others have wonderful lives but in reality almost everyone must confront hardship of some form or another. The Sherpa of Nepal believe that if they do not behave themselves during the first life on Earth their punishment will be a second life on Earth.

One only needs to study nature to realize that the natural order of things is survival of the fittest. Life is not fair and never will be. There is no free lunch. Others will try to take what you have and reap the benefits of your hard work. Success can be measured many ways and every individual needs to understand what his/her measure is. Governments can only do their best to facilitate the rule of law and to supply an adequate infrastructure to enable the efficient pursuit of normal activities. In those countries which have reasonably effective governments most citizens can lead comfortable lives without fear of starvation or assault. In those where the rule of law does not exist and government corruption is rife, a large percentage of the population lives in misery. By US standards, probably 90% of the world's population lives in poverty and this is unlikely to change. As populations increase exponentially, competition for scarce resources increases, croplands and forests diminish and life becomes still harder.

Why is it that in some regions of the world the standard of living is better than in others? In part this can be attributed to the climate and natural resources available but a larger part is the behavior of the inhabitants and the system of government. When the state of Israel was formed in 1948 after the United Nations mandate partitioning Palestine in 1947, most of the territory involved was semi-desert and underdeveloped. Today Israel is first-world with modern cities, agriculture and excellent infrastructure. The neighboring areas have progressed little. Human performance is related to intellect, diligence and maturity. All three are necessary for success. Those peoples who generally behave like small children make poor decisions and make little progress. Those who learn from education, experience and those around them are able to predict the consequences of their actions and therefore plan better and lead better lives. People who cannot think ahead are far more likely to be poor and commit crimes. Once good decisions have been made, hard work, sacrifice, passion and perseverance are necessary for success.

Americans must decide what kind of country they want themselves and their descendants to live in. Those who like to impress themselves and others with their charitable intentions and who advocate secularism, open borders, generous government welfare and permissive behavior should take the time to study the history of the Soviet Union. The result was a disaster in which few except the rulers were safe, prosperous, productive or happy. Much of Europe is approaching this position, having foolishly abdicated their national identities and basic cultures. This is irreversible. All those who favor high taxation to pay for social programs and national philanthropies should pay attention to the burgeoning public debt. It is interesting that those wealthy promoters of socialism pay as little as they can in taxes, clearly demonstrating the hypocrisy that accompanies their advocacy for the liberal agenda. America became great by hard work, self-reliance and a limited government which did not over-regulate. Abandoning these basic principles has been a great mistake.

At the heart of the issue is whether every citizen should be the keeper of both his brother and brothers in other nations. If it were left to each individual to take part of his paycheck each month and give it to strangers for unspecified purposes it is likely that very few would contribute. Why is it then acceptable for the government to take money for these purposes in the form of taxes? Part of the explanation is that since the government of Franklin Roosevelt instituted the pay-as-you-earn (PAYE) system in 1944 to collect taxes more efficiently to pay for the war, individuals never see this money. Until that time no taxes were deducted from paychecks by employers and taxes were paid annually by each individual. Not only did the PAYE system collect the revenues sooner and more reliably, but the fact that the payer never saw the money meant that less attention was paid to the burden.

The government is perhaps the least efficient administrator in terms of expending public revenues. No philanthropic or charitable foundation sends its funds to the US treasury to use for the public good. Those countries which have nationalized their industries have declined. This being so, it is reasonable for citizens to contribute the bare minimum in taxes to be used exclusively for those purposes defined in the Constitution. The vast bulk of the nation's wealth should be left in the hands of the citizens who earn it for them to spend, invest or save as they see fit.

There is nothing more dangerous to freedom than the overzealous liberal with the means to influence public opinion. Liberals fall into two general groups. On one side are those like Hitler, Trotsky, Stalin, Mao etc. who believe (with some justification) that the average citizen is simply too ignorant and stupid to make good decisions. They promote a government which controls everything in an illusory democracy where there is only one party on the ballot. On the other side are simply naive people who believe everyone is kind, fair, honest and decent and deserves a good life. These well-intentioned people believe that the government has the responsibility to take care of every need of every inhabitant. They feel good about themselves for espousing peace and goodwill to all oblivious to the fact that utopia is simply unattainable. However, with some exceptions, they want to disburse all these benefits with other people's (all taxpayers') money. The first group exploits the second group to accomplish their objectives.

Whereas the traditional religions preach that individuals should assist their neighbors in need using their own resources, many liberals pay little or no taxes and often reject the time-honored codes of behavior promoted by religions. Liberal agendas may deliver short-term advantages to the poor but in the long term it is the poor who suffer the consequences of misguided policy and excessive public debt. There are, of course, genuine philanthropists who do tremendous public good with their own money and time. Many liberals delude themselves that they are the voices of freedom. This is complete hypocrisy, the liberal political agenda is to have the central government control everything which inevitably means a loss of freedom. It is the conservative who believes in small government and minimal intervention, which is precisely what the Founders intended.

Many Americans believe that federal, state and local governments are comprised of reasonably decent men and women who genuinely wish to do well by their fellow citizens. This has never been true. From the time of Independence, politics has been corrupt. This is not because all politicians are fundamentally dishonest people, most of them are not. It is because when decent and normal people are in positions of power, control large funds of taxpayer money and their success depends on the co-operation of a large group of similar people they are tempted to make compromises and deals with the devil. Money and favors drive politicians, not the welfare of the country. The Framers of the Constitution did their best to control this sad reality but human nature has thwarted their efforts.

Politicians get elected based on promises. Many of the electorate do not take the trouble to vote at all and of those that do, few do the necessary research to determine whether the record of the candidate supports the promises he makes. The general public is spoon-fed ideas which appeal to their dreams and they naively believe that these dreams can come true. Both houses of Congress are controlled by a small number of powerful members who decide who sits on committees and which bills come up for discussion. Junior members seldom have influence, they are obliged to dance to the tune of the big dogs. These big dogs trade amongst themselves as in you support my bill and I'll support yours. The good of the country plays very little part.

It remains to be seen if any system of government can be devised which precludes abuse. Both current parties are equally guilty. It is not a question of which party is on the right path. It has come down to the pitiful choice of which is the least corrupt and self-serving. In fact political parties, like labor unions and governments, soon deteriorate into bodies which serve themselves rather than their members. It is time to take a hard look at the party system and determine whether the country would be better off without it. Once a corrupt system is well entrenched it is almost impossible to dislodge it without major revolution. Unfortunately history shows that even if this occurs, it does not take long for the revolutionaries to become corrupt. It is foolish for any voter to blindly support a party or an individual.

The current government is dysfunctional. The leaders of both parties are more partisan than rational. The members are mostly a bunch of self-serving squabblers who have accomplished little in the leadership vacuum. A strong president may do his best but in the end Congress controls the purse and the legislation so his hands are tied. This is nothing new. Pure democracy has never endured for long in any country. Inevitably politics is controlled by powerful business, labor and media tycoons who play a naïve and ignorant electorate like puppets. The corruption is pervasive at local, state and national levels and includes the judiciaries in each. Governments are and always have been a group of horse-traders doing not what is right and necessary but seeking personal and regional advantage in exchange for support. This results in compromises which do little to solve the real problems and create additional problems. The question remains as to whether there are still enough savvy and concerned citizens to outnumber the shortsighted and brainwashed to get back to reality. The politicians, judges and tycoons are ordinary men subject to ordinary temptations. The Constitution needs to be refined to minimize these temptations so that the government can truly serve the best interests of the people. Government does not need leaders who get into politics to foster the illusion of their own power and importance and increase their personal wealth. It needs patriotic men with high integrity who know right from wrong and make sound judgments based only on this.

Adults in any country are generally divided into three groups, the producers, the protectors and the parasites. The producers deliver a useful product or service, either tangible or intangible. The protectors make sure the public is kept safe and laws are obeyed, both criminal and civil, so that the producers can go about their business efficiently. The parasites are those who seek to prey on the producers and protectors and effectively steal some of their assets or acquire them via government welfare programs. Any successful country must seek to minimize the parasites and maximize the producers.

Parasites occur at many levels. The common thief simply steals directly. Far worse are the Wall Street hustlers who bilk old ladies out of their fortunes by slick marketing, the trial lawyers who chase ambulances to force huge settlements on anyone remotely involved and the corporate CEO's who bankrupt good companies while taking outrageous compensation for themselves. At the bottom are the career politicians, welfare abusers and pan-handlers who happily accept money for doing nothing.

Over the years Congress has sought to enact laws which discourage all these abuses but regrettably powerful interests and fear of restricting personal liberties have made the task difficult. The government itself is a large part of the problem. Its size and scope have grown to immense proportions creating an army of civil-servants which produces little in terms of wealth and costs a fortune to maintain.

A republican system of government is a representative democracy whereby leaders are elected by the people and there is no inherited power. This concept implies that the people, if left to their own decisions in the management of the country, would not necessarily make laws in the best long-term interests of the country. The assumption is that in certain cases the elected representatives will make better decisions. This may be so if the electorate is savvy and the elected officials are honestly only concerned with the welfare of the country. Unfortunately neither is the case. Without term limits, power is effectively inherited because an incumbent always has a huge advantage over a competitor. Even though the president is limited to two terms, there is nothing to prevent his/her spouse or other family members from becoming president and creating a family dynasty. In Congress there are no term limits and we see many members spend their lives in office and pass their seats on to their offspring.

Democracy implies that citizens decide their own affairs by common acclaim of the majority. The question is, where is the line drawn between decisions best left to the citizens and those they cannot be trusted with. If a referendum were taken on whether same-sex marriage should be legalized should the will of the majority prevail or should five Supreme Court judges make the decision? This decision is not about individual liberties, the security or financial health of the country, it is a question of personal belief and changing the definition of a word. There are many such issues and the Constitution is clear that unless specifically defined, the Federal government has no jurisdiction. These are matters reserved for the states to decide and federal judges should not be empowered to overrule the wills of the people of any state on matters outside the purview of the Constitution.

The overwhelming majority of Congress is made up of lawyers and former politicians from state and local offices. In the 117th congress there are 30 medical professionals, 9 engineers, 3 scientists, 27 farmers, 8 bankers and 10 accountants. Except for former governors and mayors, the remaining vast majority, including 230 lawyers, therefore have little or no experience in managing anything or being held accountable. Like a fanatical religious sect, Congress has developed a self-serving culture which has been very successful in indoctrinating all but the most principled members. Many a candidate has actually taken office with good intentions, only to be sucked into the quagmire of the establishment. The sad result is a group of men and women who spend taxpayer money irresponsibly and have little interest in the long-term prosperity of the nation. Many candidates running for re-election try to butter up their constituents by preaching that they are "confident the American voters are smart and will do the right thing". What they mean of course is the right thing for the politician's interests, not the country's. Most of the time their constituents reward them. To exacerbate the dysfunction of the system, the leader of each house in Congress can refuse to bring bills passed by the other house to the floor for discussion. This is absurd and totally in conflict with the procedures set out by the Constitution. Bills originating in either chamber must be ratified or not by the other in a timely manner, and if ratified, passed on to the President for signature. In addition to this, the Supreme Court should be required to sign off on every new law and every presidential decree before it can take effect, also in a timely manner.

Once in office, every politician must decide whether to support what is right and sensible as opposed to what is popular. Unfortunately, with a universal franchise, the two are not mutually inclusive. The right course of action often involves sacrifice and hardship in the short term in order to promote success in the long term. Politicians who do the right thing are likely to be voted out of office because their positions are unpopular with their constituents. The only solution to this very grave problem is single terms in office for every elected official.

The other huge problem is sheer numbers. When the Constitution was written there were thirteen colonies with a combined population of just under 4 million according to the 1790 census. The 2020 census recorded about 328 million. The original Constitution provided for no more than one Representative per 30,000 of population, excluding native born Indians and counting 3/5 of a person for each slave. The first Congress was comprised of 26 senators and 65 representatives. There were no political parties. This Congress passed the first ten amendments, known as the

Bill of Rights. With these relatively small numbers it was possible to operate with reasonable efficiency.

Today the congress has 100 senators and 435 congressmen. There are 435 congressional districts each with a population of about 754,000 representing a total population of 328 million. In the first place 754,000 people cannot have any meaningful contact with their representative and secondly, 535 people have a hard time agreeing on anything. What started off as a small group of civic-minded citizens taking a few weeks a year from their normal endeavors to address the needs of the government has evolved into a very costly behemoth of full-time politicians obsessed with the sound of their own voices. Laws are enacted which exceed the authority of Congress and appropriations are submitted with no regard to fiscal responsibility and full of earmarks to garner the necessary support. Not surprisingly this system is a disaster well on track to bankrupt the country and curtail the very freedoms it is charged with protecting.

Many learned scholars, lawyers and historians have written volumes about the Constitution and its effects on government over the last 250 years. For the average person however, the basics are quite simple. There is right and there is wrong. There are dreams and there is reality. Some dreams materialize into reality and many cannot. In the management of human affairs it is vital that both the managers and the managed understand the limitations that human nature places upon the degree to which lofty intentions can be realized. Many dream of a perfect world where everyone has a sound moral compass which directs him or her to behave considerately and put the wellbeing of the community first. Alas, this is but a dream. Humans, like every other species, are programmed for personal survival. This will never change and any system of government must take this into account.

There is also the question of how the perfect adult human should behave when living amongst others. Should he put the interests of the group before those of himself and his family? Ideally perhaps yes, but practically no. Many adults even put their own interests before those of their immediate families. In times of war there are variations but most of the time most people put their own family interests first. Most also plan only for the short term. In a perfect world every human would treat other humans with respect and consideration. This obviously must be reciprocated. Regrettably reality is quite different. Many humans enjoy subjugating and mistreating others and therefore provoke mistreatment to themselves. In general, people get the treatment they deserve.

All creatures behave according to two forces, instinct and thought. Each individual human has varying degrees of influence by each of these forces and indeed some think very little at all and survive mainly by instinct. There is also the distinction between intellect and wisdom. High intellect does not necessarily confer wise judgment. This makes governing a diverse group of individuals for the common good very difficult, even if the government were perfect.

Governments must enact laws which cover the basic principles necessary for reasonable cohabitation. These are ancient laws which are clearly defined in the Ten Commandments. Whereas the first four commandments relate to the Jewish and Christian religions, the remaining six apply to everyone. Honoring parents is wise and fundamental but not subject to legislation. Killing, committing adultery, stealing and bearing false witness are basic crimes and should be treated as such. Coveting the possessions of others is unfortunately part of human nature but nevertheless should be discouraged. Much of the discord in every country is the proclivity for one group of people to attempt to force their beliefs and customs on others. The Constitution has attempted to curtail this in the language of the 1st amendment but even this has not solved the problem. A basic freedom not only involves a person's right to believe what he wishes to, it also requires that others do not attempt to convert him to their beliefs. Presidents can lead well only by setting a good example in their own lives and by impressing upon their citizens the basics outlined in the Ten Commandments and emphasizing the importance of family, self-sufficiency, personal responsibility, honesty, integrity and hard work. These are ancient laws embedded in the various religions and pre-date our official Roman-Dutch law by millennia. They should also make it clear that no group of citizens owes anything to any other group.

There is in fact nothing in the Constitution referring to human behavior other than treason, counterfeiting and piracy. These are correctly addressed because they endanger the whole nation. Murder, theft, adultery and other behaviors commonly considered as crimes are not identified. Laws dealing with these issues were considered the premises of state legislatures. Somehow, over time, the Supreme Court has found ways to claim that the Constitution covers all forms of behavior. The basis simply does not exist.

In striving to design any form of government, it must be accepted that the average human being seems to have a proclivity for conflict. This may be part of his survival programming but it makes good government almost impossible to achieve. Most of human history involves war so it can then be concluded that war is the norm and peace is the exception. This is a sad reality. With a divorce rate of 50% it is apparent that even two humans have a difficult time living in harmony together. Even the lowly hyena has a better record than this, their unions are for life.

It is rather disappointing that after millennia of human civilization that a good and sustainable system of government has yet to be devised. Whereas tremendous progress has been made in science, medicine, engineering and the arts, humans continue to mistreat one another to everyone's detriment. Governments of any kind have always been about power. Certain humans are obsessed with it and will do anything to acquire and maintain it. Unfortunately, once acquired, it is soon abused. Many an aspiring politician begins his or her career with lofty ambitions of unselfishly serving his fellow citizens to their collective advantage. Once in office, most succumb to temptation and make decisions purely to their own advantage. Constitutions are written in an attempt to limit individual power but of course they can also be ignored or subverted.

Many people wonder how the Germans, a nation of highly educated, sophisticated and accomplished citizens, stood by and watched the Nazis abandon all semblance of democracy and decency and commit atrocities on a scale the likes of which the world has never seen before. In theory, after the First World War, Germany had a democratic republican government with conventional checks and balances. It was the general population who were sufficiently brainwashed into believing the wild promises and arrogant ambitions of the Nazi party. Whereas most of the general population did not actively participate in committing atrocities, they were guilty of putting the Nazis in power and then doing little to stop the excesses.

The Treaty of Versailles was the first catalyst in fomenting general dissatisfaction in Germany. Brokered by US president Woodrow Wilson it was a most unsatisfactory compromise between the harsh

Armistice conditions preferred by France and the more lenient terms favored by the US and Britain. It also created new borders which fragmented the German population. The Germans believed they had been forced to accept an agreement which was unjust and their politicians who signed it were vilified (some were even murdered). Hitler, Roehm and others formed the small National Socialist German Workers' Party to avenge this treaty and it gradually gained seats in the Reichstag. By 1928, however, the Weimar Republic was starting to show signs of recovery and support for the Nazis cooled. It was the ripple effect of the 1929 US stock-market crash which drove the world into depression and gave the Nazis new ammunition to assume control.

Like many revolutionaries, Hitler was a misfit who spent his early years as a lonely, frustrated and impecunious virtual vagabond in the streets of Vienna. Having too much time on his hands, he read widely and became enamored of the teachings of radical professors from the Berlin University who preached a most bizarre philosophy of the supremacy of the German peoples and their obligation to rule the world. They promulgated a rather strange theory involving the total authority of the state but unlike Marx, believed that democracy was ineffective and that the state should be in the form of a virtual dictator. Hitler detested the concepts of democracy and communism but believed strongly in state control of everything, with himself as director. The Weimar Republic was anathema to him and his whole passion was directed at its destruction. He saw nothing wrong with using German military might to slaughter and displace inferior species to make room for a glorious perfect world of pure Germans ruled by himself.   Apparently many Germans thought this was a fine plan.

Hitler should serve as a stark example of how one man can wreak havoc. His belief in his own destiny gave credence to his rants, which were judged not by their content but by the passion with which they were delivered. He pursued his goals with a cold and cunning disregard for any form of principle or moral rectitude, believing that the end justified the means. Like many politicians, he sought to convince each group of his complete dedication to its wellbeing. To the general workers and unions he promised dismantling of the industrial empires and institution of state control of industries. To the military he promised abrogation of the Treaty of Versailles and a return to German military might. To the barons of industry he promised a policy of non-interference in return for generous financial support. This last was done clandestinely. It appears that each group believed him for the most part and in the 1932 elections the Nazi party won 37% of the vote, becoming the largest in the Reichstag. After the Reichstag fire in 1933 the body was persuaded to pass the Enabling Act, giving Chancellor Hitler dictatorial powers to enact laws without the consent of the Reichstag. This should have served as a powerful lesson to all democracies but did not.

There were two strategies the Nazis used to accomplish their goals. The first was a cunning propaganda program designed to fire up passions, divide the country and promote the abuse of power as necessary. One of their first acquisitions was a small newspaper, through which they spewed forth anti-government propaganda. The key was to create a common enemy and for this they chose the Jews. They persuaded the citizens that they were victims of Jewish exploitation. Joseph Goebbels, the Nazi propaganda minister, assisted by Leni Reifenstal, a movie star and director, did a very effective job. Goebbels, born and raised a devout Catholic, also made every attempt to eradicate all religion in Germany. The second was a blatant system of intimidation, eagerly administered by vicious thugs who were extolled as heroes, culminating in the "Night of the Long Knives" in June 1934. This was the cold-blooded murder of German citizens by the ruling party, weeding out anyone who opposed or posed a threat to Hitler, including some of his close associates. Addressing the Riechstag after this, Hitler defended his actions as necessary to rid the country of enemies of the state and received effusive applause. The courts and cabinet abandoned the established rule of law and gave no opposition to Hitler declaring himself "the supreme judge of the German people" a de-facto Supreme Court of one.

Hitler's reign was notable for the fanatism it created. Many otherwise rational people were brainwashed to the point that Hitler became a god to be worshipped and obeyed without question. National Socialism replaced Christianity as a religion. Even at the very end, many of his hierarchy followed an obviously demented man and committed suicide rather than renounce him. Joseph Goebbels and his wife poisoned their six young children before taking their own lives. It is very dangerous for citizens to follow any one man. They need to support a rational policy and when a leader deviates from this or abuses his power he needs to be removed from power. It is astonishing that Hitler obtained his dictatorial powers quite legally and the Reichstag continued to exist during the first years of his dictatorship. By 1937 unemployment was virtually zero and the German economy and industry were vibrant. Within six years the Nazi party had control of almost every aspect of life in Germany, from education to vacation. Although deterred by intimidation, the general public did not raise any meaningful opposition to the complete loss of their freedom. In a little over four years the Nazis had transformed a bankrupt, weak, moribund and depressed democracy into a dynamo of industry rapidly gaining the reputation of one of the most powerful countries in the world. The average German was favorably impressed.

Conversely, it is astounding that British, French and American politicians during this period sat by and watched Germany re-arm and re-occupy the Rhineland in blatant violation of the Treaty of Versailles and even lent it the money to do so. It is a classic case of a flawed contemporary philosophy driven by public sentiment and democracies with universal franchises. These politicians, reluctant to offend their constituents, made flawed decisions and are as much to blame for the catastrophe as Hitler. They dreamed of peace while Hitler planned war. Hitler used unabashed arrogance and lies to cower the heads of powerful democracies into accepting preposterous demands. Even he was surprised at how naive they were.

The Nazis did not invent bestiality. Humans have practiced it for millennia, it is only the numbers that change. Sadly, the only animal on earth which has the ability to think for itself and deviate from instinctive behavior is also prone to sheer evil. In the USA awful atrocities were committed on slaves and Indians by educated people who went to church on Sundays. They appeared to take a certain perverted pleasure in their lynching's and mutilations. They did it because they could and the majority of virtuous people did little to discourage or stop them. There is no attempt to compare any American politician with Hitler. The history of the Nazis simply illustrates the extremes possible in the management of human affairs even when the country involved is considered first-world.

Civilization is all about the rule of law. Two things are necessary for this to be effective. Firstly, a minimum number of sensible and necessary laws. Secondly, an effective means of enforcing these laws. Congress is the only body authorized to make Federal laws. The

President and his administration are responsible for enforcing them. Under no circumstances is the President or anyone in his administration authorized to alter or disregard any provision of enacted laws passed by Congress. There will always be those who choose not to obey laws. This is due to stupidity, arrogance or both. If laws are neither enforced nor obeyed the country descends into anarchy as can be seen in most African countries today. The USA is heading in this direction with predictable consequences. Governors and mayors are responsible for making and enforcing state and local laws. The current vandalism and destruction taking place in many big cities today is a result of state and local officials restraining police from doing their jobs in order to further their own political agendas.

There are four groups other than the parties themselves which have had a profound effect on politics; powerful unions, big business, the media, and the universities. In each of them it is a small number of people who call the shots. Over the years, for different reasons, they have succeeded in influencing naive voters and corrupt politicians to the point that the USA is regressing. This decline began after the Second World War when the USA was in the privileged position of being virtually the only major economy whose infrastructure had not been destroyed by war. The new generation of baby-boomers, being raised in relative prosperity, set about repudiating the standards set by their ancestors. They believed in their superiority (a grand delusion) and sat by and watched other countries rebuild and start producing superior products. General Motors, Ford and Chrysler, heavily unionized, started to produce poor-quality inefficient cars with engines little changed from the 1930's. They wallowed in arrogant complacency while watching the Japanese eat their lunches. In 1960 the USA produced 85% of all new cars in the world! By 2013 this had dropped to 7%.

The most effective tool in the propaganda campaign promoting an agenda which overturns all the norms established over millennia is the concept of political correctness. Not unlike Goebbels' Nazi propaganda machine, it seeks to limit free speech by vilifying anyone who dares to speak against the party line. The issues of race, abortion, religious freedom, marriage etc. can only be discussed on a pro-establishment basis. The population has been coerced into believing that any different opinion is offensive to some and therefore off limits. Senior politicians, CEO's and celebrities have been toppled by simply using the wrong word, even in private conversations. Gay marriage is a good example of the effectiveness of propaganda. When Obama took office, he, Hillary Clinton and 60% of the public opposed it. After relentless propaganda by the mainstream media, in 2015 Obama, Clinton and 60% of the public support it.

Nothing in politics occurs by accident. The Democratic Party knows that most Democrats are liberal and most Republicans are conservative. Political correctness is their brainchild. By championing the liberal causes they make it embarrassing for the Republican candidates to openly oppose them. Those who do, lose the support of the fringe voters. Those who do not lose the support of their base. The basic term for the change in acceptance is brainwashing. It did not happen spontaneously. It is not the result of moral enlightenment. The mainstream media are all controlled by boards who favor and promote the liberal agenda to further their own interests.

The media and Hollywood have been major promoters of political correctness. Aside from a few isolated talk-shows, Americans are deprived of real world news. Every mainstream TV station focuses on inconsequential local topics of the day and continues coverage of each event 24 hours a day for weeks until the next catastrophe occurs. Comprehensive world news is only available on stations from other countries and to some extent Fox and One America. Very few liberals watch these. The focus on local atrocities has only escalated the incidence of these. The perpetrators are generally seeking attention and the media supply it. The correct approach would be to never broadcast either the names or images of these deranged people. The power of the media should not be underestimated. Newspaper editors over the history of the country have made and broken presidents and congressmen. This is not democracy. Regrettably the public does not seek out the facts. Liberals follow liberal media and conservatives follow conservative. Few people follow both in order to get some idea of the truth. A large majority does not follow politics at all and arrive at the voting booths completely ignorant.

The freedom of the press is one of the cornerstones of a free and open society. However, the public needs to understand that precisely because of this freedom, groups of media businesses can collude to spew out any information they please and to withhold information that does not further their agendas. Often the facts and the truth are never revealed to the public.

It is worrisome that many public places, which should be impartial, are able to promote one cause or another. Airports generally provide only CNN news, which is liberal. Who decides this? Some public schools block conservative websites and news programs on their internet servers. Colleges are generally extremely liberal. This is not education, it is indoctrination. Hotels often do not offer the Fox News or One America channels which are generally conservative. Hollywood seldom offers a conservative theme in a movie. None of this is by accident. In every court of law each side has equal opportunity to present its case. This is justice. There is no way to force citizens to research both sides of any political agenda but most certainly all public places financed by public money should offer all options or nothing at all. National radio and television stations, supported by taxpayer funds, should be absolutely neutral. They are not. Human nature inevitably causes individuals to instinctively follow a philosophy derived from one or more influences in their lives and once it becomes embedded, they are reluctant to even consider the merits of a different point of view. This voluntary blindness is a major obstacle in the application of democracy.

The Bolshevik revolution in Russia is a good example of the power of the media. Most of the funding for the party went towards various publications, the most powerful of which was the newspaper Pravda. The Bolsheviks also relied heavily on printed handouts encouraging the overthrow of the Kerensky government. Initially a small party of extremists without popular support, Bolsheviks used propaganda, strikes and intimidation to eventually give Lenin dictatorial power. The soviets, equivalent to unions, played a pivotal role. Units of the military were also subverted. A large part of the funding came from the German government, which was happy to do a deal with the devil in exchange for substantial Russian territorial possessions and Russia getting out of the war, culminating in the treaty of Brest-Litovsk.

After deposing the Kerensky government and assassinating the entire royal family, the Bolsheviks fought an ugly civil war for five years against their rivals, the "Whites." The most fanatical instigator was Leon Trotsky, a completely ruthless former agitator and rival of Lenin. As Jew who totally renounced the teachings of his faith, however, he conceded that the population would never accept him as supreme leader and agreed to work with Lenin. He commanded the Red army and was responsible for inconceivable atrocities. Trotsky made no secret of the fact that he was working towards a world controlled by communism and was quite prepared for massive slaughter and starvation to promote his dream. He was overtaken in his quest by Stalin, who wrested power from him after Lenin's death and sent him into exile where Stalin's thugs ultimately murdered him.

Three men effectively doomed Russians to seventy years of slaughter and misery far beyond anything they had suffered under the Romanov dynasty. The result was control of a huge country by a bunch of inexperienced idealistic zealots who had no problem starving and executing millions of their own people and ruining the country's economy. Three generations of Russians had to suffer through this misery. The country is still authoritarian.

At the heart of the Russian system was ruthless centralized control of everything. Citizens could only vote for the Communist Party candidates and these were selected by the party seniors to perpetuate the system. Centralized control is a guaranteed disaster as a few politicians sitting in the Kremlin cannot possibly understand in depth the needs and aspirations of different groups scattered over an immense land mass. For this reason the men who wrote the American Constitution were very clear on the matter of state sovereignty. They were quite correct.

The examples of Germany and Russia call into question the freedom of the press. On the one hand it is vital that opinions and different points of view can be freely disseminated by all means possible without fear of prosecution. On the other hand it is very dangerous to allow unrestricted distribution of lies and misinformation for political gain. Democracy relies on the will of the people based on truths. Powerful media can and do propagate lies to further the agendas of their owners. In the USA the media have always played a prominent role in the selection of presidents and members of congress. Horace Greely effectively ensured Lincoln's election. The Grahams of the Washington Post got Bobby Kennedy the democratic nomination and had he not been assassinated he probably would have become president. This influence plus the PAC system makes a mockery of the principles of democracy.

With the advent of twenty four hour news started by CNN in 1980 and now available on various cable channels, the public is bombarded with all kinds of conflicting information. There is insufficient real news to fill 24 hours a day so these channels are full of individuals and "panels" venting their own opinions and promoting the agendas of the channels' owners. Except for Fox and OAN, the news channels have become de facto propaganda machines for their owners and the Democrat party. There is no good solution to this problem other than to hold channels responsible for knowingly reporting outright lies.

As in the cases of many civilizations which were once great, over successive generations the culture and principles which enabled a country to achieve greatness are gradually forgotten. When life is too easy, standards drop and morals are abandoned. As Plato hypothesized, too much freedom leads to decline. Not too long ago a stroll down Main Street in any town in the USA would find well-dressed, polite people going about their business in a civilized manner. When the Wright brothers attempted their first flights at Kitty Hawk they dressed up in their finest suits, ties and all. They were proud of themselves. Profanity, rudeness, promiscuity, slovenliness and other ungracious behaviors were confined to the lower echelons and seldom seen or heard in good company. In the quest for "freedom" all this started to unravel in the 1960's. Although their predecessors were no less free, the generation born after the Second World War started falling apart. Every form of dress became acceptable, politeness and respect were abandoned and morals were pushed to the back-burner. Hollywood films played a large part, glorifying poor behavior and shabby dress as signs of character and individualism. Discipline in schools disappeared and educational standards dropped. The welfare programs instituted by Roosevelt and Johnson removed the incentive for gainful employment for a large segment of the population. The nation became fat and the functional family became less common. A culture of dependency emerged. In fact the net result was far less freedom, as the Federal government and Supreme Court began to dictate personal behavior, controlling speech and activities in multiple areas and getting heavily involved in social engineering.

The civil rights movement and Lyndon Johnson's Great Society programs swung the pendulum too far. In 1950 most children were brought up in traditional families. For blacks and whites, children born out of wedlock were about 17 and 2 percent respectively. According to the CDC, for 2019 the numbers were: non-Hispanic blacks 70 percent; American Indians/Alaska Natives, 69 percent; Hispanics, 52 percent; non-Hispanic whites, 28 percent, Pacific Islanders 50 percent and 12 percent for Asians. For all races combined the rate was 40 percent. This is a huge change which is not good for a civilized society. Research in recent years shows that married, two-parent families have a poverty rate of just over 6 percent compared with 36 percent for single-parent families headed by a female. The unintended consequences of Federal programs adopted to reduce poverty have been to increase dependence and reward mothers who bear children out of wedlock. The major decrease in traditional two-parent families has had a detrimental ripple effect throughout society.

The government and media may control behavior to a certain extent and skillful propaganda may dupe some, but all citizens are entitled to think and believe what they want to. The federal and state constitutions do not require citizens to like one another or mix together. They do not even require them to treat one another well. Nor can they. They simply provide a set of rules that try to ensure reasonable protections of personal freedom. If they attempt to control associations, language, access to private businesses, properties, schools and universities they are effectively contravening the terms of the constitutions which guarantee freedom in all these areas.

The concept of democracy in the literal Greek origin means people power, or rule by the people. However, in the Greek application, the people were represented by male citizens in good standing. It was assumed that they spoke for their wives and daughters as well. It is a fact that since the interpretation has been expanded to include every citizen over the age of 18, more turbulence and slaughter has occurred throughout the world than ever before. Universal franchise was adopted in the western world in the early 20th century and was brought to the rest of the world after the Second World War. The 20th century slaughter in Europe, Asia and Africa has probably exceeded all the slaughter in the world until that point. Part of this can be attributed to higher population and more destructive weapons but the root cause has been the general population democratically installing governments which soon degenerated into maniacal dictatorships and self-serving legislators.

CHAPTER 2: THE BASIC PRINCIPLES

Management in most civilized countries functions in layers. In a federation of states such as the USA, the top level is the Federal government. This is intended to set the rules which affect the country as a whole and provide a strong military, good infrastructure, basic safeguards to ensure the liberty and safety of all the inhabitants and protect the natural resources. The next layer is the state legislatures which determine the laws for issues affecting the state itself and the basic protections for its inhabitants. Below these are county and city officials who decide the details of acceptable behavior within their jurisdictions. Beyond these there are homeowners' associations, school boards and other local entities which deal with the details of each small area. The final layer is the family itself which sets the rules and morals it believes in. It is vital that each layer respects its boundaries.

There are many different opinions regarding how much power each layer should have. Should the head of a family be free to raise his children as he wishes or should a higher authority have the power to dictate this? The answer should be that other than in cases of serious abuse, the family should decide its life. If a community elects to allow prayer in its schools, should the city or state have the power and authority to ban this? Obviously the most freedom is obtained when groups decide for themselves as long as their decisions do not adversely affect other groups or contravene basic laws.

History makes it clear that all groups of humans need management of some kind. Left to themselves they revert to anarchy, stealing, raping and killing at will. This has been a way of life for millennia and is still going on today in parts Africa, South America and the Middle East where no effective governments exist. On the other hand, once some kind of government or leadership has been established, it does not take long for it to abuse its subjects to some degree. Once the leaders realize that they can enrich or empower themselves by extracting payment from their subjects in the form of money, goods or labor they rapidly escalate the payment until a limit is reached. The original forms of leadership and control involved protection. The king, emperor, chief, lord or magnate offered protection to those living on land within his control in return for a portion of their agricultural output. This often involved the leader getting 90% of the output and living in opulent luxury and the peasants living at subsistence level. It was a self-perpetuating system whereby the peasant had very little recourse. Whereas the Greeks and Romans refined the system so that certain segments of the population had some say in selecting their leaders, the rest of the world continued in a basic feudal system until the Industrial Revolution brought masses to the cities and lethal weapons to the military. In the mid eighteenth century those living in the American colonies of England decided to end the abuse the King of England and his government were subjecting them to. They rebelled, won the war and declared their independence from England. To avoid a repetition of the abuse by their own government they drafted a constitution with certain safeguards.

The American Constitution was based on the same basic principles of the English Magna Carta, the document forced upon King John in 1215 by the English feudal barons to curb the omnipotence of the throne. Many of the clauses were subsequently abandoned or repealed, but three important ones endured and remain in force today. These are the freedom of the church, the right to certain liberties and the right of due process. Of course any constitution is only a piece of paper. For it to protect the rights of the citizens and states it needs a mechanism to enforce it. The Magna Carta was largely eviscerated by subsequent kings of England because nobody had the power to stop them. The American Constitution has been whittled away by multiple small deviations because the American people did not hold their representatives accountable.

There are two schools of thought regarding the Constitution. One is that it means exactly what it says, no more and no less (the originalist interpretation). This ascribes to the theory that the Framers chose their words carefully for good reason and only these specific words apply. The other is that it was a broad document open to interpretation and successive courts and Congress were free to manipulate the words to conform to changing times and current requirements. The Supreme court justices are divided between these two approaches and this is a problem. In fact the second case has been applied to the point that the Framers would have difficulty in recognizing their document as interpreted today. The correct approach is, when changing technologies or circumstances create a need for amendments to the Constitution, this should be done in the prescribed manner, as was done with the current 27 amendments.

The first priority in understanding how this has occurred is to understand critical terms used widely by politicians but never clearly defined. The concepts of freedom, equality, poverty, equal opportunity, justice, rights, democracy, diversity and racism mean different things to different people.

The term "freedom" implies that every citizen is free to lead his or her life as he pleases. This is never the case. Individuals can never be entirely free in this sense. Even a man living alone in the wilderness must work hard to sustain himself. When humans live together, one man's freedom can be another man's constraint. Civilized societies pass and enforce laws to attempt to ensure that there are reasonable balances in permissible behaviors. Inevitably this goes beyond reasonable and leads to excessive regulation and empowers the government to virtually control every aspect of its citizens' lives. The USA has reached this point. Congress needs to allocate a certain period of each session to eliminate unnecessary and outdated laws and regulations.

Equality really cannot be applied to human beings, each one is unique and the physical and intellectual differences are boundless. We now can prove this with DNA testing. The word is used in the Declaration of Independence stating that all men are created equal. This statement has been seized upon to imply that everyone is inherently the same. This is not what was intended and is simply absurd. The Founders wished to state that everyone had equal rights bestowed by God and they enumerated these. The rights to life, liberty and the pursuit of happiness. Equal in the mathematical sense denotes the same value. This cannot be applied to humans because it depends on value to whom. Even two siblings are not necessarily valued equally by their parents. As every schoolteacher can attest to, every child is different. If all students of the same age are placed in the same class the pace of learning will be dictated by the slowest learner. This has little to do with environment and economic conditions, it is genetic.

The closest a government can come to ensuring fair treatment is covered in the 14th Amendment, guaranteeing every citizen equal protection under the law. However, this is not enforceable because of the different competences of lawyers, judges and juries. The concept of equality or fair treatment has perplexed humans for millennia. Plato and Aristotle wrestled with it and came to different conclusions. Aristotle believed that each individual should be treated differently in accordance with his or her behavior. In this way he claimed that each would be given equal consideration and get what he deserved. Plato, Aristotle's mentor, believed that everyone should be treated the same regardless of behavior. This treatment can only apply to acts the government can control, which are limited. The Russian experiment with communism has demonstrated that attempting to achieve income or wealth equality results in poverty for all, or equalization at the bottom level. The communist axiom of to each according to need and from each according to ability is nonsense. Aristotle believed the opposite, to each according to ability. This is the basis of capitalism and gives each person the incentive to perform to capacity. Inevitably this will result in a vast range of income and wealth.

The question arises as to how vast this range should reasonably be. If a schoolteacher is worth $x is a university football coach worth $20x? Certainly not. In terms of value to society, a schoolteacher is infinitely more important than a football coach. The same applies to the total compensation paid to CEO's of public corporations compared to that of the average employee in those companies. Is he 100 times smarter? Trial lawyers, Wall Street hustlers and celebrities also appear to get disproportionately high rewards considering their talents and efforts. For many of these their compensation is not based on their efforts and talents or value to society but on what the market will stand. However, in a free market economy these excesses occur. In the USA this is partially due to unions, the tort system and shareholders' apathy. It is what the culture dictates. Outrageous compensation is bound to cause resentment.

In the USA most individuals are not rich, poor or middle-class because of any racial, ethnic or religious influences. They find their places in society according to their behavior. Those that are smart, hard-working and plan ahead rise, regardless of where they started. Those that are the opposite sink to lower levels. In relatively homogeneous societies such as Switzerland, there are no slums. Even those with minimal wealth maintain their simple houses neatly and obey the laws of the land. This is not because anyone forces them to live this way, it is in their nature. Each individual has different physical, intellectual and maturity attributes. Many highly intelligent people lack the wisdom to use good judgment and behave like children. Conversely, many with limited intellectual resources act wisely and do well.

Governments cannot make everyone rich but they can make everyone poor by means of excessive taxation and poor policies. It is, of course, always those who have the least who want to "share" and if they make up a majority of the population they can elect a government which will redistribute wealth. As demonstrated in Russia, this does not turn out well. Many humans prefer their fellow citizens to have no more than themselves, as depicted in an old Russian story: A poor family owns one cow, which provides milk and fertilizer and is their only asset. One day the cow dies and the family is distraught, contemplating starvation. Miraculously, a genie appears and offers to grant the father one wish. He requests that his neighbor's cow die too!

Poverty is a relative term but is used frequently by politicians to garner votes from those who have less than others. If it is the least successful who end up electing politicians then it can be expected that these politicians will also be the least effective in the management of government. The USA has an actual definition of poverty. At this time it is an income of less than $23,000 for a family of four. How on earth was this calculated? There are innumerable variables involved. Real poverty is when a person is starving and without clothing or shelter. The USA has one of the highest rates of obesity in the world so it is hard to claim a high rate of poverty. If everyone had the same income would they all be poor or rich? Whereas it is a valid objective to raise the average standard of living in a country by means of good government policies, the "war on poverty" is a foolish illusion along socialistic lines. There is nothing in the Constitution authorizing the federal government to redistribute wealth. Each state is free to deal with its poor as it sees fit.

Giving able-bodied people handouts financed by productive people or massive borrowing is not the way to reduce poverty. Indeed this policy encourages it. If nobody gave cash to panhandlers there would be no panhandlers. The correct solution is to foster job creation by minimizing regulations and lowering or eliminating income taxes. Those unwilling to find their own employment should be required to work at whatever jobs the state dictates at a minimum wage. With more people actually earning money, the value of the currency will be enhanced and retail consumption will rise, benefitting everyone.

The average citizen has a hard time understanding economics and finance and regrettably these subjects are not taught in any depth in high-schools. Economics is a fuzzy field which depends to a large extent on psychology and for this reason it is classified as an art, not a science. The average worker is apt to resent the high salaries and bonuses paid to top executives and the dividends paid to stockholders. Reality is that without entrepreneurs willing to innovate and take high risk and stockholders willing to risk their capital, there would be no jobs in commerce and industry. These people expect high potential rewards to compensate for the degree of risk. The average employee takes no risk and when he accepts employment and it is on the basis that he accepts the agreed compensation. It is clear that most people prefer a low-paying job in a city to a low-paying job on a farm and therefore they have made their own choices. If they form unions and force their employers to raise wages and benefits beyond the point of viability, the employer will either close shop or shift his enterprise to another state or to a country where it can remain profitable.

In the macro sense, policy in large, publicly-owned corporations plays a major part in human relations.. Should the management put the stockholders, the employees or themselves first? As in politics, most corporate boards are comprised of internal directors who are also on the boards of other corporations and outside directors who are CEO's of other corporations. They make decisions to favor themselves on the basis of "you scratch my back and I'll scratch yours." Next in line come the stockholders because they have a vote in selecting directors and employees come last. Socialists may argue that this is unfair and that employees are being exploited. This is how unions became powerful. In reality however, as long as labor laws protect employees from abuse, big corporations provide millions of good jobs and employees work there of their own free will. In theory at least, high executive compensation attracts the best and motivates them to do great things.

The problem with politicians and CEO's of public corporations is that they have access to other people's money. The temptation for abuse is simply irresistible. Politicians want to get re-elected and want to seen as champions of good deeds. They appropriate large sums of public revenue for pet projects in their own states and philanthropic programs throughout the world. This strategy allows them to persuade their constituents that they are wonderful, generous and compassionate people looking out for mankind. CEO's are a little more honest, they simply allocate themselves huge salaries, bonuses and perks by persuading others on their boards that they will do the same for them. In both cases this misuse of public funds is blatant exploitation and abuse of public trust. In the cases of the President and Congress, there is nothing in Constitution authorizing the use of treasury funds for anything other than those purposes clearly defined. A president may be applauded for his initiatives in spending billions to alleviate some world crisis but in fact he has no authority to do this unless it is directly related to the safety or welfare of American citizens. The USA is the most indebted country on earth simply because its government has squandered hundreds of billions of taxpayer dollars on foolish wars, social hand-outs and unauthorized philanthropy. Wars are only justifiable when the safety of the US is threatened and philanthropy is best left to voluntary contributions from foundations, businesses and individuals.

The term "equal opportunity" is preached by politicians. This is also nonsense. Everyone has different opportunities depending on many factors. All federal and local governments can do is to provide a consistent and effective system of justice, basic education for all, a well maintained infrastructure and a financial system which encourages maximum effort to succeed and avoids taxes and regulations which impede progress.

Justice is linked to the concept of equality and is understood as fair treatment, but of course fair is open to interpretation. The concept of justice depends on the philosophy of those to whom it is applied. In his book The Republic, Plato discusses the matter at length. There is no distinct definition. Governments, through the making and executing of laws, try to be fair in most circumstances but even this does not necessarily guarantee fairness in the minds of the judged. We frequently are told that "the rich must pay their fair share of taxes." This sounds good to the poor who will benefit disproportionately but is it really fair when those in the top 1% of incomes pay 37% of the income taxes? These people could argue that every adult should pay the same tax regardless of income and everyone should benefit from tax-funded programs equally. The current system is the exact opposite. The problem is that fair in its true sense is impractical in this example and so we have an inherent unfairness in order to make the country viable. Different cultures have very different ideas on justice as exemplified by comparing classical Roman-Dutch law to the Moslem Sharia law. This becomes a problem when two very different cultures live in the same country.

The term "right" implies the uncontested privilege of receiving something from another, tangible or intangible. What must be understood is that for this to be true, the other party, be it an individual, a group or a government body, must agree with his/its obligation to deliver this. The word has no basis if the giver does not agree with the principle. The Declaration of Independence states that each citizen has the rights to Life, Liberty and the Pursuit of Happiness. This is a noble theory but forms no part of the Constitution. The Bill of Rights binds the Federal Government to treat its citizens in certain ways. Nowhere in the document is there specified a right to charity, "free" healthcare, "free" education etc. Of course no government service is ever free, taxpayers must always supply the funds. Politicians and the media throw out the word "right" frequently when there is no established entity obligated to supply this right.

Democracy must be defined. If it is to function well it must rely on voters to be sensible, well-informed and more concerned with the general well-being of the nation than with their own well-being. If the electorate were to be confined to citizens meeting these criteria the voter roll would be very small, perhaps 10% of the adult population and this would be more correctly described as aristocracy (rule by the best). On the other hand, universal suffrage or democracy is bound to result in disaster. Most adults are selfish, poorly informed and easily influenced by smart politicians and corrupt media. In our current system of universal suffrage, Congress has an approval rating of less than 10% which confirms the failure of the system and yet voters continue to re-elect most incumbents. The pitfall in limiting the electorate to adults who meet certain qualifications such as education, income, property ownership or tax payments is that they would then have the means to perpetuate the exclusion of those who do not meet the criteria and this would generate resentment.

The system adopted by the Founders was in fact a representative aristocracy and was indirect, meaning that individual voters could not vote on every issue that required attention. Only male land-owners over 21 years of age could vote in general elections. They were divided into groups according to where they lived and could vote for a representative to go to Washington periodically to vote on issues on their behalves. This was for two good reasons. Firstly, sheer numbers would make direct voting impractical and expensive. Secondly, and more importantly, in certain instances the majority of voters cannot be relied upon to vote in their own communal long-term interests as can be seen in the California referendums. Regrettably, elected representatives themselves cannot be relied upon to vote for the long-terms best interest of the country as a whole either. They want to be re-elected and therefore vote to please their constituents or financial supporters. This makes the system inefficient and basically corrupt. In many elections the vote is very evenly divided, with the winner garnering very little over 50%. This means that almost half the electorate disapproves.

Voting is a serious business and affects the well-being of a country for generations. It should be a privilege which has to be earned. It should be hard, not easy so that only those who take the trouble to educate themselves on the issues and candidates actually vote. Simply being born or naturalized in the country are inadequate qualifications. The first problem which must be solved in the USA is verification of citizenship on the voter registration rolls. The current system simply requires a signature declaring citizenship, no proof needs to be submitted. The USA has resisted any system of national identification on the grounds that it is the first step in creating a police state. In today's world of massive fraud and ID theft, a biometric ID system would solve many problems. In the absence of this, a birth certificate, naturalization certificate or passport should be required to register and a photo identification should be presented at the polling booth each time a vote is cast. This is fundamental. Mail-in voting should be restricted to those who submit proof that they have no means of voting in person.

The next is the franchise. The fairest way to arrive at a reasonably mature and educated vote is to institute a basic eligibility test during the registration process. This would involve questions in English on the Constitution, basic civics and the functioning of government, government responsibilities, taxation, finance, government debt and the budgeting process. Free courses should be offered in these subjects and they should be taught in all high-schools. This gives everyone equal opportunity to qualify and weeds out those who are too lazy or stupid to deserve a vote. Southern states had a short test on these lines but it was oral and used to exclude blacks because it was not administered equally. For this reason eligibility tests were ruled unconstitutional and abolished during the Civil Rights movement. This was the wrong solution.

The tests should be set and administered by the Federal government and be in written form and the same for everyone.

The current US franchise is a disaster which has resulted in a congress consisting of self-serving incompetent legislators who cannot agree on anything. Special interests and gerrymandering have led to the election of persons incapable of administering a public toilet. It is an embarrassment to the country when these people are making public appearances and ridiculous statements. When random interviews of the public are conducted by the media regarding knowledge of government and current affairs it is clear that the majority are woefully ignorant and misinformed. With this kind of democracy it is not surprising that the Federal government is a bloated, ineffective, expensive mess.

It is obvious that democracy cannot function in other walks of life so it is surprising that anyone believes it can work for government. Imagine a military operating on a democratic basis whereby every soldier voted to elect the officers and these officers depended upon soldier support in the prosecution of their duties. Imagine schoolchildren electing their teachers and requiring them to accede to their demands. Imagine a large business allowing the employees to elect a board of directors. None of these would work. This is why powerful unions destroy good companies.

The barons of industry do not want strong men in Washington. They want people who are beholden to them and can be manipulated to pass laws and dictate policies which suit their own interests. With no restraints on campaign contributions, these barons are able to effectively buy Washington.

Politicians do not want an informed and savvy electorate which will hold them accountable. They love stupid, ignorant masses which are easy to brainwash and manipulate. For this reason they promote a universal franchise with no safeguards . They have also worked hard to dumb-down the public education system so that American children are far down on the list compared to other civilized countries. Some even suggest lowering the voting age to sixteen. If anything, with most people now living longer, the age should be increased to the original twenty one. Most eighteen year olds have never lived outside their parents' homes and know very little of the realities of life. Furthermore, politicians are seldom held accountable for deviating from the platform which got them elected. Each candidate should publish his or her platform and if at any time he or she votes in conflict with this the seat should go up for re-election. Politics at every level has always been corrupt. Bribery and patronage have played a part throughout history. There is little likelihood that these can ever be entirely eliminated but a well-informed and savvy electorate and term limits can at least make it more difficult to abuse the system.

The modern liberal philosophy preaches that "diversity" is essential in all walks of life. The interpretation of this means that any group anywhere must be comprised of many races, religions, and nationalities. It is "immoral" to form an Italian club where only Italians are allowed to join. Workplaces, sports, universities etc. must all include all types of people regardless of their suitability, eligibility or ability. Historical figures who were undeniably white must be played by blacks in Hollywood productions in order for the cast to be diverse. This strategy is supposed to promote unity but it completely neglects the powerful forces of nature. There is no evidence that the policy provides any benefit to anyone. On the contrary, it is an egregious infringement on basic liberties and the freedom of association. Skin color, ethnicity, race, religion are not qualifications for inclusion in any group except in those cases where the position justifies it, for example a Catholic priest must be Catholic. Diversity cannot be an objective. If it occurs as the result of needed skills, qualifications, character and behavior there is nothing wrong in this.

The term "racism" is used widely in every type of circumstance to imply that someone is being mistreated simply because he or she is a member of a certain race. In fact these claims are not really about race, they are about skin color. To start with, in today's world, racial lines are blurred. Most people are a vast blend of many races which is clearly demonstrated by DNA testing. Notwithstanding this, race has been simplified by the media and politicians into two groups, white and everyone else. Only the whites are ever accused of being racists. The problem with the concept of racism is that it can be used effectively to explain the cause of any action or behavior unacceptable to the person in question. If a person is fired, reprimanded, passed over for promotion etc. because of incompetence or other valid reasons, the door is opened for an accusation of racism. There is no defense and the term is widely abused. Individuals and businesses are petrified of lawsuits and therefore reluctant to take actions which would be normal and reasonable. Race has become a tool of the left to create division and anger in order to polarize the electorate.

The popular definition of a racist is someone who believes one group of people is "superior" to another. We must then define superior. Better football players? More honest? Stronger? Taller? Smarter? The measures are endless. Nobody really thinks how the term should be applied, it is accepted as vague. It is time for the term racist to be expunged from the English vocabulary, its use benefits no-one. Nor should race be a question on any survey or application. It is not a qualification or disqualification for anything.

Not surprisingly, if asked to define the term racist, many different answers would emerge. Most people would agree that everyone is unique and has differences other than skin color. Each race has evolved over the millennia in its own environment and has developed traits which allowed it to survive. These are instinctive and cannot be rapidly changed by change of environment, education etc. There are also very wide variations between individuals and groups within each race. Strangely, blacks are all considered as one group although Africa has innumerable different tribes with very different cultures just like any other continental group. Then there are innumerable mixtures of races. Barack Obama is considered black, but genetically he is no more black than white. All creatures learn to judge other creatures by their behavior, which is vital for survival. However, by necessity they judge by group behavior, not individual behavior. If 90% of pit bull dogs are vicious, people are wary of all pit-bulls although this may be unfair to certain good-natured animals. They are not wary of pit bulls because of their brown fur. They are wary because they bite. Once bitten, twice shy.

The media frequently quote statistics implying a certain group is being mistreated because of race. This is nonsense in today's society. By this philosophy every group should conform to the national census figures, for example only 13% of football players should be black and 64% of airline pilots should be white. Different races have different talents. If 80% of football players are black and 95% of airline pilots are white this means that blacks are better players than whites and whites make the best pilots. We are told a disproportionate percentage of black make up our prison populations. People do not commit crimes with statistics in mind.

The statistics show the facts. If a the percentage of blacks in prisons is greater than their percentage of the population this simply means as a group blacks commit crimes at a higher rate per capita than others.

Distinction between groups of humans is not only about race. Groups disagree and fight one another over very minor issues even when all are of the same race. The Hutus fight the Tutsis in Rwanda. The Shiites fight the Sunni in the Middle East. The North fought the South in the Civil War. Humans somehow always find reasons to disagree and persecute one another.

It can be argued that judging individuals by group standards in inherently wrong and unfair, and this is true. Reality, however, is that this is the instinctive rationale simply because one cannot predetermine if an individual will behave differently than the majority of that group. Profiling is instinctive. Numbers also play a part. If one stranger enters a group he is likely to conform to its standards and behavior. Once a large number accumulate, they are likely to revert to their traditional customs and in fact try to convert their hosts to these customs.

Martin Luther King is remembered for his "I have a dream" speech on the Washington mall in which he declared he dreamed of the day "when a man would be judged not by the color of his skin but by the content of his character." In fact his dream has always been true, that is exactly how groups are judged. The skin color or other distinguishing feature merely identifies a person as a member of that group. If the majority of the group behaves in a certain way, all members are presumed to behave this way. The USA has attempted to legislate for basic behavior and this is impossible. A fair society should have no laws involving race, just as the First Amendment prohibits any law affecting religion. Perhaps the First Amendment should be expanded to include race. Affirmative action, racial quotas, special dispensations for college entrance, jobs promotions or positions are all attempts at social engineering in which the government has no business. People will judge for themselves and this is one liberty that cannot be infringed upon. It is inherently wrong and immoral for the government to legislate different treatment for certain groups regardless whether it is to their advantage or disadvantage. The common language of the USA has always been English and there is no justification for the government to favor certain groups by making official business available in Spanish or any other language at taxpayer expense.

People judge one another by innumerable criteria, race is only one of them. Height, weight, build, facial features, accent, talking and walking speed, posture, clothing, behavior, intellect etc. are all instinctively taken into account and determine the way people interact with one another. Sometimes the initial judgment is proved incorrect by subsequent experience. In the end all humans are subject to the judgment others end up giving them. Very few are capable of judging themselves as others see them.

The "blacks" have become a special group eligible for special privileges. The justification is that their ancestors were mistreated and the current generation is entitled to redress. They comprise approximately 13% of the population but garner disproportionate attention. Special advantageous treatment was initiated by the whites during the civil rights era and over time blacks have come to expect it as their permanent right. It has indeed had the desired effect of eliminating the discriminatory Jim Crow laws and given blacks equal access and acceptance in society, which all citizens should be entitled to. The perpetuation of these special privileges however has not been beneficial to anyone. In a free and "equal" society no group of able bodied citizens should receive special treatment, positive or negative. The blacks cannot have it both ways. If they consider themselves "equal" then they cannot expect any advantageous treatment.

The whole concept of a free and fair society is tied to making laws which benefit the majority without disadvantaging minorities. This is a delicate balancing act, but when there is doubt, it is the majority that must prevail. This concept has now been convoluted to the point that the majority must dance to the tunes of the minorities. The general electorate is reluctant to object for fear of being branded racist, homophobic, etc. 90% of the population is probably affected by the actions of the 10% who are championed by the media and wish to impose their views and customs on everyone else. It seems that the majority is supposed to be very sensitive to offending the delicate feelings of the minorities without feeling offended themselves when their customs are curtailed. The basic premise of democracy is that the will of the majority should prevail. The Bill of Rights protects everyone from abuse by the government. There is nothing in the Constitution to protect hurt feelings. Therefore if more than 50% of the population supports a policy then the remainder must accept it or seek to change it at the next election.

It is an interesting statistic that according to US Census data, only 5% of precincts which traditionally vote Republican are less than 50% white and about 65% of Republican house seats are in districts which are over 70% white. In contrast, of those districts voting Democrat, 49% are more than 50% minority. It was the Democrats who championed slavery, spawned the Klu Klux Klan, resisted reconstruction and instituted the Jim Crow laws. The Republicans ended slavery, passed the 13th, 14th and 15th amendments and initiated the civil-rights movement under Dwight Eisenhower. It is therefore surprising that the vast majority of blacks support the Democrat party. It can be said that the Democrat party is indeed the choice of minorities and as the minority population increases more rapidly than the white population, unless the whites unite in opposition, the country will eventually be controlled by those making up current minorities. While on the surface there may appear to be no downside to this, Americans must consider if they want to be ruled by politicians who do not share their culture or heritage. This is not very different from losing a war and being occupied by a foreign power.

The 2020 civil unrest has highlighted the degree to which race has been exploited. The Covid 19 epidemic and resulting lockdown caused huge unemployment, meaning many citizens had nothing to do. The prolonged restraining tactics of one white police officer which caused the death of an unarmed black man in Minneapolis ignited a firestorm of emotion and indignation which was rapidly exploited by subversive groups in the name of racism. The idle public took the bait and went on the streets, disrupting traffic, burning looting and destroying. The old cries of systemic racism within police departments were chanted. It is not coincidental that both the virus and the unrest were hugely beneficial to the Democrat party and its members exploited the unfortunate situation in the hopes of deposing Trump.

The police have been placed in an untenable position. If they do their jobs as trained they risk accusations of racism and may face criminal prosecution. No-one appears to state the obvious that firstly one should not break the law and secondly, when caught breaking the law one should obey the police and refrain from resisting arrest. It should be made clear that resisting arrest, accosting police or threatening them in any way could result in dire consequences including death. As previously mentioned, statics show that blacks are arrested at a far higher rate than other races when taken as a percentage of their respective populations. This not due to racism but simply the fact that blacks commit more crimes than others on a per capita basis. There are many reasons for this but the most obvious is the breakdown in the black family and resultant number of young blacks raised by their mothers in poverty. Only the blacks themselves can remedy this.

It is not coincidence that certain countries have contributed much to science, technology, medicine and art and others have contributed little. Just examining the Nobel prizes gives some insight. The USA has 349 recipients, United Kingdom 316, Russia 27, China 8, Argentina 5 and Brazil none. Progress is dependent on both the culture of the population and the type of government they choose for themselves. The USA has the lion's share principally because its culture and government promote innovation and many innovators immigrate there to take advantage of these. Regrettably, increasing regulation and litigation have caused much of the manufacturing to move to more hospitable countries. Most of the jobs derived from innovation are in manufacturing.

There are also the concepts of liberal and conservative when describing political philosophy. In broad terms, the liberal is idealistic and believes that all humans are wonderful and well-intentioned but ironically they believe in big government and very progressive taxation to fund a host of social programs which implies that most people are too lazy or stupid to look after themselves. The conservative believes in reality, personal responsibility, high moral standards, minimal government regulation and low taxation. In recent history, starting with the French Revolution, the worst atrocities visited upon mankind have begun with liberal agendas. In the USA, a number of the modern liberal presidents have been hypocrites with low moral standards who enriched themselves via politics, cheated on their wives and lied frequently to the electorate.

Liberals preach freedom but they are the ones who promote government intervention which restricts freedom. It is liberals who object to prayer in schools, national ID cards, red-light cameras etc. in the name of freedom. The ALCU has been the force behind many laws which we do not need and obstructing laws that are beneficial.

Since the evolution of homo sapiens, human beings have struggled to behave themselves reasonably. It is easy to imagine how wonderful the world could be if every one of us was honest, kind, compassionate, generous, industrious etc. Songwriters over the ages have composed lyrics to this effect and it is indeed a commendable dream. Sadly, it will never happen. For this reason humans need management of one kind or another and over the millennia they have tried just about every form of it. A large part of the problem is selfishness and lack of consideration for others. A tragic result is broken families, poverty and perpetuation of the problem. The secularization of the population has contributed to the breakdown in basic morals and norms.

From the days of the cavemen two forces were recognized. The first, a terrestrial and visible leader whose job it was to manage the behavior of those within his sphere of influence. This leader was simply the strongest and/or smartest in the group and he controlled by force or common acclaim. His management could be good, bad or mediocre. The second was a spiritual force or belief which exercised invisible control and served to explain phenomena which were otherwise inexplicable. Often the terrestrial leader invoked the authority of the spiritual force to control his subjects.

Some form of religion has always played a part in human behavior. It seems that mankind needs to worship something. The danger is that it will be another human. The classic religions preach a set of rules which promote honesty, decency, compassion and respect. The USA was founded by Christians who used the Judeo/Christian laws revealed by Moses in the Ten Commandments. Other religions have similar laws. Historically government and religion have been closely intertwined but the instances of excess and abuse led the Founding Fathers to wisely prohibit the Federal government from passing any laws with respect to religion, but they had no intention of abandoning it. It was accepted that in the family circle, in schools and indeed in government and business, adherence to religious principles promoted a healthy and successful citizenry. The breakdown in the family unit, the high divorce rate and the dismal academic performance of American public school students today can all be attributed in large part to the abandonment of traditional values.

The Ten Commandments constitute a set of logical rules which were developed over the centuries to promote a code of behavior likely to permit humans to live together in harmony. Regardless of religious beliefs or lack thereof, these rules can be defended as reasonable. Throughout the ages, however, both the religious leaders and the adherents have preached but not practiced them. Indeed, the Bible, the Koran and other religious teachings have been misinterpreted and misconstrued to suit the desires of individuals. Religion, or a code of behavior, should never be promulgated by force, it should expand by example and common sense. Alas, almost all religions have had periods in their histories in which powerful leaders have promoted war and condoned atrocities. It is still occurring today. It is the human character that desires to force its will upon others. However, religions certainly play a part in building solid communities with decent codes of behavior. It should not be forgotten that the first thing socialist and communist governments do when they seize power is attempt to stamp out religion. A secular society is far easier to corrupt and control.

Throughout history there have been dissatisfied subjects with and without justification. The vast majority of humans are reasonably content if they have adequate food and water, some form of shelter from the elements and can live without constant fear of bodily harm. However, even if these basic needs are satisfied, human nature leads all of us to make comparisons and if we perceive that others are in a more favorable position than ourselves, we become jealous. There is no cure for jealousy.

The other human failing is the inability to handle power responsibly. Almost every human seeks power over other creatures, human and animal. For the average person this does not extend beyond immediate family, pets and livestock, but for those in positions to dictate to larger numbers of people the temptation to abuse this power is usually irresistible. There is no cure for this either.

In the management of their lives, humans have always been divided into two groups, the rulers and the subjugated. Normally the rulers were a minute percentage and their primary objectives have been their own welfares. The moment they realized that they could profit from the labors of others the temptation to exploit their positions became irresistible. The subjugated masses remained in poverty. In instances when the rulers abused their subjects to a point that death was preferable to their existence under those conditions, revolutions occurred which started the cycle again.

Society at the time the Constitution was written was very different from today, both in philosophy and composition. Until the advances in science and medicine in the last century, nature weeded out the feeble of mind and body via starvation, disease and war. This is no longer the case and the general population on average is now weaker, less intelligent and older. In the USA this is particularly evident due to excellent medical care and the welfare system. In 1776 the voting population was predominantly homogeneous and Christian. Today it is diverse in all respects and what appeals to some offends others.

In the late 18th century most of the population lived off the land. Farmers must work hard and plan well ahead. They also tend to be independent and largely self-sufficient. The franchise was limited and voters were men of means who had accomplished something in life. They were not naive and voted for candidates whom they believed were competent to make and execute laws which were necessary and just. Although newspapers and other printed matter played a part in elections they did not have the insidious influence the media has today.

CHAPTER 3: THE CONSTITUTION

In 1765 Britain imposed the Stamp Act on the Colonies in order to raise money to pay for governors and judges. This met with strong resistance and was followed by the Townshend Acts in 1767 and 1768. These imposed tariffs on commodities not readily available in the Colonies with the objectives of raising revenue. Not surprisingly these acts were met with outrage, including the burning of the English ship Gaspee in 1772 because the colonists had no representation in the English parliament. Following this, all tariffs except those on tea were repealed. This tariff was retained to make it clear that Britain had the right to tax the Colonies as laid out in the Declaratory Act of 1766. By then, however, conditions in the thirteen English colonies of the New World had reached a point where the majority of leaders and the general population believed that they were being abused by the English king George the third. The imposition of the Tea Act in May 1773, which re-enforced the tax on imported tea, was the final straw. This act was seen to contravene their colonial rights to local control of tax issues, and the cry rose throughout the colonies of "no taxation without representation". Matters came to a head in December 1773 when a shipment of tea was dumped into the Boston harbor in what became known as the Boston Tea Party. The English responded by closing the port of Boston and revoking the self-governing status of Massachusetts. This incensed all thirteen colonies and in order to co-ordinate resistance they formed the Continental

Congress which convened its first meeting in Philadelphia in September 1774. They resolved to take the situation into their own hands and effectively took control from the royal governors. Britain responded by using its regular army in Massachusetts to confront the state militia and fighting broke out in April 1775, starting the Revolutionary War. In July 1776 the Continental Congress formally declared an independent Republic of United States free from any English control. This involved a carefully worded document primarily drafted by Thomas Jefferson and subsequently edited and approved by the 56 members of the Continental Congress. The single page, hand-written document was simply titled "The Unanimous Declaration of the thirteen united States of America".

The Revolutionary War was fought at great risk and expense to rid the country of English control. George Washington was unanimously elected to lead the military campaign. He commanded a ragged army of state militias and federal troops, poorly trained and equipped with scant financial support from the new federal government. After a series of losses and great hardship, with the aid of the French fleet, English general Cornwallis was defeated at Yorktown in October 1781. George 3rd had become weary of this expensive and protracted conflict and agreed to peace terms, culminating in the Treaty of Paris signed in September 1783.

After the war had ended, the government of newly formed United States of America drafted a very good Constitution which was ratified by all the states between December 1787 and January 1791. Arriving at a document which satisfied the varying demands of thirteen diverse independent states was no easy task. It came down to north versus south, with the institution of slavery being a major stumbling block. The southerners also envisaged a predominantly rural economy whereas northerners favored more industrialization. As with all such documents, compromises were made which paved the way for further conflict at some time in the future. There was understandable concern that the new government would eventually evolve into another version of the English domination with the president declaring himself king and therefore great care was taken to structure a constitution with safeguards to prevent the Federal government from ever becoming massive and intrusive and abusing its citizens again. The Framers worded it as carefully as possible, but over the years it has been misconstrued and manipulated to the point that the Federal government has incurred a huge national debt which continues to rise and it has weaseled its way into almost every aspect of Americans' lives. Some kind of control and tax has been applied to almost every aspect of personal and commercial life. The Constitution has been studied and interpreted by thousands of scholars and over the years it has been amended twenty seven times. It is time to take a candid look at our present situation and see how far we have strayed from the safeguards the Founders wisely incorporated. Predictably, over the years, scholars and judges have sought to read the document according to their predetermined philosophies and desires and have construed the words to conform to these.

Constitutions are a set of rules addressing basic human behavior. This is primarily to control the actions of the politicians, not the average citizen. They are drafted based not on topical circumstances but on the psychology of the human mind. Whereas fashions and fads come and go, basic human behavior for any group changes little over the ages. The ancient Greeks had to deal with the same problems that exist today. For this reason a good constitution should not be amended constantly according to advances in technology, fashion or popular thinking. The normal legislative process takes care of these. Right and wrong do not change. However, where there is lack of clarity or potential for abuse, changes are necessary.

The Constitution is a few pages of paper. The rules and regulations stipulated therein can be strictly followed, somewhat followed or completely ignored. It is no better than the extent to which it is adhered. All three branches of government are responsible for adhering to the Constitution which they swore in their oaths of office to uphold. All three are guilty of ignoring or manipulating the words to suit their own agendas. The Framers intended the Supreme Court to be the last level of protection but even this has failed.

The Declaration of Independence set the stage for the Constitution. Jefferson drew heavily on the concepts promulgated by the 17th century English philosopher John Locke. Locke, and others before him, believed that humans were all endowed with a basic understanding of right and wrong which some called natural law. Jefferson used this concept to convey that every human was created equal in this sense and in an ideal world had equal unalienable rights.

"We hold these truths to be self-evident, that all men are created equal, that they are endowed by their Creator with certain unalienable Rights, that among these are Life, Liberty and the pursuit of Happiness".

This implies that these rights come from God and not man. This may be so, but He has left it to man to recognize them, which man has done a very poor job of. Of course rights involve more than one person and one man's right is another man's obligation. This requires that both parties recognize the pact and laws try to ensure this. On the other hand, the laws of necessity must be recognized. If a man is being attacked, he must have the right to defend himself even if this results in the death of his attacker and even though his conscience and law prohibit killing. In fact there is nothing in the Constitution guaranteeing the rights to Life, Liberty and the Pursuit of Happiness.

It is indeed idealistic to believe that all humans are born with an equal sense of justice. Humans, like all creatures, are programmed for survival. This can be attributed to God or to evolution or both but survival rules behavior regardless of natural law. A starving man will steal food to survive and kill to defend himself. Primitive societies living a subsistence life care far less about the niceties of etiquette than civilized societies. Instinct is strong and cannot be easily or rapidly changed. In addition to these traits, the sad truth is that certain humans under certain conditions are prone to inflict the most horrendous atrocities upon those within their power, be it their own people or their enemies. The Framers of the Constitution realized this.

Most of the prominent citizens involved in drafting a new constitution were educated men of English descent. They now had a unique opportunity to devise a system of government for themselves and create a set of laws and checks and balances so that American citizens could pursue their dreams with minimal restrictions whilst treating their fellow citizens with consideration and respect.

Although some of the men involved had legal expertise, this was not the primary requirement. What they most needed was a profound and candid knowledge of human behavior and history. They had to examine themselves and take into account the lessons of history and their own experiences with other men to fully understand all the possible ways that power can be abused. They then used their legal talents to compose a system of government and a set of laws and procedures to explicitly and unequivocally cover all these potential hazards.

At the heart of this endeavor was the need to understand the workings of the human brain. Psychologists have analyzed human behavior extensively, but it is interesting to compare the brain to a modern computer. A computer has hardware which dictates its capability for processing information. Depending on this it can process faster or slower and can store more or less information. This hardware requires a basic set of instructions which directs it to do certain things when given specific inputs. This is the operating system or software, and different suppliers such as Microsoft and Apple use different systems. Once the hardware and operating systems have been defined, the computer will behave in a consistent way dependent on the input of the operator. Like the computer, the brain has evolved according to necessity and continues to evolve. Computers have proliferated to accomplish many different tasks in business, aviation, industry etc. Humans born in different regions of the world also refined both their "hardware" and "software" over millennia in order to survive. Once born with certain hardware and software, the only things a human can change are the operator inputs. This means that the same input to two different humans will not necessarily produce the same output. Each human is unique but groups of humans taken collectively display certain similarities both in physical appearance and behavior. Based on their personal experiences and the study of history, including religion, the Framers had to work out a system of government which could both take into account behavior of different groups and ensure harmony and progress. However, at the time, the white population of the country was reasonably homogeneous, being mainly from the British Isles and North Western Europe. It was predominantly Christian and as a group, had much in common. This situation has changed dramatically and the current government must address the problems and needs created by a population with very diverse attributes and philosophies.

A prerequisite of the Constitution was the desire to preserve the independence of each state whilst giving a central authority the powers to deal with matters that affected all the states jointly. There was strong opposition to any system which included the means to create a monarchy or any other inherited or privileged positions and titles. The states were intended to remain de facto separate countries in all but certain areas of common interest clearly defined in the Constitution. This was a good strategy and served the country well until Federal politicians found ways to abuse it. Both the Federal government and state governments (Article IV, section 4) were set up as republics, meaning that the head of state was elected directly or indirectly. The Founders wanted no more kings or emperors.

The Founders understood that in order to avoid the abuse of power by their own government, they would need to devise a system with checks and balances so that no one person or small group could ever seize control. They worked very hard on this and gave it a great deal of thought, drawing from history and their candid assessment of the human mind, recognizing all its talents, desires and failings. They came up with a very good document, somewhat similar to the British Magna Carta, and this became the initial Constitution. Not surprisingly, the various states had issues with certain clauses and ratification was protracted. At the heart of the controversies were the philosophical differences in culture between northern and southern states. The north promoted progress in commerce, industry and finance and generally opposed slavery whereas the south envisioned a rural, agrarian nation where slaves were indispensable. In order to explain and extol the document, Alexander Hamilton, James Madison and John Jay took it upon themselves to publish a series of "papers" in the New York press under the pseudonym Publius. These became known as the Federalist Papers and played an important part in the ratification process. On June 1st 1788 the required quorum of nine states had ratified the Constitution and after another two followed the formation of the Federal Government commenced.

The first Congress, comprised of 26 senators and 65 congressmen, after much deliberation, wisely added the first ten amendments known as The Bill of Rights in

December 1791. These addressed the various freedoms which were to be preserved by the Federal government in every state.

Contrary to common belief, the Constitution guarantees only a few rights to individual citizens. These are the Writ of Habeas Corpus, due process, freedom of religion, speech and assembly, to bear arms, freedom from unreasonable search and seizure, citizenship, to vote and equal protection under the law. Everything else is left to each state to decide as long as the aforementioned rights are not abridged.

Aside from the English and European population, the founders also had to deal with Africans and the indigenous groups. Recognizing all the differences and the possible behaviors was not an easy task but they did the best they could. In an effort to avert most of the social and political problems experienced by traditional forms of government they set out to design a system which would give the new country a decent chance of preserving liberty for its citizens while also creating prosperity. They therefore drafted the Constitution to formalize the conditions under which the government would be elected and could operate.

It must be understood that the free peoples of the thirteen original colonies had developed very different ideas on many issues. The northern colonies had few blacks but many religious sects. They had harsh winters to plan for and deal with. The southern colonies were mainly English protestant, relied on black slaves for farm labor and had very hot and humid summers and mild winters. These differences and others led to different lifestyles and core values. In drafting the Constitution, compromises had to be made between northern and southern states, one of which was the system of the Electoral College for selection of the president and vice-president. The slave states maintained that slaves were not citizens and therefore could not vote. Nevertheless they persuaded the northern states that in calculating the number of representatives each state could send to Congress, that each slave should be counted as 3/5 of a person, a bizarre formula to say the least. This meant that in real terms, the southern states would have a disproportionate number of congressmen compared to voters. This also gave them a disproportionate number of electors. By design, the combination gave the South a distinct advantage. This was a compromise between north and south in order to form the union.

Each state desired its own independence in all respects except for those which affected the Republic as a whole. Each had been founded and settled by groups with different ideas and social priorities and wanted to preserve these. The states were not even necessarily aligned on many issues but they realized that if they were to maintain their independence and protect themselves in the future that they had to combine forces. They were very concerned about the dangers of a powerful central government which could restrict their freedoms, tax them unfairly and in effect land them back in exactly the same predicament they had just escaped from. On the other hand, they chose to give the Federal government certain powers to enforce the freedoms granted by the Constitution to preclude the possibility of state governments abusing their powers. This proved to be controversial because it effectively empowered the central government to control the internal functions of each state to a certain degree, beyond the necessary common interests of defense and trade.

The Constitution and Bill of Rights were deliberately drafted to be short, clear and simple. To protect the independence of each state, the Federal Government was constrained to a very narrow range of powers. These were deemed essential for the common good of all the states. The 10th amendment makes clear that

"The powers not delegated to the United States by the Constitution, nor prohibited by it to the States, are reserved to the States respectively, or to the people".

This is one of the most important clauses in the Constitution because it constitutionally limits the power of the Federal Government to interfere in the internal affairs of each state beyond those authorized by the Constitution. The Founders recognized that each state should be administered according to the voters' choices in that state and that this could create different cultures for each. Citizens would be free to move between states in order to accommodate their preferences and each state could learn from the successes and failures of the others.

There are those who believe that due to the passage of time the Constitution should be amended to reflect modern conditions. In fact the basic principles enshrined in the document have not changed at all. The words used in the Constitution were carefully chosen and the Supreme Court should not be at liberty to rule for broader interpretation. A good legal document is normally written explicitly to be precise and unambiguous and for the most part, the Constitution meets these requirements. It is written in simple English, readily understandable to anyone proficient in the language. It was never intended to be "interpreted" by various Supreme Court justices. It means what it says and the justices' responsibilities are merely to decide whether the cases under consideration meet its requirements or not. The only case for intervention is where there is a lack of clarity, as in the General Welfare clause of Article I, Section 8 or a definite need for solutions to specific problems.

The Constitution was very well designed to allocate only certain defined powers to each branch of the Federal government and to ensure effective input from responsible citizens. In the Federalist Papers, Federalist 45 discusses the relationship between the Federal and State governments. James Madison wrote:

"The powers delegated by the proposed Constitution to the federal government, are few and defined. Those which are to remain in the State governments are numerous and indefinite. The former will be exercised principally on external objects, as war, peace, negotiation, and foreign commerce; with which last the power of taxation will, for the most part, be connected. The powers reserved to the several States will extend to all the objects which, in the ordinary course of affairs, concern the lives, liberties, and properties of the people, and the internal order, improvement, and prosperity of the State."

Federal taxes were intended to mainly fund the areas as Madison described. This is precisely why the Constitution defines the limited powers of the Federal government. The great flaw in the scheme was allocating to the Federal Supreme Court the power to decide exactly what the language of the Constitution meant.

Article 1, section 1 of the Constitution makes it clear that **all** legislative powers

"shall be vested in a congress of the United States, which shall consist of a Senate and House of Representatives."

Sections 2-7 deal with the elections and procedures of Congress. The House of Representatives was to be elected directly based on the population of each state.

The election process was left to the states to decide but Congress retained the right to intervene. The Senate was to be elected by the state legislators. To give balance to the states with small populations, two senators were to be elected for each state regardless of population. These two bodies together formed the Congress and had sole power to make laws and allocate federal funds.

Sections 8-10 define most of the powers allocated to Congress. It is instructive to read these powers carefully and then compare the reach of today's Federal Government into the affairs of each state. Nowhere in the Constitution is Congress empowered to involve itself in health, education, abortion, emergency relief, charitable donations of taxpayer money, welfare, retirement, foreign aid or any other issue not clearly authorized.

The first part of Section 9 was included at the insistence of the southern states and reluctantly accepted by the north. This effectively gave protection to slavery for 20 years. This clause prohibited the Federal government from passing any law to prohibit the importation of "persons" until 1808. In preparation for ending importation, in 1794 Congress passed the Slave Trade Act which prohibited outfitting and constructing ships for the slave trade. In his 1806 annual address President Jefferson denounced the slave trade as a violation of human rights and in 1807 Congress passed an act prohibiting the import of slaves, to take effect in 1808 to abide by the Constitution. The southern states were aware that the northern states in general did not condone the practice and so to avoid conflict the subject of owning slaves was simply never raised in the original Constitution. It is indeed quite astounding that educated Englishmen ever condoned the practice. No decent human being should feel at peace whilst considering another as his property and treating him or her as an animal. In the slaveholders' minds however, blacks and native Indians were wild savages and therefore not due the normal consideration due to "men". The slave period will remain a sad blemish on the otherwise impressive history of the USA. Probably nobody felt good but Southerners closed their consciences because they were dependent upon slave labor and without it they could not work the large farms they had acquired.

The separation of powers was important to ensure that no one branch could dominate. The price for this was potential gridlock whereby any one branch had the capability of thwarting the desires of the other two. This indeed frequently occurs and either nothing is done or a compromise is reached which pleases nobody. Presidents are judged by their accomplishments in office but this is not necessarily fair. Some presidents have a Congress of their own party and can get things done. Others have most of their initiatives blocked by Congress. The lucky ones have a Congress which advances the correct agenda and all the President has to do is give his signature and get the credit.

Article II defines the rules for election of the President and Vice-president and enumerates their powers and responsibilities. The President and Vice-president were to be elected indirectly via a body of electors designated by each state equal to the number of senators and congressmen allotted to that state. The manner in which these electors were to be chosen was left to the legislatures of each state. The votes of the electors of all the states were combined and the person receiving the most votes became President. The Vice-president was the person who received the second most votes, regardless of party. The rationale behind the Electoral College system was that the Framers of the constitution believed that the members of Congress could not be trusted to elect the best men for these positions by adopting the English parliamentary system. They felt that a group of men sitting together frequently would be subject to subterfuge amongst themselves and appoint men who suited their own agendas rather than the public good. The Electoral College was a group equal in number to Congress who never sat together and therefore, theoretically could not collude. In practice it is a clumsy and flawed system which should be eliminated. 10 presidents have won election with less than 50% of the popular vote. In the cases of Lincoln, Wilson, Nixon and Clinton, the percentage was closer to 40.

The original text reads:
"Each State shall appoint, in the Manner the Legislature thereof may direct, a Number of Electors

*equal to the whole Number of Senators and
Representatives to which the State may be entitled in the
congress: but no Senator or Representative or Person
holding an Office of Trust or Profit under the United
States, shall be appointed an Elector"*.

The Electoral College system has been the subject of
considerable debate.
Constitutionally there is no requirement that citizens get
involved in the election of the president and vice-
president. The state legislatures are empowered to
appoint the electors and, once chosen, each elector is
free to vote as he pleases. In practice, today citizens in
each state vote for a ticket of president and vice
president and except for Maine and Nebraska, the pair
that receives the most votes receives all the votes of the
electors of that state. Sets of electors are chosen by
each party and are expected to vote for that party's
candidates if it receives the majority of votes. 26 states
have laws requiring the electors to vote for their party's
candidates and in theory, electors of the other states
may vote as they please but seldom deviate from party
lines. Two states, Maine and Nebraska, do not have a
winner-take-all system and allocate electors according
to the vote in each congressional district except for the
two senatorial electors who are chosen by the state as a
whole. This would seem to be a more rational system
whereby each district rather than each state chooses its
president. This means each elector has a duty to vote the
will of his precinct which would result in a much more
balanced electoral college. Historically the rural

districts tend to vote conservative and the big cities liberal. This is because big city dwellers receive the bulk of government welfare. Except for Maine and Nebraska, in reality each state votes for the presidential ticket but the number of electors in each gives highly populated states far more influence than sparsely populated states. This is mitigated to some extent because every state has two senators so that in states with small populations the number of residents per elector is lower than in highly populated states. The two extremes are demonstrated by Wyoming with about 200,000 citizens per elector and California with about 700,000 citizens per elector. This means a voter in Wyoming has more influence than a voter in California, which is inherently wrong. In practice, unless it is a very close election, this has little impact because Wyoming only has 3 electors. In states with one or more very large cities, which traditionally vote democrat, the city vote overrides the votes of the rest of the state.

This is a flawed system but the alternatives all have detractions too. The Founders did not predict that the country would divide itself into just two parties and therefore did not deal with party politics in the Constitution. The party system has rendered the Founders' intentions regarding the electoral college futile. Electors were supposed to independently vote their best choices for the country, not the party. As long as only two parties exist, it can be argued that a popular vote would be a better system, notwithstanding the fact that most voters do not necessarily vote rationally. When more than two parties get involved this system has major problems as can be seen in countries where this exists and coalitions must be formed to govern. A short lived coalition between the Nazi party and the German National People's Party put Adolf Hitler in power in 1933.

The President is responsible for executing the laws enacted by Congress and is the Commander in Chief of the armed forces. He also has the power to appoint ambassadors, ministers and judges to the Supreme Court. The President does not have the power to make or change laws. Beginning with George Washington however, presidents have by-passed Congress by issuing Executive Orders. In fact there is nothing in the Constitution specifically authorizing this authority, it has been assumed by broadly interpreting the language of Article II, Section 1, clause 1 which states

"The executive Power shall be vested in a president of the United States of America."

At first it was used mainly for the President to define how a law passed by Congress was to be interpreted and enforced but it gradually evolved into de facto law-making by the President. This has become necessary due to the frequent gridlock in Congress along strict party lines and the inability of Congress to do its job and get necessary legislation passed. The fault lies in the system, whereby congressmen and senators no longer vote according to their personal convictions but simply as the party dictates. The party line is directed at gaining or maintaining power and the needs of the country play little part. Executive orders are subject to review by the Supreme Court and from time to time they are struck down as unconstitutional. However, this very much depends on the composition and zeal of the court and modern presidents have effectively used them to make and change laws and to fail to enforce laws which their oath of office required them to enforce.

Constitutionally the President has limited powers but practically he is the leader of the nation and must be chosen carefully. Aside from being a person of demonstrated integrity and with proven leadership qualities, he must be wise. He must appoint his cabinet ministers based not on friendship or the size of political contributions but on their records and experiences in appropriate positions in each field. Presidential decisions must be based on complete and accurate information from ministers and advisors. A CEO is no better than those around him and the President is no different. The framers did not stipulate any qualifications for the office of president other than born in the USA and age. Over the years the voters have elected presidents across the spectrum from generals with proven leadership qualities to those who had not been in charge of anything. Any other institution or business would require certain credentials before being eligible for the top position and the lack of this for the highest office in the land has proved to be problematic.

Article III sets out the procedures for the Supreme Court and its powers and responsibilities. The Supreme Court was to be the highest court in the land, with judicial powers similar to those of the English House of Lords. Its members were to be nominated by the President and confirmed by the Senate. Members could hold their positions for life and were supposed to be independent of party or other influences. They were to pass their judgment based solely on the academic interpretation of the law and the provisions of the Constitution. The number of justices was to be decided by Congress. The original number was six, which automatically gave at least a two-thirds majority. This was expanded to ten at one point to account for the growing number of judicial circuits and eventually was reduced to the nine who sit today by the Circuit Judges Act in 1869.

Regrettably, the Framers did not devote a great deal of time to the composition, procedures and precise duties of the Supreme Court. It seems that they saw it as the least-complicated and least influential branch of government which would only rarely be called into action. In fact very early in the life of the new nation this court became involved during the nullification disputes and this set the stage for its disproportionate power ever since. The Founders did not provide any safeguards to counteract a rogue Supreme Court. The only mechanism in place to remove a justice once appointed is impeachment by the House.   This can only be invoked for "misbehavior" not for misjudgment. No justice has ever been impeached.

The Supreme Court justices were intended to be the custodians of the Constitution. Collectively they are responsible for ensuring that Congress can make no law which deviates from the terms and rights specified in the Constitution. The language in the Constitution is not open to interpretation, it is in clear English. For circumstances not envisioned by the original framers there is a clear procedure to amend the Constitution. The body was to also serve as the court of final appeal in criminal and civil cases. In practice it has made rulings far beyond its authority and has accorded itself dictatorial powers. The Founders intended it to have purely academic duties, comparable to a panel of scientists evaluating a scientific issue. Over time the court has made rulings which the other two branches of government have been impotent to repeal and which the general public strongly opposed. The public can boot the President and congressmen from office by the electoral process but no-one can remove a justice except by impeachment. It can be said that the Supreme Court as it has evolved is the greatest threat to freedom and democracy. Ironically the Court has become partisan and used the Constitution to thwart its intended protections, common sense and will of the majority. Presidents come and go but justices remain for life. The greatest impact a president may have is his selection of justices during his term.

The entire Federal Justice Department has expanded far beyond what was intended by the Constitution. Originally there were only three crimes which justified federal involvement, treason, counterfeiting and piracy. Today the list is unending and federal judges can overrule state judges' decisions in certain cases. Big businesses are held hostage to a confusing and lengthy list of laws and regulations and the cost of litigation has soared to the point that in many instances when these businesses are challenged by the Justice Department for some real or unproven infraction, they find it preferable to pay huge fines rather than spend years and millions of dollars in court. The details of these settlements are not made public and billions of dollars flow to state and federal coffers without any transparency. In some cases fines are justified but in many it is simply a case of government extortion. There should be no question of corporate guilt, corporations are inanimate and incapable of breaking laws. If laws have been broken then those officers in charge of the corporation should be held liable as individuals.

The Founders were well aware that a direct democracy would be a disaster and therefore they examined the different systems that had been practiced by various governments since the Greeks first gave their citizens a vote. They absolutely did not want a monarchy as they had seen how England's king had broad powers to abuse the system. They decided upon a representative democracy in a layered structure but which differed from the English parliamentary system in that the

President and Vice president were effectively elected by the voters via the Electoral College and the President was free to appoint his cabinet, ambassadors and Supreme Court judges "*by and with the Advice and Consent of the Senate*" from private citizens of his choosing.

.

As intended, this was a pretty good system, taking into account almost all the shortfalls of the human character. However, it was not totally bulletproof and before long, ambitious and corrupt men in the Federal government and private sector found ways to twist and distort the language of the Constitution to gradually transfer more and more power to themselves. This was cunningly pursued over a period of time, inch by inch, so that the voting public never quite realized what happening. Often, changes and amendments were presented as beneficial and an increasingly complacent and apathetic public enthusiastically endorsed their own gradual subjugation.

The Founding Fathers knew that it would be dangerous to make elected offices full-time jobs with attractive compensation and benefits. They knew that if they did, the average man would succumb to the temptation to work towards securing his position rather than serving the public good. For this reason, apart from the Supreme Court justices, all offices had a time limit after which re- election would be necessary. To avoid sudden drastic changes, the periods were tiered, two years for the House, four for the President and six for the Senate. However, the number of terms any candidate could serve was not specified. It was assumed that after doing his civic duty, a member would be only too happy to return to his normal life as soon as possible.

It was understood that each elected official would pursue his own full-time career and simply take a few weeks each year to attend a session of Congress. He would get no salary or benefits and would receive only a per-diem allowance to cover expenses for the days spent in Congress. From 1789 to 1815 this per diem was fixed at $6. From then it was gradually increased and in 1855 the system was changed to an annual salary of $3000. This was a big mistake because it gave the means to make politics a profession. This salary was gradually increased until by 1955 it had reached $12,500. From then onwards it increased rapidly and in 2021 it is $174,000. The position has now also become a full-time profession, with expensive staffs, offices, travel expenses etc. A congressman now costs the taxpayer over $1,200,000 per year and a senator $3,300,000 per year in allowances and expenses. They also have other attractive perquisites. The Capitol is now occupied by self-serving representatives who collude with one another to pursue their own agendas for their personal benefits. Their public duty plays no part in their deliberations.

This current system also gives an unfair advantage to incumbents over competitors, not to mention that in order to remain in office, incumbents must start campaigning for the next term at least a year before elections instead of attending to the county's business. For a country $28T in debt there is no justification for huge allowances and perks for Congress. Most executives of major corporations only have staffs of one and members should have no need of more. Once they leave office, presidents can make millions writing books and effectively selling access by means of outrageous speaking fees. These are powerful incentives completely unrelated to the intended goal of service to the country.

The current system is at the root of many of the failures of democracy. If representation in Congress can be seen as a lifelong career with power, money and perquisites it will attract candidates for the wrong reasons. They will not suffer the consequences of their votes. The only reason anyone should present himself for a position in Congress is to serve the country for the good of all. The terms should be limited, the salaries modest and the perquisites eliminated. This will result in only sincere patriots with their own means of support presenting themselves for these positions.

It is indeed instructive to examine the credentials of individuals who present themselves as candidates for the presidency. Most would not be considered for any executive position in the private sector. It is absurd that men and women who have not demonstrated outstanding performances in leadership, accomplishment and impeccable personal behavior should even consider themselves for this office. In fact they can and do and sometimes get elected. We hear from starry-eyed liberals that our system is wonderful because anyone can become president. Sadly this has been proved correct. It should not be so. Only persons who have demonstrated the above qualities and had broad experience in management, finance and world affairs should be eligible.

The system is so entrenched now that even well-intentioned new congressmen and senators are soon indoctrinated to the self-serving philosophy. Nothing gets done by logic, it is all about favors and re-election. It is one of the rare cases where experience is a liability as far as the electorate is concerned. There is very little difference between the Democrat and Republican parties, they both sing from the same hymnbook. They are equally corrupt. In reality the public would be far better served if parties were prohibited and candidates ran on their own platforms and voted according to their own philosophies.

This sad situation is further corrupted by blatant bribery. Businesses and groups of people with special agendas of their own can contribute vast sums of cash in various ways to members of Congress in return for political favors. Congress has coined a more obscure term for this bribery and it is known as lobbying. This term has its origins in the centuries old practice of British citizens wishing to seek favors with members of parliament accosting them in the lobby of the Houses of Parliament. Many members of Congress become lobbyists after their terms expire as this is a far more lucrative and influential position. Furthermore, in order to ingratiate themselves to their constituents, members routinely insert special appropriations into important bills which have absolutely no connection to the bill and benefit only their own states or constituencies. These are known as earmarks. Most members engage in this so there is no objection. We now have an auction system where votes in Congress go to the highest bidder and democracy is a faint illusion. In the 2020 election it is estimated that the Democrat campaign spent $8.4 billion and the Republican campaign $5.3 billion, almost three times the amount spent in 2016. The winners rewarded their major contributors with lucrative public appointments for which they were generally totally unqualified. This is precisely the result the Founding Fathers wished to avoid.

CHAPTER 4: THE TESTS

It did not take long after the formation of the Union for the Constitution to be tested. The major issue was the right of each state to nullify any law passed by Congress which it deemed to be outside the powers granted to Congress by the Constitution. These attempts to preserve the powers intended for the states were frustrated by the fact that Article III, section 2 of the Constitution, states:

"The Judicial power shall extend to <u>all Cases, in Law and Equity</u>, arising under this Constitution, the Laws of the United States..."

This could be construed to give the Federal Supreme Court ultimate authority to be the final arbiter in interpreting the meaning of the Constitution. This broad interpretation effectively gave a small number of unelected judges the power to trump any state law. This was absolutely not what the Framers intended, they merely wanted final judgment on compliance. To further confound the problem, the Constitution did not specify the number of judges who would make these decisions nor what majority would be required when determining the reach of the Constitution. It turned out that there are 9 judges and a simple majority can rule on every case. This effectively means that in certain cases where the court is evenly divided, one unelected judge can make a momentous decision! This is totally in conflict with the principle of democracy and not very different from a dictatorship or supreme monarchy.

In addition to this, Article VI of the Constitution states:

"This Constitution, and the Laws of the United States which shall be made in pursuance thereof; and all treaties made, or which shall be made, under the authority of the United States, <u>shall be the supreme law of the land</u>; and the judges in every state shall be bound thereby, anything in the constitution or laws of any state to the contrary notwithstanding".

This is known as the Supremacy Clause and has been used to justify the right of the Federal government to impose its laws on the states and to nullify state laws.

There is a certain ambiguity to this because any laws made by Congress must be in "pursuance" of the Constitution, which clearly defines the areas in which the Federal government can involve itself. If these limitations have been stretched, as they have been, then the Supremacy Clause extends federal law into areas never intended.

The first test of this flaw came in the Kentucky and Virginia Resolutions of 1798 protesting the Alien and Sedition Acts. Two of the original Framers, Thomas Jefferson and James Madison argued that the states have the right to interpret the Constitution and can declare federal laws unconstitutional when the Federal government exceeds its delegated powers.

"Resolved, that the several States composing the United States of America, are not united on the principle of unlimited submission to their general government; but that by compact under the style and title of a Constitution for the United States and of amendments thereto, they constituted a general government for special purposes, delegated to that government certain definite powers, reserving each State to itself, the residuary mass of right to their own self-government; and that whensoever the general government assumes undelegated powers, its acts are unauthoritative, void, and of no force: That to this compact each State acceded as a State, and is an integral party, its co-States forming, as to itself, the other party....each party has an equal right to judge for itself, as well of infractions as of the mode and measure of redress."

Unfortunately other states did not agree and asserted that only the Federal courts had the power to interpret the Constitution. In 1813 Virginia again challenged the powers of the Supreme Court to override state court decisions regarding constitutionality but was overruled by the Supreme Court, which argued that its powers were clearly defined in Article III of the Constitution. It can be argued that Jefferson and Madison, both involved in the drafting of the document, would never have accepted a document which effectively stripped the states of their sovereign rights. Over the years in fact the Supreme Court has been able to manipulate the words to suit the politics of the day which has resulted in the Federal government acquiring for itself powers never intended.

These rulings effectively eviscerated the original protections for state autonomy which the authors of the Constitution believed they had secured. From then onwards, the door was open for the Federal government and the Supreme Court to force whatever laws or regulations they desired upon the states. Had the Court upheld the intended powers granted under the Constitution many of the future problems would have been avoided.

The rot began fairly soon after the first generation of the Independence era died out. The original voting requirements were based on property ownership and age. The original Constitution did not address voting rights, these were left to each state to decide. The state legislatures believed that to ensure a responsible and involved vote, only those males above the age of twenty one and owning a certain amount of property should be eligible. The rationale was that if a man was not smart or diligent enough to accumulate any property then he had no business voting. It was assumed that if his wife had an opinion she would communicate it to him. This was not majority rule and nobody intended it to be. The politicians didn't take long to work out that the young impressionable voters who had no property to lose would be easier to deceive. By about 1820 the franchise had been expanded to include all tax-paying males over twenty one in most states. By the 1850's almost all financial restrictions had been eliminated and all (white) male citizens over twenty one could vote. This had mixed results. The populace was happier in believing that all adult males had equal representation but on the other side, a more naïve electorate could be more easily manipulated.

As early as 1812 the Governor of Massachusetts, Elwood Gerry, had discovered a means of manipulating the electoral districts to give advantage to his party. He re-drew the lines for one particular district in such a bizarre way that the resulting area on the map resembled a salamander. The Boston Gazette seized upon this and coined the term gerrymander. This distortion has continued throughout the states and can be used by the party in power to give advantage to itself or to promote the causes of racial, ethnic and religious groups. Because of this, many seats in Congress are uncontested and the incumbent has only to fear opposition from another contender within his own party.

Aside from the gerrymandering, the concentration of populations in the big urban centers of the country mean that these small geographical areas have an undue influence in the number of congressmen and electoral votes they control. In the "winner takes all" system, a state may be 90% for one party geographically but lose to the other because of the urban vote. To exacerbate this problem, there are now a large number of residents, mainly in urban centers, who are not citizens and therefore cannot vote. These are official resident aliens, children under 18, felons and illegal aliens. They are counted in each census and they play a part in determining the number of representatives and congressional districts in a state. One congressman represents about 700,000 residents. This means an urban area with 1,400,000 residents, only 700,000 of which are citizens, will get two representatives whereas a rural area with 700,000 residents, all of whom are citizens, will get only one. In effect the vote of the urban citizen is then worth twice the vote of the rural. As the urban areas tend to be Democrat strongholds, this situation is favorable for the party.

Gerrymandering and citizenship questions came before the Supreme Court in July 2019 involving the requirement on the 2020 census form to include the citizenship of the respondent and the ability of the party in power to gerrymander precinct boundaries. The court sent the citizenship question back to the Trump administration for further clarification and declined to get involved in gerrymandering, claiming this was the precinct of the states.

Recently some states have examined the possibility of changing the formula for determining the drawing of precinct lines from the existing, based on total population, to a system based on the number of eligible voters. This would exclude children below voting age, resident aliens and illegal aliens. In states with large numbers of these groups this would have a profound effect. Traditionally, the party in power draws lines to give itself the best advantage. The formula above would favor the Republican party as most aliens live in the large cities. Notwithstanding the logic, this will be a tough sell.

The franchise has been further expanded over the years by the 14th, 15th, 19th, 23rd, 24th and 26th amendments in which the Federal government gradually took over the states' rights to decide who could vote. Predictably, this has resulted in an increasingly more socialistic society and an electorate which is far easier to manipulate.

In Federal elections many voters now focus on issues entirely irrelevant to the efficient workings of the Federal government and good policy. The subjects of abortion, gay rights, religion in public places etc. play no part in the powers delegated to the Federal government by the Constitution and they are not important in keeping the country safe or prosperous. These are state matters and voters in each state should make these decisions. Instead of educating the public on important national issues, the media concentrates on these divisive matters and the candidates are obliged to confront them. Many an excellent candidate has lost simply because he or she stood on principle.

CHAPTER 5: THE INDUSTRIAL REVOLUTION

The Founders could not envisage the Industrial Revolution and therefore did not include any language in the Constitution to address the possible effects it may have on the economy and human behavior. As we know, the effects were tremendous and advances in science and technology continue to play a major part in the lives of everyone. Inventions such as the steam-engine, the cotton gin, the harvester, the automobile and the aeroplane changed life drastically. Until the 1830's, most of the population relied on the land for their livelihood. Land was the most common asset and those who amassed large tracts of productive land were generally the wealthiest. However, unless sold, land was an asset that had to be worked and crops had to be sold to produce a cash income.

The railway system was the first of the great industries, spawned by the enhancement of the steam engine to produce rotary motion by Scottish engineers Watt and Boulton in the late 1700's. By the 1830's trains started transporting goods and people in the USA. Transport by rail vastly reduced the time and cost of moving goods and people and its proliferation created another huge industry, the manufacture of steel. Those who invested in these industries soon became wealthy beyond anything previously possible for the common man and by cunning maneuvering and often predatory tactics, huge fortunes were amassed. The discovery of oil and its uses in heating and in the automobile industry created another bonanza for the tycoons. The barons of industry and Wall Street soon began to collaborate and integrate to seize control of much of the economy, creating monopolies which stifled competition and bankrupted farmers and small businesses. Their exploitation of labor spawned unions which soon became powerful enough to disrupt production if their demands were not met.

No-one in government was quite sure how to address these new problems. On the one hand, the USA was founded on freedoms and had prospered promoting the laissez-faire approach to business. Entrepreneurs were prepared to take risk and were entitled to profit from their ventures. New businesses created jobs for many and boosted the economy as a whole. On the other hand, if these businessmen chose to band together and control prices and by various means both legal and illegal monopolize segments of industry, this was harmful to both the citizens and the economy.

In an effort to protect the public, in 1890 Congress passed the Sherman Antitrust Act. The first two sections lay out the intent.

Section 1:

"Every contract, combination in the form of trust or otherwise, or conspiracy, in restraint of trade or commerce among the several States, or with foreign nations, is declared to be illegal."

Section 2:

"Every person who shall monopolize, or attempt to monopolize, or combine or conspire with any other person or persons, to monopolize any part of the trade or commerce among the several States, or with foreign nations, shall be deemed guilty of a felony."

Not surprisingly, the tycoons, politicians and labor bosses who controlled the local, state and national agendas had little appetite for enforcing these laws and little changed until Theodore Roosevelt assumed the presidency.

Industry had another important effect on the country as people moved from the farms to the cities and towns to take up employment in manufacturing. The cotton gin, combine harvester and tractor reduced the need for manual labor on farms which added to this migration. Once in the cities, people were subjected to different influences and voted accordingly.

CHAPTER 6: THE CIVIL WAR EFFECTS

The Civil War changed the country drastically. It was a war in which the Southern States did not seek control of the whole country, they merely wanted to secede from a union whose government they found to be in conflict with their own interests, much as the thirteen original states had sought independence from English rule. Each state had entered the Union voluntarily with the understanding that it could secede without prejudice at any time. The contrary argument is that all the states jointly agreed to a union and any deviation would require the consent of all parties. In declaring their independence the Southern States neither sought nor expected to go to war. In fact the term Civil War is a misnomer for the South, it was a war of independence. It is the essence of democracy that a large group of people have the means to decide their own fortunes. There was nothing in the Constitution prohibiting secession or slavery other than the moratorium on import of slaves and at such time the country felt that there should be, the Constitution could and should have been amended by the prescribed process.

The causes of the Civil War are a subject of considerable disagreement but it can said that whereas the question of expansion of the practice of slavery to new territories was the catalyst, the actual war was triggered by the secession of the southern states and their declaration of an independent confederacy. They feared that the new Republican administration would not only prohibit the taking of their "property" to the new territories and thus ruin their opportunity to expand and prosper but would also abolish slavery in existing slave states. The flames of abolition had been fanned by the book Uncle Tom's Cabin and by the 1857 Supreme Court Dred Scott ruling. This declared that blacks were not citizens and therefore did not qualify for constitutional protection and that the Federal government had no power to regulate slavery in territories added since the formation of the union. This decision infuriated a large segment of the population and even today is regarded as one of the worst rulings of the Supreme Court and a good example of how this body can and does distort the intent of the Constitution.

Until this time the country had been careful to have a balance between slave states and free states so that the Senate was evenly divided on the issue. The balance was maintained until 1850 when California was admitted. There was no new slave state available and so it was agreed that it should send one pro and one con senator to Washington. After this the balance was upset by admission of more free states which added to the anxiety of the slave states.

The Confederacy drafted its own constitution which was very similar in most respects to the original document but taking into account lessons learned over the past seventy years. Two of the most important changes were the elimination of the General Welfare clause and giving the President line-item veto authority in any bill presented for his signature. The latter is a most important power which has been brought before congress several times but has never received the votes necessary to pass both houses. These two changes corrected the major flaws in the original Constitution.

Although abhorrent in principle, in reality slavery is relative, not absolute. Any time one person has power over another there is potential for abuse. Most people are under the control of others in some form or other. An employee is typically controlled by a boss who dictates hours of work, dress-code, behavior etc. A Moslem woman is owned by her father or husband and must obey him. A person drafted into the military effectively becomes a slave. He must follow orders without question, dress, eat, sleep and behave as prescribed and if he chooses to escape, can face death. It all depends where the line is drawn. When a person is physically restrained and abused and not permitted to make any personal decisions affecting his or her life then the line has been crossed. Amazingly during both world wars Germany, Japan and Russia used prisoners as slave labor to the point that many were worked to death by design. Slavery still exists in Africa today. Probably most of the world population has ancestors who were enslaved, it was a common custom to enslave one's vanquished enemies in ancient cultures.

Aristotle was in favor of a form of slavery. Not unreasonably, he believed that a certain segment of the population needed close supervision and management for their own good and also for the good of the community. Those unwilling or incapable of providing for themselves can generally be employed gainfully by others who can direct them. In this way they can have a sense of personal accomplishment, learn skills and provide for themselves. The remuneration may not be in cash, but can be in food, lodging, clothing, medical attention etc.

We do not know the percentage of slaves in the southern states who were abused but certainly abuse occurred as it does any time one human being has absolute control of another. It is likely that many slaves were treated reasonably and did not have awful lives. Perhaps with a phased-in approach of personal freedom and some form of monetary payment the system could have been gradually rectified without ruin to the owner or slave. This would have given both parties a transition period and have avoided the destructive animosity created by the war. This is in fact what occurred in most of Europe as the feudal system was slowly modified to democracy with mixed results. The Industrial Revolution played a major role in this transition as populations moved from farm to city.

In 1860 Abraham Lincoln was elected president and was faced with the escalating crisis which his predecessor, Buchanan, had done little to avert. Lincoln's election was somewhat surprising considering his qualifications for the office. Having endured a rough childhood with less than two years of formal

education, he read law and practiced as a country lawyer in Illinois. He served as state legislator and was elected to Congress in 1846 where he served one term in the Whig party. He ran for the US Senate in 1858 but lost to the powerful Stephen Douglas. With his imposing stature and engaging charisma he was able to win the 1860 Republican presidential primary against formidable opponents William Seward and Salmon Chase. Lincoln was elected rather unusually.
The new Republican Party platform proposed no interference with slavery in the existing slave states but promoted the opposition to slavery in the new territories. The field was split four ways between Lincoln, Douglas, Breckinridge and Bell. Lincoln won with less than 40% of the popular vote with an unprecedented voter turnout of 81.2%. He garnered 180 of the 303 electoral votes for a solid victory.

Before Lincoln assumed office, but after seven southern states had already seceded, the Corwin amendment to the Constitution was passed by Congress and (prematurely) signed by president Buchanan in an attempt to defuse the slavery crisis. It stated:

"No amendment shall be made to the Constitution which will authorize or give to Congress the power to abolish or interfere, within any State, with the domestic institutions thereof, including that of persons held to labor or service by the laws of said State".

It was then submitted to the state legislatures for final ratification. Lincoln tacitly supported this amendment and at his inauguration he sought to allay the fears of the South, saying: *"Apprehension seems to exist among the people of the Southern States that by the accession of a Republican Administration their property and their peace and personal security are to be endangered. There has never been any reasonable cause for such apprehension. Indeed, the most ample evidence to the contrary has all the while existed and been open to their inspection. It is found in nearly all the published speeches of him who now addresses you. I do but quote from one of those speeches when I declare that I have no purpose, directly or indirectly, to interfere with the institution of slavery in the States where it exists. I believe I have no lawful right to do so, and I have no inclination to do so."* Civil war interrupted the ratification process and the proposed amendment was abandoned. Had it been ratified, the 13th amendment would not have been possible and the power of the federal government to interfere in state politics would have been severely restricted. .

Lincoln was strongly opposed to any dissolution of the Union for strategic reasons and, more importantly, because the Federal government stood to lose over half of its tax revenues. The bulk of federal revenues came from tariffs and the Confederacy had a number of major ports. As Commander in Chief, he resorted to using his army to ensure its integrity, thereby initiating a civil war. He also temporarily suspended the right of habeas corpus in contravention of Article I, section 9 of the Constitution. In order to pay for the war, Lincoln decided to levy a tax on income in contravention of the same section 9. The constitutionality of such a tax was questionable but Lincoln was successful in persuading the Union Congress to pass the Revenue Act of 1861 which levied a 3% tax on income above $800 per year regardless of source. This type of tax effectively penalized citizens for their productivity and was repealed in 1871. The temptation was too great however, and in 1894 Congress passed a flat rate Federal income tax which was subsequently (and correctly) ruled unconstitutional by the Supreme Court because the Federal government had no authority to tax individuals in each state.

Article 1 Section 9 of the Constitution reads as follows:

"No Capitation, or other direct, Tax shall be laid (unless in Proportion to the Census or enumeration herein before directed to be taken)".

This means that any direct taxes (paid by individuals or businesses to the Federal government) could only be levied in proportion to the populations of each state. This effectively prohibited Federal income taxes.

Hungry for more and more revenues, in 1909 Congress passed the 16th amendment to the Constitution which allowed the Federal government to tax the income of individuals and businesses. This was ratified in 1913 and the rates and complexity have increased exponentially since then. The Federal government now had a means of confiscating unlimited portions of the fruits of its citizens' labor and by making the system ever more complex, also had a means of controlling behavior.

The taxing of income has had very serious effects on the economy and productivity of the country. In seeking to please influential friends and businesses in return for votes, Congress has manipulated the tax code with loopholes and exceptions, giving special treatment to certain groups in various ways. The progressive nature of the tax has resulted in the top 1% of earners paying 37% of the taxes and the bottom 50% paying nothing. Companies and individuals must make business decisions based not on logic but on how to avoid excessive taxation. Many companies and individuals simply relocate to other countries with more sensible tax systems. The Internal Revenue Service has become a behemoth with the power of the Gestapo and an army of tax lawyers and CPA's makes a huge income preparing taxes for companies and individuals because few normal people can understand the rules. Notwithstanding this convoluted tax system, the Federal government has spent prodigiously without any attempt to limit expenditure to income and today finds itself $28T in debt.

The Civil War, like all wars, had far reaching effects all over the world. Not only did it annihilate half a million of the nation's young men and destroy billions of dollars worth of the nation's property and infrastructure but it also bankrupted the South and created huge debts for the reunited Union. In refusing to honor the Confederate bonds issued during the war and considering its own war debt, the Union now faced a credibility problem which resulted in severe inflation and devaluation of the dollar. It was a war based on serious misjudgments on both sides with catastrophic consequences. Probably the most serious mistake the South made was not military but financial. In seeking to raise the price of its "Cotton Bonds" the South restricted the flow of cotton to England, creating severe unemployment there. The English quickly found other sources, the bonds became worthless and the South was unable to get additional financing to fund the war. The Union occupation of the port of New Orleans further restricted the export of cotton and this sealed the fate of the South.

The Civil War also gave rise to three more amendments to the Constitution, the 14th being the one most litigated. During his first term, in 1863, Lincoln gave the famous Emancipation Proclamation which was largely symbolic because it sought to declare slaves free in the ten rebellious Confederate states where the Union government had no enforceable jurisdiction. It was an Executive Order, not a law passed by Congress and derived its authority as a military order by the Commander in Chief. It placed the abolition of all slavery as an objective of the war and gave hope to those slaves in the states still unoccupied by Union forces. The Proclamation did not offer any compensation to slave owners. This proclamation was driven less by any compassion for the slaves than by the military objective of encouraging slaves to flee and thus disrupt the South's economy. The slaves in the five slave states which stayed in the Union (Delaware, Kentucky, Maryland, Missouri, West Virginia,) were not freed by this declaration. In April 1864 when the outcome of the war was certain, the Union Senate passed the Thirteenth Amendment which formally abolished slavery and involuntary servitude everywhere. After strong opposition had been quelled by unabashed political maneuvering and outright bribery, it was subsequently passed by the House and became part of the Constitution in December 1865. It was the first of three Reconstruction amendments. It could be argued that it was indeed unconstitutional to pass any amendments without the bona fide participation of all the states as the Union government had never recognized the secession of the Confederate states. Having lost the war however, these states were in no position to oppose the acts.

The amendment was short and simple:

Section 1. *"Neither slavery nor involuntary servitude, except as a punishment for crime whereof the party shall have been duly convicted, shall exist within the United States, or any place subject to their jurisdiction".*

Section 2. *"Congress shall have power to enforce this article by appropriate legislation".*

This amendment created a problem for Republicans in the re-unified country because former slaves could now be counted as whole persons instead of the former bizarre 3/5 formula enshrined in the original Constitution. This had the effect of increasing the number of representatives in the House from former slave states. They solved this by adopting the 14th Amendment, which made citizens of former slaves and gave them the right to vote. It was assumed that they would all vote Republican.

The 14th Amendment was adopted in July 1868 after bitter opposition by southern states. Eventually these states were forced to ratify it as a condition of regaining representation in Congress. The first section has given rise to many of the landmark decisions of the Supreme Court. It states:

"All persons born or naturalized in the United States, and subject to the jurisdiction thereof, are citizens of the United States and of the State wherein they reside. No State shall make or enforce any law which shall abridge the privileges or immunities of citizens of the United States; nor shall any State deprive any person of life, liberty, or property, without due process of law; nor deny to any person within its jurisdiction the equal protection of the laws"

. The last phrase has been used to justify all kinds of activity and has been the tool used most in litigation involving this amendment. The second section gave full voting privileges to all male citizens above the age of 21. The third and fourth sections dealt with eligibility for public office for persons who had engaged in insurrection and the treatment of war debt.

Notwithstanding terms of the 13th and 14th amendments, the Republican congress was concerned that southern states would find ways to discourage or prohibit blacks from voting. Fearing a loss of their majority, after more maneuvering, the 15th Amendment was ratified in March 1870. It was very simple:

> **Section 1.** *"The right of citizens of the United States to vote shall not be denied or abridged by the United States or by any State on account of race, color, or previous condition of servitude".*

> **Section 2.** *"The Congress shall have power to enforce this article by appropriate legislation".*

As can be seen from this series of events, none of these acts was in fact because the Republican Party had the welfare of the slaves as a priority. It was all about preserving party power. The passages of these amendments were accomplished by various pressures, they were not voluntarily supported sufficiently to have passed and would certainly have never passed if the

Civil War had not compromised the power of the southern states.

The war had a profound effect on the whole country for several generations. It is likely that had Lincoln not been assassinated, he would have taken a kinder and gentler approach to the South. His successor, Vice-president Andrew Johnson, was a different character and while giving lip-service to the new policy regarding former slaves, did little to enforce it, for which he was impeached. His successor, Ulysses Grant, resorted to martial law in the southern states to protect the newly bestowed rights of blacks. It is disappointing that Southerners refused to accept reality and continued to abuse blacks and this intransigency ensured that they would pay a high price for the war in many respects. This created tremendous animosity and delayed the resurgence of the Southern economy.

President Grant is not admired to the extents of presidents like Washington and Lincoln but in fact apart from being the general who won the war, as a president he was confronted with an very divided country with a mountain of post-war baggage. A kind and just man, Grant must be commended for taking up the cause of justice for all citizens. Unlike politicians today, he died a poor man but his funeral elicited one of the largest outpouring of respect accorded any president up to that time.

CHAPTER 7: THE PROGRESSIVE AGENDA

In 1901 a new type of president burst on the scene.
Following President McKinley's assassination in
September of that year, Vice-president Theodore
Roosevelt assumed the presidency and won a second
term in 1904. At 42, he was the youngest man ever to
hold the office. Although not tall in stature, he was a
bull of a man imbued with a boundless exuberance and
energy. Coming from an affluent background he
initially supported the existing free-enterprise system,
believing that government should stay out of business.
He was elected to the New York state legislature at the
age of twenty two, but once in office it did not take him
long to realize that state legislatures were controlled
largely by big corporations and labor and party bosses
who had little interest in serving the needs of the
common man. After investigating the situation more
thoroughly, he revised his philosophy and concluded
that the Federal government should involve itself in
several new areas in order to reign in excessive power
of the large corporations, curtail abuse of factory
workers and institute regulation of freight charges by
the railroads to ensure that farmers were not exploited.

His philosophy was further influenced when he was
appointed Commissioner of the Civil Service by
President Benjamin Harrison. He realized that the civil
service was staffed according to the "spoils" system
whereby the party in power appointed cronies to key
positions regardless of merit and at each change of

administration, competent people were fired to make room for these. Entrance exams were rigged to favor party candidates and the whole system was corrupt. Roosevelt did his best to correct these abuses but he found the system so entrenched that his actions had minimal effect.

Roosevelt got another insight into the world of corrupting influence when he was appointed Police Commissioner of the City of New York. Having befriended several investigative reporters who alerted him to the situation, he was shocked to find the degree of control the labor bosses exerted over the police. Blatant and pervasive bribery up to highest levels gave labor immunity from laws and provided them with substantial income in the form of "protection" money. The New York Democrat machine, Tammany Hall, pretty much controlled local politics and was the major recipient of local and federal patronage. Roosevelt risked his job in trying to correct the situation but received little support from Republicans because his actions threatened their seats. He learned another lesson about politics.

Roosevelt was the quintessential extrovert. With his impressive presence, a mouthful of diverging teeth and booming voice, everybody loved him. He was quick to enlist the support of all the major publications and after serving as Police Commissioner he was elected Governor of New York and subsequently served as Vice-president to McKinley. He was the first president to set up regular press briefings at the White House. He realized that the means to persuading other legislators to support his agenda was to get the press to fire up the public to put pressure on their representatives. He was very successful with this strategy and during his two administrations he was able to address many of the issues he believed essential to the continued prosperity of the country. He was fortunate in that during this period there were a number of excellent investigative reporters who drew the attention of the public to the corruption and supported Roosevelt's agendas to correct the situation.

The impetus for this new "progressive" agenda, named The Square Deal, was to a large degree supplied by the evolving effects of the Industrial Revolution which were rapidly changing lifestyles throughout the civilized world. In fact the turn of the century found the USA quite prosperous after the 1892-3 depression. In Roosevelt's and other prominent Republicans' minds however, the free-enterprise system practiced heretofore had given rise to an unhealthy monopolization of the country's wealth by the big corporations. There were few labor laws in place and factory workers were at the mercy of their employers. The workplaces were unsafe in many instances and workers had no recourse for reducing accidents and improving unhealthy conditions. The corrupt state legislators made no efforts to alleviate the situation, owing their seats to the very tycoons exploiting it.

The major challenge in the early 20th century was to decide how much regulation by the Federal government was necessary to protect the public from abuse and predatory practices by ruthless businessmen and labor bosses. Americans were generally opposed to any tendency towards socialism but they recognized that the historical laissez faire system needed some limits. The difficult task was to determine how much and what type of regulation effectively prevented abuse without stifling innovation and productivity and creating a government behemoth. In principle this was the responsibility of the states, but in practice their legislatures were so corrupt that nothing was done. Roosevelt struggled with this and eventually concluded that the Federal government had to act. Unfortunately, once the government started down this road it was inevitable that eventually it would create over-regulation and drive businesses to more hospitable countries. The USA, created as the land of the free, is now one of the most regulated countries on earth.

The big problems were and still are money and patronage. Roosevelt did his best to lessen the effects of these but was strongly opposed by both parties. He was further thwarted when Congress voted to prohibit the Secret Service from investigating corrupt businesses, senators and congressmen. Every well-intentioned politician must face the fact that corruption in one form or another is a time honored method of doing business. From the day he is sworn in, pressure is brought to convert him to the system, usually with rapid success. The only hope to at least reduce this corruption is to limit all presidents, legislators and judges to single terms so that no-one can establish a prolonged influence on the affairs of the citizens. This of course precludes the rare honest and talented men from continuing their good work but it is the price that must be paid.

Despite strong Republican opposition, Roosevelt was successful in creating a Bureau of Corporations to bring some order to corporate and labor abuse. He was the first president to vigorously enforce the 1890 Sherman Antitrust Act, bringing 40 antitrust suits against such large conglomerates as Standard Oil and the Northern Securities Company which controlled three of the largest railroads. He supported the gold standard, and initially favored protective tariffs and lower taxes. During his administration Congress passed the Meat Inspection Act and the Pure Food and Drug Act. He also involved himself in creating standards for health and hygiene in public schools and the care of dependent children. Being an avid naturalist, he promoted conservation of natural resources and added 5 more national parks to the system during his tenure. The Antiquities Act of 1906 facilitated the creation of many more national parks and monuments.

Roosevelt was convinced of the potential and efficiency of hydro-electric power in a rapidly expanding electrification of the entire country. He correctly predicted that if nothing was done to secure the available sites on the nation's major rivers, smart tycoons would step in and acquire these lands to set up private generation systems or re-sell the land at huge premiums. He therefore instigated a program for the Federal government to take possession of these sites so that the entire water system of the country could be responsibly integrated and controlled. In 1902 he signed The Reclamation Act which created the U.S. Reclamation Service, later known as the Bureau of Reclamation, to promote the use of the country's water systems for irrigation of arid lands, flood control and power generation.

Theodore Roosevelt was one of the very few presidents who genuinely worked to do good for the country throughout his terms but even with his energy and high popularity he found many of his correct initiatives thwarted or diluted by his own party. The concept of party politics should be examined. On the one hand, parties enable like-minded voters to concentrate their resources and talents into powerful blocks. On the other hand, these blocks quickly become too powerful and undermine the principles of democracy. In order to secure funding, the parties sell their souls to tycoons who demand compensation in the form of legislation favorable to their interests. Decent men elected to protect the public interest are outvoted or subverted by party bosses. There is only one solution to this major problem, which is to take the big money out of politics at every level. Whereas this may be possible for direct funding, it would be unconstitutional and unwise to put any restraints on individuals' rights to free speech. Tycoons would continue to be free to own and influence every form of propaganda and it would be up to citizens' groups to counteract inaccurate information.

Despite his profound influence on correcting some of the nation's wrongs, many of Roosevelt's initiatives were blocked by the pro-business Republicans in Congress. They did not want to alienate the major contributors and believed that he was going too far with his progressive agenda. He reversed himself on some issues after a time in office and sought to lower tariffs and make up the income from progressive income taxes. He also supported employer liability legislation, direct election of senators and a post-office saving system (later occurring as the Savings and Loan industry).

It is interesting that then and still today the huge labor unions have never been subjected to anti-trust litigation. As large entities controlling entire industries they are just as dangerous as large corporations. The reason they have escaped is simply that politicians are too beholden to union leaders and cannot afford to alienate them. Today, with strict federal labor laws dictating work hours, safety practices, worker discrimination, workers' compensation in case of injury and minimum wages the need for unions must be questioned. In a free society every worker is free to choose his or her employer and in doing so, accepts the compensation package that is agreed upon. If either the employee or employer chooses to terminate the deal he should be free to do so.

If a group of workers at any one facility seeks to bring attention to management to any issue regarding their employment they are at liberty to do so. There is nothing unfair involved.

Roosevelt had very clear ideas on immigration and being an American, which politicians and citizens today should take note of. This philosophy should apply to citizens of all races and creeds. He made the following statement in 1907:

"In the first place, we should insist that if the immigrant who comes here in good faith becomes an American and assimilates himself to us, he shall be treated on an exact equality with everyone else, for it is an outrage to discriminate against any such man because of creed, or birthplace, or origin. But this is predicated upon the person's becoming in every facet an American, and nothing but an American ... There can be no divided allegiance here. Any man who says he is an American, but something else also, isn't an American at all. We have room for but one flag, the American flag ... We have room for but one language here, and that is the English language ... and we have room for but one sole loyalty and that is a loyalty to the American people."

In 1909 Roosevelt was succeeded by William Taft, his friend and hand-picked successor. Weighing over 300 lbs, Taft was a big man but gentle and caring. His preferred field was the judicial system and he had previously served as a circuit judge on the Federal bench and governor of the Philippines. He also was disillusioned by the cronyism and corruption in the courts and did his best to bring about improvement, with limited success. He was less vigorous than Roosevelt in promoting the "progressive" agenda and this led to a rift between the two men. The big issue for Taft was to continue Roosevelt's efforts to reduce tariffs. The eastern manufacturers favored high tariffs to give them price advantage over foreign competition but the rest of the country opposed tariffs because they inevitably led to higher prices and allowed local businesses to reap unreasonable profits. The Old Guard Republicans in Congress fought hard to retain the tariffs which benefited their contributors and the new Progressive faction supported Taft. The Constitution provided that the bulk of Federal revenues should be derived from tariffs and excise taxes, so if tariffs were to be reduced, the shortfall would need to be made up from other sources. This led to the drive for income and inheritance taxes.

Taft had to negotiate with party bosses to proceed and the resulting legislation, the Payne-Aldrich Act, was a compromise which impressed no-one. Roosevelt had disappeared for a year of hunting in Africa, but upon his return when he learned of Taft's actions on the tariffs and in firing his forestry chief who had spearheaded the conservation efforts, he lost confidence in Taft. In frustration, having previously declared that no man should serve more than two terms as president,

Roosevelt ran against Taft at the 1912 Republican convention and lost. He then made the unwise decision of forming a new party, The Progressive, with a plank which included many of his previous initiatives and some new ones, one of which was a government program to take care of the sick, aged and unemployed who were unable to care for themselves. This split the Republican party and enabled the election of the Democrat Woodrow Wilson.

CHAPTER 8: WILSON ERA AMENDMENTS

In 1913 Woodrow Wilson took office as President. He was an academic and former professor and president of Princeton University. As president of a very elite institution, he caused considerable consternation amongst the board of trustees by attempting to dismantle the rich-man's club heritage and open the campus to the general public. In1910 he was quite surprised to be approached by the New Jersey Democratic party boss, "Sugar" Jim Smith, to run for governor of New Jersey, and with solid backing from his promoters, he won. After less than two years as governor, these same promoters persuaded him to run for the presidency. After considerable horse-trading behind the scenes to get the Democratic nomination, he was elected in 1912 with 40% of the popular vote in a four-way race, much like Lincoln. Both his election to governor and president were greatly facilitated by New Jersey tycoons who saw in him a useful puppet who could be manipulated to further their business agendas.

After election to president he surprised his backers by adhering to his strong moral principles and advancing his own agendas. One of his closest friends and advisors was "Colonel" Edward House, a wealthy Texan bon vivant who had been instrumental in delivering the electoral votes of Texas. It is worrisome to supporters of the democratic process that House, unelected and without any formal office in the government, played a very strong role in Wilson's decision making and even served as Wilson's representative at the Paris conferences. Wilson himself described House as his "second persona". Whereas presidents are quite entitled to seek and act on good advice from knowledgeable people, when a single unelected and unofficial person exerts undue influence this is dangerous.

Wilson was an enthusiastic promoter of Roosevelt's Progressive Movement, going far beyond what Roosevelt had intended. The son and grandson of Presbyterian ministers, he was probably the most pious president. He was also the most educated, having earned a Ph. D. in Political Science at Johns Hopkins University. Wilson believed the Federal government should see to every need of its citizens, effectively relegating them to incompetent fools. He was an avid student and great admirer of the English parliamentary system, believing that the executive powers should be vested in the leaders of the majority party in the form of prime-minister and cabinet ministers who were elected members of parliament. Paradoxically, although he believed in fair and respectful treatment of all citizens, he was an ardent segregationist, believing that the black and white races were better off going their separate ways. During his administration several major pieces of legislation were passed which continue to have a profound effect. Many of these were initiated by Theodore Roosevelt. In his first term he presided over ratification of the 16th, 17th, 18th and 19th amendments, the Federal Reserve Act, the Federal Trade Commission

Act, the Clayton Antitrust Act and the Federal Farm Loan Act.

The 16th amendment gave the Federal Government the power to tax the incomes of individuals and businesses, which enabled it to spend considerably more of the nation's money as it pleased and to redistribute wealth. The Founding Fathers were well aware of the great temptation for the government to by one means or another confiscate increasing proportions of the nations wealth. To protect against this, Article I, section 8 of the Constitution stipulates:

"The Congress shall have Power To lay and collect Taxes, Duties, Imposts and Excises, to pay the Debts and provide for the common Defence and general Welfare of the United States; but all Duties, Imposts and Excises shall be uniform throughout the United States".

This section continues and lays out the areas in which Congress can involve itself in the use of this money. The Founders were determined to create a fair and just system whereby the government could not treat different segments of the population differently and thus establish classes. They were totally opposed to any form of income tax, realizing that this would soon lead to progressive rates which took from some to give to others. They reinforced this in section 9:

"No Capitation, or other direct Tax shall be laid, (unless in Proportion to the Census or enumeration herein before discussed to be taken)".

The 16th amendment directly reversed this:

"The Congress shall have power to lay and collect taxes on incomes, from whatever source derived, without apportionment among the several States, and without regard to any census or enumeration".

This was a huge mistake, giving the Federal government direct access to a substantial amount of additional money. From 1850 to 1900 federal spending averaged $300 million per year and by 1901 it had reached $588 million. It increased rapidly in the next 50 years, reaching $52 billion in 1951. The 2019 budget was $3.65 trillion with a deficit of $985 billion and national debt of $22 trillion. Income taxes in general are bad, but progressive income taxes are inherently wrong and contrary to the principles of freedom set out in the Constitution guaranteeing equal treatment under the law. The established religions have never required their adherents to contribute on a scaled basis. Everyone is assessed at the same percentage. Progressive income taxes pave the way for wealth redistribution by the government. Inevitably this leads to vote-buying programs which take money from productive citizens to give to unproductive citizens and in doing so, ensures the votes of these citizens. At the point when more people receive money than contribute, the party supporting these programs is assured of majorities until the money runs out.

It did not take long for the President and Congress to dip their fingers into this treasure chest. From a starting top rate of 7% of income over $4,000 in 1913, by the 1930's this had jumped to 63% under Hoover and then to 90% under Roosevelt. In fact, Roosevelt issued an executive order to tax all income over $25,000 at 100% which Congress subsequently repealed. Instead of boosting the economy to end the Depression, this confiscatory tax prolonged it until the start of the war and even today is regarded as unfair and counterproductive.

In the original law, in order to keep the system as simple as possible, interest expenses were tax-deductable for both individuals and businesses. This included interest for home loans. At that time it was almost irrelevant because less than 1% of the population earned more than $4,000 and therefore paid no tax at all. As incomes increased with inflation, more and more people became liable for income tax and these could take advantage of the interest deduction. It was never intended as a policy to facilitate home ownership but by degrees became a major factor in a person's decision to take a mortgage to purchase a home. It can be reasonably argued that it inherently unfair for all those without mortgages to partially fund the mortgages of others.

The erosion of the Constitution was further facilitated by the 17th Amendment, ratified in 1913. This changed the system for the election of senators. The Constitution wisely decreed that two senators should be elected by the legislatures of each state. This ensured that senators would be relatively free from bribery and corruption by businesses and individuals and a majority in each state legislature would need to support the election. The Senate was intended to be a rationalizing body to temper the excesses the House may be tempted into. The problem was that as the Industrial Revolution created huge and powerful businesses and labor groups, state legislatures became puppets for tycoons, party and labor bosses. The correct solution would have been to clean up the state legislatures by means of term limits and campaign financing reform. Instead, the populist movements garnered sufficient support to change the Constitution. The 17th Amendment changed the system so that senators would be elected directly by the citizens of each state and therefore be subject to all the same temptations as the congressmen. This had the effect of rendering Congress more prone to legislation that favored their own re-elections rather than considering the benefits to the country as a whole.

The 18th amendment, prohibiting the manufacture, sale and consumption of alcohol, was a clear intrusion into private lives which was not authorized by any language in the Constitution except by very broad interpretation of the General Welfare clause. After strong pressure,

Wilson supported women's suffrage which culminated in 1920 with the 19th Amendment and added millions to the voter roles. Women tended to be more liberal than men and this was beneficial to the Democratic party promoting the liberal causes.

After running for his second term on the platform of keeping the USA out of World War One, in 1917 Wilson reversed himself after Germany attacked US shipping and tried to incite Mexico to attack the USA. He then inserted himself into the armistice negotiations and personally participated in the Paris Accords where he insisted on the inclusion of his famous Fourteen Points and the creation of the League of Nations. There was no easy solution. The result was a disaster whereby the League of Nations, which Wilson saw as the answer for perpetual world peace and the treaty of Versailles, which dealt with Germany, were rejected by the US Congress on party lines. The arbitrary redrawing of frontiers without regard for ethnic populations and the rape of Germany via reparations set the stage for World War Two.

It can be argued that the USA should either have openly allied itself with Britain and France prior to World War 1 or stayed out of it altogether. If Germany had known up front that any attack on France would bring the might of the USA against it, the Kaiser and Austrian Emperor Franz Josef and their generals might have reconsidered. Alternatively, if the USA had remained neutral, it is likely that the European belligerents would have concluded a far different armistice which would not have given rise to the second war. Wilson's naïve crusade to instill American-style democracy throughout the world via "self determination" was the genesis of many of the world's problems today. The chaos in the middle-east, Africa and Asia are largely the result of Wilson's departure from previous wise policy of not involving the USA in the affairs other nations.

Wilson took advantage of his newly formed Federal Reserve Bank to borrow billions of dollars by way of Liberty Bonds to finance the war effort, which commenced the grand debt of the United States. The Federal Reserve was a controversial issue because the average American had deep mistrust of both the bankers and the Federal Government. Since the Revolution, various schemes had been tried, none of which solved the problems of economic volatility in trying times. The Federal Reserve was a compromise, a spread of 10 regional national banks with the head of each on the central board of directors. By controlling interest rates and the money supply it sought to stabilize the financial systems. Whereas in principle this seemed like a good idea, in practice it gave the Federal Reserve, a non-elected group of directors, incredible powers to manipulate the economy. It failed to bolster the money supply in 1929 resulting in multiple bank failures.

CHAPTER 9: THE MONEY GRAB

The thirteen colonies broke away from England primarily because they objected to excessive taxation over which they had no control. Governments and rulers have always taxed citizens in some form in order to perform certain necessary functions and eventually to live in luxury themselves. The rulers did not earn this wealth themselves and therefore had little incentive to restrain the taxation. Inevitably this led to taxing as much as the citizens would tolerate and resulted in irresponsible spending, eventually going into substantial debt, as the USA has done. Even the ancient Babylonians in Mesopotamia foresaw the problems this would create and wisely passed laws that required the settlement of all debts periodically. In the book of Deuteronomy there is reference to cancellation every seven years. These customs were for the good reasons that the peasants, or the general public, could not produce crops or be available to fight if their lands and assets were expropriated by creditors. The same applies today. A population which is taxed excessively and heavily indebted is less productive.

Modern governments discovered another means of taking from their citizens. In printing paper money which is simple to do but has zero intrinsic value, governments can effectively steal value. In a perfect system, a value would be determined for all available goods and services. The amount of money printed would represent the value of the combined value of these. This is not possible in the real world for many reasons, so the banking system is faced with a difficult balancing act. National banks are supposed to be independent and make decisions regarding the printing of money based on sound financial principles. Inevitably they are influenced by the government in power at the time and end up manipulating the system.

Any paper currency is only a measuring device. It is a simply a standardized version of a promissory note. It gives a convenient means of transacting business using a common measure just like selling sugar by the pound. However, somewhere the currency must be tied to a constant, just as the modern pound weight standard is preserved by a platinum cylinder in the Standards Department of the British Board of Trade. If there is no fixed standard, the pound could be any amount of sugar, depending on the whim of the seller. Gold had been the most common standard because it is relatively rare and difficult to come by and it does not corrode. It has an intrinsic value as a commodity.

Unless in the form of gold, diamonds, or other rare entity, money is not wealth in itself. It is worthless if the underlying commodity or service is not present. The real wealth of a country is its products and services which can be used domestically amongst its residents and exported in exchange for other goods or services. The system would be far more stable under a strict barter system, it would just be very cumbersome and inconvenient to administer.

The value of goods or services depends on the demand for them. The most volatile are agricultural products which are subject to seasonal variations in climate. In a short-crop year prices rise and when there is a surplus prices fall. Farmers are perennially prone to react to these fluctuations in exactly the wrong way. Looking at short year prices, they overproduce for the next year, causing prices to drop. Looking at surplus year prices, they under produce for the next year, causing prices to rise. This creates a vicious cycle. Over the years the federal government has sought to reduce this instability by destroying crops, hoarding and mandating minimum prices, all at taxpayer expense. None of these methods has been successful for anyone except the farmers.

Other goods and services are subject to price fluctuations for different reasons. If there is a shortage of persons in a profession, the price for these services rises. Some professions such as legal and medical intentionally limit the number of practitioners in order to maintain high prices. They do this by making it difficult to enter the university programs and by requiring an extremely long and expensive qualification process before being admitted to the profession.

For millennia a country obtained wealth by two means: it produced it using its own labor and natural resources or it stole it from other countries during war. In fact the major causes of many wars were simply to acquire wealth in the form of goods, labor and territory. The basics have not changed.

The majority of the population has very little understanding of economics and finance. It is not the intent to delve deeply into these subjects here, but some fundamentals are important. Paper money can be and is used to manipulate the economy. In its very basic form, assume ten people each produce equal amounts of different products each day and that all products have the same unit value. At different times each person needs the products of the others. During a period of one month each produces a hundred units of which he sells ninety and then buys ninety units from the other nine. The total number of units is 1,000. They decide to print 1,000 bank notes, each entitling the purchase of one unit. In this way they can use the notes instead of bartering the units. If on any day A needs a unit from B but B does not need what A produces, he can accept a note from A and use this to buy a unit from C. If, suddenly, D clandestinely forges 100 notes there are now 1,100 notes representing 1,000 units, eventually it requires 1.1 notes to purchase a unit causing inflation. Conversely, if E has a house fire and loses his 100 notes, only 900 are left to represent 1,000 units, so each now costs 0.9 notes, causing deflation.

Managing the money supply is a difficult balancing act for the central bank. Having too little money in circulation causes deflation, causing buyers to delay purchases in the hope that prices will fall. This creates a recession. Having too much money circulating causes inflation, causing people to spend all they can quickly for fear of price increases. As has been seen in countries like Argentina and Zimbabwe, if governments cause the central bank to print far more money than is needed, rampant inflation occurs and the economy is ruined.

Under the classical gold standard, inflation was almost zero. In the USA between 1880 and 1914 inflation averaged 0.1% per year. The First World War changed everything as the major belligerents resorted to inflationary financing to fund the war. Facing massive outflows of its gold reserves to the USA to pay war debt, Britain abandoned the Gold Standard in 1931 and one by one other countries followed. At its formation in 1913, the Federal Reserve Bank paid citizens $20.67 per ounce of gold delivered which had been the price since 1834. Seeking to stimulate the moribund economy by prohibiting the hoarding of gold, Franklin Roosevelt unilaterally removed the dollar from the gold standard in 1933 and basically forced US citizens and foreigners to turn in all their gold currency to the Federal Reserve in exchange for paper money at the historical value of $20.67 per ounce. This was accomplished by Executive Order 6102 on April 5th, 1933. It forbade the hoarding of gold coin, gold bullion and gold certificates within the continental United States. This effectively made it a crime for any individual, partnership, association or corporation to possess gold. Astoundingly, no strong objections were raised although this was a clear abuse of the authority granted to the President by the Constitution. It was outrageous to tell citizens they could not own a valuable commodity.

In 1934 Congress took this one step further by passing the Gold Reserve Act which required that all the gold and gold certificates held by the Federal Reserve be surrendered and turned over to the US Department of the Treasury to be stored at Fort Knox. It also outlawed private possession of gold except for artistic purposes and changed the price of gold from the historical $20.67 to $35. This devaluation of the dollar effectively created a 75% increase in treasury holdings and short-changed the citizens and creditors by devaluing their paper money by 43%. Once free from the requirement that paper dollars or dollar credits could be redeemed by citizens in gold at a fixed rate, the Federal Reserve could print paper money at will, and did so.

There is divided opinion regarding the desirability of a world gold standard or any other type of monetary common denominator. On the one hand it preserves the value of a currency but on the other side it limits the tools a country may have to deal with various crises. There is no question that many countries have totally abused these tools to great detriment of their citizens and creditors. Looking at the big picture it would seem that some types of constraints need to be placed on governments and although not perfect, the Gold Standard is a good equalizer. Allowing currencies to float randomly according to the debt obligations and perceived risk factors in each country is not in the interests of the average citizen. It allows governments to devalue the currency at will which decreases the buying power of incomes and savings. It is indeed a form of theft. Individuals and businesses get into the currency markets and move money between currencies based on fear or rewards which again causes volatility in exchange rates. The big investment houses make billions each year on currency trading.

Countries can now manipulate the interest rates on the sovereign bonds in order to facilitate borrowing by their treasuries. A currency whose bonds are considered high-risk must offer a high interest rate. This trickles down to general financing within the country and stifles investment. To compound the problem, in certain cases, foreign investors may consider the rewards worth the risk and buy the bonds which results in over-valuation of the local currency. This in turn stifles exports and exacerbates the root problem of excessive debt.

With the rapid expansion of the internet and online services the world has almost reached the point where paper money has become obsolete altogether. Transactions are simply a question of electronic impulses flashing around the world at the speed of light. The swipe of a credit card instantly moves abstract "money" from one account to another by merely adjusting the balances of each accordingly. This is fast, convenient and so far, reasonably safe. The question then arises as to what will prevent governments or hackers from manipulating the system. This would be equivalent to printing excess banknotes or forging them successfully. The answer is that hackers already accomplish cyber-theft to some extent and credit-card companies must absorb this by charging higher interest rates.

Despite all the technical innovations, in times of uncertainty the average citizen wants something tangible in hand. They rush to troubled banks to withdraw their funds in hard cash and if the banks cannot come up with sufficient cash, panic ensues and the crisis escalates rapidly, as occurred during the Great Depression. Therefore it is imperative that not only must the country maintain a system involving actual cash but the central bank must maintain sufficient cash reserves to stave off panic. The Federal Reserve is responsible for ensuring this happens.

Economics is a fuzzy field. It involves both basic finance but also must take into account psychology. Ten different economists will have twenty different theories. When people are scared they seek safety for their assets and throughout the ages gold and other rare commodities have served as instruments of refuge. These cannot be multiplied at will, each takes labor and capital to get out of the ground which means these commodities have intrinsic value. In unstable economic times, as occurred in the Great Depression, people will buy and hoard gold, silver, diamonds and other rare items. This takes money out of circulation and these people buy less of staple items which keep the economy going, thus prolonging the depression. By forcing the population to give up their gold, Roosevelt effectively put cash back into circulation and people used it to buy various other things. As a temporary expedient this strategy could be defended but in the long term it gave rise to heavy inflation and devaluation.

After two world wars, the USA had secured a considerable amount of Europe's national gold and cash in reparations and repayment of war debts. It was now in a position to dictate international fiscal policy. Under the Bretton Woods Agreement of 1946, the US dollar replaced gold as the international reserve currency but other nations could redeem their dollar holdings in gold at $35 per ounce. In 1964 the restriction on American ownership of gold certificates was relaxed for private investors although these certificates could not be redeemed for bullion. However, in 1971, facing ever-increasing foreign trade deficits and loss of confidence in the dollar, President Nixon abrogated the fixed conversion option for other nations and let the price of gold float, which immediately started rampant inflation and devaluation of the dollar. By 1975 Americans could again buy and hold gold freely and they did. By 1980 the price had risen to a peak of $674 reflecting the high inflation during the Carter years, but as the economy recovered it settled back down to around $300, still a huge devaluation of the dollar from the original $20.67.

The Bretton Woods agreement produced two other entities, the International Monetary Fund (IMF) and the Bank for Reconstruction and Development, later to be known as the World Bank. These were to be based in Washington and sought to bring some order to the movement of capital between nations. This effectively gave the USA unprecedented control over world finance. One of the chief architects of the Bretton Woods agreement was the controversial economist John Maynard Keynes. The immediate net effect of the war and agreement was the increase in value of the US dollar against other participants' currencies. From 1850 until the First World War one pound sterling was worth 5 US dollars. By 1950 the rate had dropped to 2.85. Today it is around 1.3. In looking at the actual buying power of the US dollar, up until 1933 an ounce of gold could be purchased for $20.67. Today it costs $1500 and has been as high as $1800. If citizens had stashed their dollars in a safe in 1913 and removed them in 2019 their buying-power would have effectively decreased by a factor of about 75 if we consider gold a consistent measure of value.

Under a fixed standard, citizens can save with confidence and make plans accordingly. Businesses do not need to build in correction factors to their projections and inflation is near zero. In the workplace annual raises would not be given unless the employee is producing more. Gold, platinum or any other rare and durable element cannot be randomly produced or multiplied.

The Federal Reserve would like people to believe that a certain amount of inflation is somehow a good thing. This is simply an illusion. Most people now expect an annual raise in their salaries in order for them to feel that they are making progress. In fact at best they are breaking even and most of the time they are losing purchasing power because the real inflation is higher than the raise they received. Inflation is simply a form of theft. Countries and individuals would be far better off without annual raises and without inflation.

Individuals, businesses and governments can do various things with money. Each has different objectives and these determine the health of the economy. Individuals can spend, save or hoard money. Under the gold standard hoarding was a valid strategy as no value was lost and no risk was taken other than the possibility of theft. Without the gold standard, inflation discourages hoarding of cash, which is one of the reasons the gold standard was abandoned. Depositing the money in a bank normally ensures its safety but the earnings are low or zero. Investing in bonds and equities gives higher returns commensurate with risk. As most people are unwilling to take high risk they end up getting returns on their savings which are less than inflation which means their savings gradually lose buying power. For this reason many do not save at all and spend their money before it can lose value. Many economists believe this is a good thing because it encourages spending and discourages saving.

Businesses can pay out profits as dividends, re-invest in the company or a combination of both. They can hold their free cash in banks or other investment instruments in their base country or in other countries. The public can invest in public corporations by purchasing stock. The price of the stock theoretically depends on the predicted success of the corporation. In practice however stock prices are influenced by many factors, legitimate and spurious. Major stockholders can buy or sell large blocks, lawsuits can result in huge settlements and even bankruptcy. Local and world politics play a fuzzy part. Technology also renders some products wildly popular and others obsolete. Equities, while offering huge potential rewards, involve commensurate risk..

Governments can tax their citizens to a greater or lesser extent and spend the tax revenues on various services and projects of their choosing. Too often these projects serve only political expedients and are not in the long-term interests of the country. The most beneficial projects are those which improve the infrastructure and thereby increase the comfort and efficiency of the citizens. These are solid assets which endure. Money spent on wars, foreign-aid, disaster relief and social hand-outs is essentially wasted and no long term benefits accrue to the general population. It can be argued that this money is used to buy American goods and services but this does not alter the fact that the end-products are of no value to the country.

Individuals and businesses are likely to handle their money to their best advantage and make decisions which benefit themselves. If they retain a good proportion of their earnings they have a strong incentive to produce. If the government confiscates too much in taxes and fees, productivity is diminished and there is strong resentment. Governments are normally extremely inefficient in their use of money. In all cases the money goes somewhere, but under government control it can be squandered in various ways with little lasting benefit to the citizens. Government's primary responsibilities are defense, infrastructure and protection of the environment. When governments become bloated, an unhealthy proportion of the country's wealth goes to pay for government employees, most of whom produce nothing tangible.

A good example is the President himself. He spends half his first term campaigning for his second term and in the process, flies in a Boeing 747 with his entourage regardless of distance. At the destination airport, all flights in and out are suspended for several hours even though the presidential party never goes through the terminal. Traffic on the roads he will use is halted for hours and millions of man-hours are squandered. It is estimated that Air Force One costs $182,000 per hour when in use and of course has substantial costs when on the ground. No other head of state comes anywhere close in privileges. The President, who should be setting the example for good fiscal policy, instead is the most blatant example of government waste and abuse. Trump is well aware of this but is constrained by law and the Secret Service to follow the protocols in force.

CHAPTER 10: WAR, DEPRESSION AND MORE WAR

There are seldom any winners in war. The costs in treasure and lives are never compensated by gains in territory or temporary social changes. The perpetrators do not consider the long-term consequences of occupying someone else's land and with the exception of the Americas and Australia/New Zealand, most countries are occupied by their historical peoples. The First World War created the platform for a complete rearrangement of the world stage. It was a most foolish war, started almost by accident after a sequence of minor events triggered reaction because of strategic alliances. After the assassination of Archduke Ferdinand and his wife at Sarajevo, Austria-Hungary declared war on Serbia despite the misgivings of an aging Franz Josef. Russian generals persuaded a weak tsar Nicholas to enact full mobilization of its forces on its western border. Against his better judgment, a nervous and ambitious Kaiser Wilhelm II of Prussia allowed his generals to persuade him to pre-empt a possible pincer movement by Russia and France by quickly eliminating France. The result was a disaster for everyone, the only possible winner being the USA. Even it paid a high price in blood, but gained considerable power and gold. To a large extent this war set the stage for the Great Depression and the second war.

The war had another important effect. Historically, anyone who could make it to the shores of the North American continent was welcome to stay simply because the country needed people. Most of the influx to the east coast came from Western Europe and to the west coast from China. In 1921, due to excessive immigration after the First World War, Congress enacted the Emergency Quota Act limiting immigration to those from northern Europe who were likely to have similar cultures to Americans. The quota was 3% per year of the population of each of these nationalities already in the USA. This was intended to be a temporary solution to a flood of immigrants.

In 1924 Congress enacted the Johnson-Reed Act which included The National Origins Act and Asian Exclusion Act which limited the annual number of new immigrants to 2% from each country who were living in the USA at the time of the 1890 census. It forbade the immigration of certain nationalities who were considered ineligible for eventual citizenship because of major cultural differences. No foreign national could enter the country without a valid visa obtained at the US embassy in the country of origin. This act was intended to preserve the cultural composition of the US and continued in force until 1965. It made complete sense.

The causes of The Great Depression can be traced to several factors both material and psychological. The sudden and unexpected outbreak of WW1 sent shock-waves through the world and stock-markets and bonds took a major hit at the time. The Dow Jones Index fell to 53 but recovered as the war progressed, boosted by the war economy and vast inflows of payments and reparations from the European participants. Amazingly, US and UK banks lent Germany the cash to pay the reparations. Unjustified optimism caused stocks to become over-valued, with the Dow reaching 381 in 1929 before crashing spectacularly. It is widely accepted that the US stock market crash was the catalyst which led to the Great Depression. Stock markets had existed long before this, with periodic spectacular crashes but this crash was extreme. Unscrupulous traders drove short-sales and investors took fright. After the war boost petered out and the involved nations surveyed their enormous debts there was an expected contraction of trade throughout the world as each country tried to protect its own industries. The US public had also highly leveraged themselves, taking advantage of easy credit from banks. The expanding power of the trade unions made it difficult for employers to lower wages to remain competitive and so they resorted to massive lay-offs to remain solvent. This had a snowball effect and about 25% of the US workforce became unemployed and unable to service their debts. By 1932 the Dow had dropped to 41 and did not regain its 1929 peak until 1954, albeit in severely devalued dollars. The run on the US banks caused over 2000 to fail as the fear escalated and the credit markets contracted instead of expanding. It can be argued that the newly formed Federal Reserve Bank could have mitigated the panic by injecting cash into the system but it did not.

The basic concept of stock ownership involves the purchase of part of a business which either delivers attractive returns or is expected to deliver these in the future. For a savvy investor who understands the particular business and the risks, the market is an attractive option. The evolution of the system has produced a multitude of variations which have led to unpredictable volatility, and, as in 1929, complete melt-downs. The average investor does little research and follows the crowd, giving snowball effects to prices. Short-trading, futures options, derivatives and margin purchases exacerbate the volatility. Large institutional investors have sufficient buying power to influence prices regardless of financial health of companies. Today computers trade in nanoseconds based on minor fluctuations. Most of the safeguards put in place after the Great Depression have been removed, setting the stage for the 2008 financial crisis.

Herbert Hoover is commonly regarded as the President who failed to solve the problems created by the crash during his administration. The facts paint a little different picture. Hoover, an orphan Quaker who lifted himself up by his own bootstraps, was the first student to go into residence at Stanford University. He graduated with a degree in mining engineering and made a fortune in mining endeavors all over the world. Being a humanitarian, as World War One took Europe by surprise, he led the effort to get all stranded Americans safely home, using his own funds when necessary. With his leadership and organizational skills proven, he then formed the Commission for the Relief of Belgium (CRB) to supply vital food and medical assistance to Belgium after the German army had devastated the country. All this aid was supplied by voluntary contributions from individuals, corporations and governments. He went on to serve as head of the US Food Administration during the war. Wishing to give back to the country which had given him opportunity, he agreed to become Secretary of Commerce after the War in the Harding and Coolidge administrations. He easily won the Presidential Election of 1928 and set his sights on making the Federal Government more efficient. He was the first of only three presidents to donate his salary to charity. (The others are Kennedy and Trump)

The Great Depression was not of Hoover's making but he did all he could to lessen the effects. He signed the Smoot-Hawley Tariff act which backfired as other nations retaliated with their own tariffs on American goods. He initiated many programs to generate employment and offer relief. However, it can be argued that whereas in general his strategies were correct there was no quick fix and time ran out for his re-election. A disillusioned public booted him from office in 1932 and elected Roosevelt.

Franklin Roosevelt is regarded by many as the president who got the USA out of the Great Depression and instituted various social programs which benefited the country as a whole. Roosevelt was from a wealthy New York family and rode the coat-tails of his very popular fifth cousin, Theodore Roosevelt. He gained the support of the unions, Tammany Hall and the powerful Joseph Kennedy which assured him of victory. He repaid Kennedy by appointing him ambassador to Great Britain. Once in office, Roosevelt set about consolidating his position by forming an unlikely coalition of the labor unions, liberals, minorities, Southern whites and the poor receiving government support. The "bosses" in the big cities rallied their voters largely because they were the recipients of billions of dollars in Roosevelt's unemployment relief schemes and federal patronage. This proved to be a winning coalition which got Roosevelt re-elected three times and delivered Democrats to the White House in all but nine elections from 1932-2012. Democrats also controlled both houses of Congress for the majority of this period.

Roosevelt actually continued many of the programs initiated by Hoover and received the credit. He expanded government spending on social and public works programs, telling the public not to worry about the exploding debt, saying "after all, we owe it to ourselves". This was not quite correct, as most citizens did not have the cash to purchase government bonds. Reality was that all the citizens owed it to a few citizens, companies and foreign countries. All this spending did not actually end the Depression, it took the Second World War to get everyone back to work again, also at government expense. The war production also brought in billions from the Allies who purchased American arms.

In reaction to the devastating effects of bank failures after the stock market crash of 1929, in 1933 Roosevelt signed the Banking Act, a culmination of efforts by Senator Carter Glass and representative Henry Steagall, to separate commercial and investment banking. It also created the Federal Deposit Insurance Corporation to insure the money in each account up to a certain amount. Beginning under the Clinton administration, the separation requirements have been abandoned, in part leading to the 2008 crisis.

The Second World War was even more foolish than the First. Roosevelt, together with the English, French and Italian governments, sat by and watched Germany become a virtual military dictatorship under Hitler. Despite dire warnings from his ambassador in Berlin, he did nothing to avert this catastrophe. Whereas Nazi militarization and rearmament were in flagrant violation of the Treaty of Versailles forced upon Germany by Woodrow Wilson, none of the signatories tried to enforce it. This remains astounding. The USA never became a member of the League of Nations and never signed the treaty as the majority of the country was strongly opposed to a second involvement in European affairs. While watching Germany descend into anarchy and vigorously re-arm, the other nations reduced their militaries. When war became a certainty in 1939, Roosevelt realized the necessity of preparing for US involvement and instituted conscription and conversion of industrial production to military production.

Despite the warm friendship between Roosevelt and Churchill, as the war was drawing to an end, Roosevelt found himself at odds with one of Europe's most astute statesmen. At the conference in Yalta in February 1945, the main issue was the composition of the post-war spheres of influence of the victors. Notwithstanding Churchill's advice and requests, Roosevelt naively believed that Stalin would honor the agreements made at the conference, particularly regarding the post-war status of Poland. Of course Stalin already occupied Poland and much of Eastern Europe and had no intention of returning them to independent democratic republics, thereby setting the stage for chaos in a divided Germany and subjugation of Eastern Europe by the communist regime. In fact then and still today, the real enemy was Russia, and it is astounding that the US naively failed to realize this, but in fairness the only way to dislodge Russian influence from these territories would have been further military conflict which nobody wanted.

At the time of Yalta the war was effectively over. Roosevelt, however, felt that Russian forces were still vital to a speedy victory and was reluctant to resist Stalin's demands. In fairness, Russia had provided the bulk of the manpower and suffered the greatest losses in defeating Hitler. It can be argued that Russia won the war for the Allies, albeit with huge contributions of armaments from the USA. With access to the best American and German technology and shortly thereafter nuclear bomb technology from the Rosenbergs, Russia was in a position to thwart the western opposition to the spread of communism. This led to the loss of China, the Cold War and the complications of Korea and Vietnam. It remains a problem in dealing with Africa, South America and the Middle East.

Both World Wars were completely unnecessary and should never have happened. With the communications and sophistications created by the Industrial Revolution it should have been possible for statesmen to resolve their differences in a logical and mature fashion to be fair to all. In fact, the wars began because of gross misjudgments by educated people who should have known better. They had far-reaching effects, effectively ending the superiority England had enjoyed for almost three hundred years, bankrupting most of Europe and relocating most of the western gold to the USA to pay reparations and for military materiel supplied to the Allies. This gave the USA unprecedented leverage over world affairs, as by controlling the money it could control the politics.

As the only combatant whose country had not been devastated by bombs and military action, for the USA the Second World War provided the impetus to greatly expand the manufacturing capability and effectively end the depression by getting everyone back to work. The increase in production during the war, instituted by Roosevelt, was astounding and demonstrated to the country that it could perform beyond anyone's expectations. Roosevelt was not experienced in manufacturing but his exhortations to do what others considered impossible were realized. Although very costly in terms of lives and treasure, this war effectively positioned the USA as the world's pre-eminent superpower. The USA also gained significant advantage in the fields of science and engineering by offering sanctuary, and to some, immunity to the sharpest minds in the world. Aside from Einstein and Fermi who sought sanctuary before the war, in 1945 Operation Paperclip the US brought in 1500 German scientists, engineers and technicians to both bolster its own rocket and military programs and to deprive Germany and Russia of the talents of these people.

A common threat brings people together and the USA astonished even themselves at the incredible quantities of war equipment and supplies that were produced for US and allied use. It can be claimed that this productivity was one of the major contributors to allied victories. The need for arms also finally got everyone back to work including women and blacks previously excluded from industrial production. The Depression was finally over. The victory resulted in the USA becoming the leading world power militarily and economically and as such, in a position to pressure the European nations to give "independence" to all their colonies and dismantle their empires. This was one of Roosevelt's objectives. In fact this policy led to destabilization of former colonies which continues today. The entire African continent and Middle East are in turmoil. It is ironic that in all the former colonies where the indigenous population was granted "independence, the resulting instability and mismanagement has led to mass migrations of these people to the very countries which had colonized them. Europe must now deal with hordes of refugees flocking to escape the misery of their own countries.

As part of the tremendous expansion in manufacturing to supply arms for the war, for the first time many women entered the workforce and performed admirably. When the war ended, many of these women continued to work outside the home, effectively increasing the workforce permanently. When more people are available for the same number of jobs, the price of labor drops. This is not immediately perceptible because of inflation but the net result has been that today many families depend on the income of both spouses to live comfortably. The cultural revolution of the 60's and 70's is very likely due to the fact that many of the post-war children grew up in homes where no parent was present during the day. The steady breakdown of the family unit is probably also due partially to this.

The other far-reaching effect of the second war was reaction to the Nazi and Russian genocides. These differed from prior mass killings in that they were not instigated for military reasons or for retribution, but were cold-blooded, calculated attempts at extermination of particular groups of the countries' own citizens. Whereas previously most of the world's countries were nationalistic and gave preference to the majority tribe or race, a new doctrine emerged encouraging strong protections for minorities. The 14th amendment to the US Constitution, like the legal systems in most other countries including Germany, sought to give every citizen equal protection under the law. As evidenced in the US and Germany, the law can be ignored. Most western democracies decided that additional safeguards were needed and encouraged both unrestricted immigration and special protection for minorities. This sentiment, together with other factors, led to the passing of the various Civil Rights Acts and subsequent acts to curtail discrimination in every possible circumstance.

The concept of special protection is noble in principle and indeed the language of the Civil Rights Acts simply prohibits discrimination based on race, color, religion, sex, or national origin. This applies to everyone. The problem this creates is that it provides a legal tool for anyone who feels mistreated to sue the offending party, regardless of whether the offense arose from one of the enumerated factors or not. The end result is that minorities are in a position to thwart the will of the majority which is contrary to the basic principle of democracy.

CHAPTER 11: THE NEW DEAL

By all accounts, Franklin Roosevelt was a man who waited to see which way the wind was blowing before making decisions. A charming personality allowed him to conduct press briefings with entertaining anecdotes without answering any questions. He was reluctant to commit himself to any course of action but was adept at presenting a most amenable posture while agreeing to nothing. He had few close men friends but enjoyed the company of various women with whom he spent considerable time. Shortly after taking office, Roosevelt presided over two more amendments, both ratified in 1933. The 20th dealt with the timing of the terms of elected officials and the procedural matters and the 21st repealed the 18th, thus ending prohibition. Franklin Roosevelt greatly enjoyed the power the office of president offered him. Like many who are raised in luxury he sought political favor from the masses by promoting their causes using borrowed money. This ensured his continuing support in elections and he was the first president to test the number of terms a president could serve. He died in his fourth term, after which Congress wisely passed the 22nd amendment in 1947, ratified by the states in 1951. This limited all future presidents to two terms. Roosevelt also sought to pack the Supreme Court with candidates who were likely to interpret the Constitution in his favor. He lobbied for an increase in the number of justices via his Judicial Procedures Reform Bill of 1937. This bill was defeated but nevertheless, Roosevelt was able to appoint 8 new justices during his 12 years in office, giving him considerable leeway to implement his New Deal. During this time the court substantially changed its interpretation of the Constitution which facilitated Roosevelt's agenda. It also guaranteed that the Court would rule liberally for many years to come. This influence on the composition of the Court was a major reason for the 22nd amendment.

The New Deal saw the passage of a number of bills which were intended to both end the depression and bring the Federal Government into the lives of citizens. Whereas the original Constitution and Amendments sought to limit the Federal government to issues of state, Roosevelt believed that it should also play a role in providing services and dictating behavior to individuals. To the naïve voter, money and services from the "government" are somehow free. To those who pay no taxes indeed they are. Parts of the New Deal were continuations of Hoover programs under new names. One of the most far-reaching programs was Social Security.

Roosevelt took office at the height of the Depression and wisely appointed a group of experienced economists and bankers to advise him on how best to deal with the problem. One of the first actions taken was to abrogate the gold clause embodied in many national and international contracts. This clause sought to insure against currency fluctuations by stipulating payment could be made in cash or gold at the creditors' discretion. In order to stimulate the economy and get folk to start spending, Roosevelt's advisors recommended devaluation of the dollar to cause inflation and raise prices, particularly of farm commodities. In order to accomplish this the gold clause had to be abandoned. In the case of international debt this was a serious breach of contract and eventually the case was referred to the Supreme Court. The court correctly rejected the case which was one of the reasons Roosevelt attempted to add more justices.

Roosevelt was instrumental in passing the Social Security Act of 1935 when the Depression was still in full swing and many older people were suffering. Although charitable in intent, in fact there is nothing in the Constitution authorizing Congress to get involved in the affairs of individuals or in effect imposing a forced retirement scheme upon them and their employers. While undoubtedly attractive in the short term and likely to garner votes, this scheme is a pyramid type operation whereby today's workers do not save for themselves directly, but pay for today's retirees. Since this door was opened, the concept has been expanded to include payments for healthcare, disabilities and various other cases to the point that it is now an unsustainable behemoth. Total Social Security expenditures in 2013 were $1.3 trillion, 8.4% of GDP and 37% of all government expenditures. To make matters worse, the excesses in the SS trust fund and other social programs have been converted to federal bonds and form a large part of the unfunded liabilities of the Federal government. There are now two parts to the national debt: that part which is owed to the public and the part which is owed to government trust funds for social programs from which the government has borrowed. Many countries have mandated retirement schemes but the smart ones involve individuals contributing to their own accounts which bear interest and accumulate for their own use after retirement. Again, any charitable services are for the states to decide, not the Federal government. For most recipients, Social Security is not a hand-out but simply a return of their own and their employers' contributions. Those who die before their actuary ages are short-changed. Those who live beyond this age receive more than their contributions.

The constitutionality of the SS Act was in fact challenged and came before the Supreme Court in 1937 under Helvering vs Davis and Steward Machine Co. v Davis. However, the issue was not the broad constitutionality of the principle of mandating a pension for people in their old age or other benefits but was limited to whether the payroll tax was a suitable use of Congress's taxing power. The court decided that it was. Article I, section 8 of the Constitution provides that

"The Congress shall have the Power To lay and collect Taxes, Duties, Imposts and Excises, to pay the Debts and provide for the common Defense and general Welfare of the United States......."

The term "general Welfare" is unfortunately open to all kinds of interpretation and is at the root of many of the abuses of public funds. Strictly speaking, the judges should have read a little further in section 8 and they should have concluded that nothing is mentioned regarding the right of Congress to get involved in old-age pensions. If it is not mentioned then Congress has no jurisdiction. The term "general Welfare of the United States" was intended to cover benefits to the states, not individuals.

The two Supreme Court rulings that affirmed the constitutionality of the Social Security Act were rationalized as follows:

- In *Steward*, "[*It*] *is too late today for the argument to be heard with tolerance that in a crisis so extreme the use of the moneys of the nation to relieve the unemployed and their dependents is a use for any purpose narrower than the promotion of the general Welfare* ". The dissent claimed that the social security act went beyond the powers that were granted to the Federal government in the Constitution. They argued that, by imposing a tax on employers that could be avoided only by contributing to a state unemployment fund, the federal government was essentially forcing each state to establish an unemployment-compensation fund that would meet its criteria, and that the

Federal government had no power to enact such a program.

- The *Helvering* decision, on the same day as *Steward*, upheld the program because "*The proceeds of both [employee and employer] taxes are to be paid into the Treasury like internal-revenue taxes generally, and are not earmarked in any way*". That is, the Social Security Tax was constitutional as a mere exercise of Congress's general taxation powers.

This is not true. The taxes are specifically dedicated to Social Security and any excesses are placed in a trust fund for future payments to this program. Trust fund cash is converted to treasury bonds which earn interest at the prevailing rate and theoretically become part of the national debt. From its inception until 2014, there was flow into this trust fund. This was supplemented from 1984 onwards by taxing the Social Security payments to seniors whose income exceeded a certain threshold. It is estimated that by 2015 the receipts will be less than the outlays and the trust fund will need to redeem the bonds and eventually will be depleted unless changes are made to the program.

These two decisions were to some extent influenced by Roosevelt's plan to pack the Supreme Court by effectively adding 6 more judges who would presumably vote in his favor. By approving these parts of his New Deal before the court-packing plan could be voted upon, the pressure to approve it was diminished.

This is another case of the Supreme Court second-guessing the intent of the Constitution and manipulating the words to suit their desired outcome. All civilized societies recognize that certain safety nets are necessary to care for and protect certain segments of the population. Traditionally, extended family has shouldered most of this burden. When this has not been possible, the original English system involved workhouses for the able-bodied indigent and single mothers unable to provide for their children and this was the original system in the USA. These were never intended to be attractive options and were considered solutions of last resort. This was for the valid reason that every able-bodied person was encouraged to provide for himself and his family. Those too old or frail to work who have no family to care for them and no assets or income must be cared for somehow, but this was and should have remained a state responsibility.

The Industrial Revolution combined with the great dust-bowl years in the midwest had a major impact on the number of people requiring assistance. Before this, a large percentage of the population lived on farms with extended family members who provided support. They were largely self-sufficient in food and shelter except during the extended drought which gave rise to the "dust bowl" in the 1930's. The huge shift to the towns and cities and the prolonged drought disrupted this system and left many in dire straits.

Before the Great Depression each state had some measure of assistance in place and also relied heavily on charitable institutions. The Depression overwhelmed these resources temporarily and the relief by the Federal government should have been temporary. As Roosevelt himself proclaimed in his State of the Union address in January 1935
"The lessons of history, confirmed by the evidence immediately before me, show conclusively that continued dependence upon relief induces a spiritual and moral disintegration fundamentally destructive to the national fiber. To dole out relief in this way is to administer a narcotic, a subtle destroyer of the human spirit". . . . . Notwithstanding this, he signed the Social Security Act in August.

At its inception the payroll tax was 2% of the first $3000 in earnings. In 1966 president Johnson added the Medicare system and today the combined payroll taxes are a total of 15.3% of the first $113,700 in earnings. In other words, the maximum contribution has increased by a factor of 290. None of these programs is the business of the Federal government. Each state is empowered to institute its own program to provide for the old and needy. It does not make any sense for the Federal government to collect money and then allocate it to the states for disbursement. If each state had its own system this would be far more efficient and over time the best strategy would become evident.

1937 saw more efforts by Roosevelt to increase the power of the presidency. When the court-packing plan was thwarted, he proposed adding significantly to the staff of the executive and consolidating federal agencies under cabinet members. This was opposed initially but after negotiations and amendments, in 1939 the Reorganization Act was passed. This not only added presidential staff but more importantly created the Executive Office of the President. This effectively reduced the power and authority of the cabinet and created two distinct bodies within the executive, those in the EOP and those working directly for the President. This permitted the President to conceal policy making behind the claim of executive privilege.

The Reorganization Act gave rise to Executive Order 8248, with the basic objectives defined below:

"There shall be within the Executive Office of the President the following principal divisions, namely: (1) The White House Office, (2) the Bureau of the Budget, (3) the National Resources Planning Board, (4) the Liaison Office for Personnel Management, (5) the Office of Government Reports, and (6) in the event of a

national emergency, or threat of a national emergency, such office for emergency management as the President shall determine".

This effectively consolidated executive powers in the office of the President.

The Franklin Roosevelt administration had various other long-lasting effects on the country. A major player in some of these was his wife, Eleanor, Theodore Roosevelt's niece. Early in the marriage Franklin entered into a relationship with Eleanor's assistant, Lucy Mercer. When Eleanor eventually discovered this she offered divorce, but Franklin's mother threatened to cut him off financially and he knew this would adversely affect his future in politics so the couple decided to remain married as de-facto business partners. Having abdicated her position as a wife, she became driven in the pursuit of social justice and spent the majority of her time traveling the country promoting various causes and cajoling Roosevelt to act upon her recommendations. It is not the business of the Federal government to force charities upon its citizens. It must confine itself to enacting reasonable laws to protect the safety of the people and ensuring that these laws are enforced uniformly and justly. Charity is the premise of individuals and private businesses.

As the wife of the President, Eleanor was effective in strongly promoting the causes of the poor and the blacks and as a result of this, many blacks were won over to the Democrat party. This began a trend which continues today whereby over 95% of blacks consistently vote Democrat. To avert a crisis regarding the treatment of blacks in the military and war economy, Roosevelt reluctantly signed Executive Order 8802 on June 25th, 1941. Part of this was:

"Whereas it is the policy of the United States to encourage full participation in the national defense program by all citizens of the United States, regardless of race, creed, color, or national origin, in the firm belief that the democratic way of life within the Nation can be defended successfully only with the help and support of all groups within its borders;"

"Now, Therefore, by virtue of the authority vested in me by the Constitution and the statutes, and as a prerequisite to the successful conduct of our national defense production effort, I do hereby reaffirm the policy of the United States that there shall be no discrimination in the employment of workers in defense industries or government because of race, creed, color, or national origin, and I do hereby declare that it is the duty of employers and of labor organizations, in furtherance of said policy and of this Order, to provide for the full and equitable participation of all workers in defense industries, without discrimination because of race, creed, color, or national origin..."

This was not law, but an administrative order which formed the basis for the Civil Rights movement and subsequent laws including the Civil Rights Act of 1964 signed by Lyndon Johnson.

CHAPTER 12: TRUMAN AND EISENHOWER

Vice President Harry Truman assumed the presidency after Roosevelt's death in April 1945. A self-proclaimed small-town boy, his self-effacing, homey personality was in stark contrast with his predecessor. He presided over the end of the Second World War and set about returning the nation to normal. Often referred to as the "accidental president" Truman, like Wilson, was co-opted into public office by a corrupt party boss, in his case Jim Prendergast. A most reluctant candidate to serve Roosevelt as vice-president, Truman's strong work ethic, incorruptible principles and willingness to make difficult decisions rapidly won him the respect of Congress and American citizens. Having endured back-breaking work on his family farm and bankruptcy at his haberdashery Truman understood real life. He served honorably as an artillery commander in the fiercest battles of World War 1 and knew the horrors of war. Perhaps no prior president was less prepared and more challenged (Roosevelt kept him largely in the dark) but Truman rose to the occasion and put his heart into serving his country.

Perhaps no new president faced more daunting problems than Truman. However, being a true patriot, he did his utmost to make honorable decisions which served America and the world best. At the Potsdam conference regarding post-war agreements with Churchill (and later Atlee) and Stalin he found the

Russian leader intransigent and was unable to make any meaningful progress. He had to make the historic and very difficult decision to use nuclear force against Japan but after exhausting all other options he gave the order and took full responsibilty.

During his tenure the question of prayer in public schools came before the Supreme Court. The First Amendment clearly states that

"Congress shall make no law respecting an establishment of religion, or prohibiting the free exercise thereof; or abridging the freedom of speech, or of the press; or the right of the people peaceably to assemble, and to petition the Government for a redress of grievances."

This says nothing about prohibiting religion in public places etc., it simply makes it clear that the Federal government cannot involve itself in religion by making laws affecting it. There is nothing in the Constitution referring to separation of church and state. On the contrary, church was a big part of life at the time of independence and this extended to free expression of religion regardless of venue. There is room for clarification however. As worded, the language implies that all religious practices are permissible and Congress cannot make laws prohibiting them. This would mean that if a particular recognized religion historically practiced the stoning to death of a woman who committed adultery then its adherents would be free to do so. There is no clear solution to this but each state is free to make laws it considers appropriate for its residents.

One of the first challenges to the free practice of religion came in 1948 in the Illinois public school system. The case was brought by Vashti McCollum, an atheist, objecting to her child being required to attend classes in religion. Whereas the Illinois Supreme Court had upheld the school's right to offer these classes, the Federal Supreme Court ruled as follows:

"The facts show the use of tax-supported property for religious instruction and the close cooperation between the school authorities and the religious council in promoting religious education. The operation of the state's compulsory education system thus assists and is integrated with the program of religious instruction carried on by separate religious sects. Pupils compelled by law to go to school for secular education are released ... in part from their legal duty upon the condition that they attend the religious classes.

To hold that a state cannot consistently with the First and Fourteenth Amendments utilize its public school system to aid any or all religious faiths or sects in the dissemination of their doctrines and ideals does not ... manifest a governmental hostility to religion or religious teachings. ... For the First Amendment rests upon the premise that both religion and government can best work to achieve their lofty aims if each is left free from the other within its respective sphere".

Despite the vague language, the conclusion was that McCollum won and the classes were ruled unconstitutional. Religion is a major part of history and the Bible is the most widely read book in the world. The majority of Americans are Christians and no harm can be done to non-Christians by learning history and the tenets of the Christian religion, the principles of which form the basis for the US form of government. The simple solution would have been to make classes involving religious instruction voluntary for those students who preferred not to participate.

Today the Gallup poll estimates that in the USA, 77% of inhabitants consider themselves Christian, 18% do not have specific religious identity and 5% are non-Christian. 77% is a pretty solid majority and if the concept of democracy is applied, the members of this group should have the right to decide where and when Christian customs can be practiced in each state. Others are free to participate or not. No-one is harmed. It is astounding that the 77% did not rise up in revolt to preserve rights that had existed since the formation of the Union. Eight Supreme Court justices ruled that one atheist could curtail the rights and privileges of 150 million Christians.

There is another aspect of the religious debate which is now coming before the courts. If a business establishes a dress code, is it obliged to hire someone who refuses to meet this code because of religion? The case came up regarding the Moslem head scarf. In a free country a private business should be free to hire and fire whom it pleases. There are now so many restrictions instituted by the Federal government that business are scared to hire and fire. The unintended consequences actually hurt the majority. The next question is what constitutes a religion? A prankster in Indiana has created the Church of Cannabis and has secured non-profit tax status from the IRS based on the concept that this is a religious entity. This is a fine example of how absurd the thinking has become.

Harry Truman set a different direction for US foreign policy in instituting the Truman Doctrine in 1948. This was in reaction to the rapid spread of communism after the Second World War, a situation to some extent created by Roosevelt at Yalta. Truman's philosophy held that the US should support any regime or revolutionary force which opposed communism regardless of the form it took. This resulted in US involvement with dictators and terrorists in many countries without regard to democracy, human rights or any other quality. As can be seen still today in Cuba, the policy had little effect and served in many cases to create monsters.

The four terms to which Franklin Roosevelt was elected caused Congress to consider the question of term limits for the office of president. The original Constitution placed no limits on terms and in theory a person could hold the office for life, not unlike a dictator or king. In 1951 Congress wisely ratified the 22nd amendment which limited future presidents to no more than two elected terms. Unfortunately this did not extend to the members of Congress.

Truman was succeeded by Republican general Dwight Eisenhower in 1953. In addition to having first-hand experience of the devastation and atrocities committed in Europe, Eisenhower also took careful note of the infrastructure Hitler had created which had enabled Germany to conduct the war so efficiently. One of these was the autobahn system. Eisenhower initiated the Interstate road system, a wise use of taxpayer money which substantially increased the efficiency and enjoyment of the US citizen and tourist. It also provided needed employment to the thousands of people seeking work as a result of the termination of war. Eisenhower retained the high taxation instituted to pay for the war to reduce the debt and improve infrastructure. Although this caused mini-depressions, financially the country did well, with almost no inflation and debt kept to a minimum. The price for this was tepid GDP growth but despite this, the Dow Industrial Average almost doubled during the 8 years of his administration.

No amendments were made to the Constitution during the Eisenhower presidency but several events had a profound effect on the country on his watch. In 1956 he used the power of the US post-war financial leverage to effectively blackmail France and Britain into giving up the Suez Canal, which they had built and paid for, to Egypt. This started the unraveling of British influence in the Middle East and Eisenhower reportedly regretted his action. He ended the Korean War with an unsatisfactory armistice which continues today and during his administration the Cold War with the Soviet Union continued despite his hopes that after the death of Stalin in 1953 relations would improve. In striving to contain the spread of communism, he involved the US in Cuba, Vietnam and Africa with disastrous results.

His administration saw the onset of the civil-rights movement and the Supreme Court ruling on segregation. The Brown vs Board of Education regarding desegregation of public schools was one of the most controversial cases brought before the Court. It rendered a unanimous decision on May 17th, 1954 ruling that segregated schools were unconstitutional. Ten states tried to use nullification and interposition to declare this decision outside the authority of the Federal Government. The Supreme Court however rejected these attempts, citing the Equal Protection clause of the Fourteenth Amendment. The clause, which took effect in 1868, provides that

"no state shall deny to any person within its jurisdiction the right to equal protection under the law".

This clause is very clear and provides that every person shall be judged and protected by the same laws in the same manner. There is nothing in the Constitution relating to education and there is no mandate that any state be required to provide it. Notwithstanding this, the Court determined that black students were harmed by the segregated system even if all other aspects were equal, which they were not. No-one raised the opposite argument that all students would be harmed by forced desegregation, which they were. The Brown case was slow to have effect but in the end it set the stage for the civil Rights Acts of 1957 and 1964.

After Arkansas governor Orval Faubus used his national guard to defy the federal law requiring admission of black students to white schools, Eisenhower placed the guard under his command and sent federal troops into Arkansas to force white schools to comply. This created great hostility by Southerners who saw it as a blatant infraction of the democratic process. If a referendum had been taken in the state there is no doubt that the majority would have opposed the integration by force.

In September 1957 Congress passed the Civil Rights Act which sought to protect blacks from disenfranchisement by southern legislatures. Senate majority leader Lyndon Johnson, realizing that the act in its original form would seriously harm the Democratic Party in the South, sent the draft to the judiciary committee, where it was considerably weakened to appease southern concerns. The act established the Commission on Civil Rights and the office of Assistant Attorney General on Civil Rights.

In 1960 the Supreme Court ruled that government employees could not indulge in any form of public prayer and no religious symbols could be displayed on government property, arguing that the government could not be seen as endorsing any particular religion. This is a far stretch of the 1st amendment and completely in conflict with the freedom of speech clause. The Founders had no intention of prohibiting public prayer, indeed it was a major force in all the colonies. The majority of the population was Christian, and the establishment clause of the 1st amendment serves only to preclude a repeat of the actions of Henry 8th whereby all of England was forced to belong to Church of England. The main Constitution does not authorize Congress to involve itself in religion at all but the 1st amendment clause was added at the behest of Maine to ensure that religious freedom would be clearly protected.

There is an inherent misinterpretation and conflict regarding individuals who are public employees making any reference to religion in presentations to any group in the line of business. On the one hand, freedom of speech permits them to say anything they please. On the other hand, those who believe in separation of church and state would like to prohibit them from mentioning religion. Jesus Christ is probably the best known individual in the world, it is absurd that his name cannot be mentioned by public employees.

The Second Amendment has come up for close scrutiny as well. It states

"A well regulated Militia, being necessary to the security of a free State, the right of the people to keep and bear arms, shall not be infringed".

This had nothing to do with hunting, it was all about the right to protect oneself and maintaining a well-armed citizenry to both provide additional military force in case of outside attack and to provide an opposing citizens' military force in case any president were tempted to use the army to suppress the citizens, as Lincoln and Eisenhower did. It is very clear and very important. The high incidence of crimes involving guns cannot be blamed on the guns, it is a cultural problem provoked by Hollywood, dysfunctional families and a perverted yearning for notoriety by disturbed individuals.

CHAPTER 13: KENNEDY AND JOHNSON

In 1960 senator John Kennedy was elected president in a very close race with vice-president Richard Nixon. The son of wealthy Boston tycoon Joseph Kennedy, he had never worked in the private sector and at 43, became the youngest man to be elected president (although Theodore Roosevelt had assumed that office at the age of 42). Kennedy fired up the young generation with his youth and good looks, greatly facilitated by his vivacious wife Jacqueline. The White House assumed an aura of fantasy and after Kennedy's death became known as Camelot, the mythical castle of King Arthur and his knights of the round table. Totally inexperienced at management, Kennedy embraced the dreams of many to create the perfect society and save the world. Although his tenure was cut short by his assassination in December 1963, his administration set in motion a number of initiatives which his successor, vice-president Lyndon Johnson, put into place. Both Kennedy and Johnson took the progressive agenda to new levels by involving the Federal government in areas neither contemplated nor authorized by the Constitution.

During the civil-rights movement of the 1960's, President John Kennedy called the existing immigration quota system prescribed by the Johnson-Reed Act of 1924 "nearly intolerable" and promoted a change. After his assassination, President Johnson signed the Immigration and Nationality Act of 1965. This was a major departure from the philosophy held since the founding of the country and the 1924 act in force until then specifically excluded Latin Americans, Asians and Africans and favored northern and western Europeans who had the same culture as the vast majority of Americans. This act abolished the 1924 national origins quota system and replaced it with a preference system based on skills and family relationships. Kennedy had figured out that the white electorate was fairly evenly divided between Republicans and Democrats, and to win the presidency he needed the support of the blacks. Whereas historically it had been the Republicans who had freed the slaves and enacted the 13th, 14th and 15th Amendments giving blacks equal rights, by having brother Bobby aid in the release of Martin Luther King from jail, Kennedy gained black support. This probably tipped the scales in his favor in the very close contest with Nixon. Johnson was aware of this and continued to woo blacks by supporting this act.

Surprisingly the authors of the act, Senator Hart and Congressman Celler, supported vigorously by Ted Kennedy, were successful in convincing Congress and many citizens that this major shift in immigration policy would not affect the ethnic composition of the country or its culture. This was at the least disingenuous and more likely a blatant distortion of the truth, but the Act passed both houses with bi-partisan support. This Act has had a profound impact on the ethnic mix to the point that at current rates of immigration it is estimated that non-Latin whites will be a minority by 2042.

Historically almost 100% of blacks and over 70% of Latinos have voted Democrat and this is likely to continue. As a majority of women also vote Democrat, this gives the party a strong advantage.

Once the act became law there was a movement to actively recruit candidates from Africa and other countries to come to the USA to study and learn the ways of America, funded by various American philanthropists including the Kennedy family. The theory was that in doing so, these individuals would return to their mother countries and bring American customs and culture to their own people. Obama's father was one of these. In fact, once exposed to the good life paid for by others, few returned to their countries and instead became residents and eventually citizens of the USA.

It is surprising that the Congress of 1965 supported this act. The country was founded and developed by Northern and Western Europeans and had become successful under their management. Introducing large numbers of immigrants from different cultures and failing economies was unlikely to benefit the country. The family member provision of this law meant that once one person had been approved for immigration, a geometric progression ensued for other family members to obtain immigrant visas and the flood gates were open. Furthermore, the country did not need more people, it was doing very well with the existing population. The only valid argument for any immigration is to acquire exceptionally skilled people who will embrace the existing culture, raise the standards of technology and productivity and allow the country to advance and produce superior products and services. However, this assumes that equally skilled and talented people are not available in the country, which is not necessarily the case. In the quest for "diversity", many universities give preference to foreign students when considering admissions and thereby deny these critical opportunities to their own citizens.

The original Founders and early immigrants had made great sacrifices and taken considerable risk because they wished to escape the crowded and constraining influences they experienced in their native countries. For this reason they wished to maintain the culture they had developed and keep the population at reasonable levels. The 1965 law opened up immigration to peoples unlikely to assimilate. Supporters of the law claimed that the "diversity" created by having to deal with many different cultures was beneficial to the country. There is no evidence of this and indeed racial, ethnic and religious divisions are now more pronounced than ever.

The pitfall of the current system and the uncontrolled illegal immigration is that within the next few years the founding culture will be overwhelmed and will abdicate control of the country to a coalition of other cultures. This is irreversible and its consequences should not be underestimated. Those countries with a majority of mixed races have not realized their potential and never will. Most of South and Central America falls into this category. The current policy has the same result as losing a war and being occupied by a foreign power except no shots are fired and the process takes much longer. There are even those who believe there should be no borders throughout the world and everyone should be free to travel without restriction and live and work where they please. Imagine the result if this came to pass. It is equivalent to opening up one's home to all-comers. Within a few days one would be outnumbered and lose control and from there the house would be rapidly overcrowded and eventually no-one could live there in reasonable comfort. Of the approximately seven billion people on earth, probably six billion of these would like to come to the USA "to lead a better life." Should they all be welcomed?

Supporters of indiscriminate immigration claim that the USA needs more citizens. This is not the case, the country is already severely overpopulated in many regions and the infrastructure is overburdened. It is not necessary to have a GDP that continuously increases. If everyone is happy and comfortable the GDP can be static with no downside. It is also claimed that low-skilled immigrants are necessary to perform work that citizens will not do. This is also untrue. As long as citizens can choose to work or not and receive government handouts for not working, they will not take jobs at the pay rate new immigrants are prepared to. If able-bodied citizens were denied welfare as long as any jobs were available the immigrants would not be needed.

The Immigration and Nationality Act and uncontrolled illegal immigration have had a particularly large impact on employment for blacks. Employers quite naturally seek the employees who do the best job for the wage being offered. With the welfare programs instituted during the Great Society, able-bodied adults are not obliged to take strenuous jobs at low wages. Since the 60's, many of the jobs traditionally filled by blacks are now done by Mexicans and other immigrant nationalities. Surprisingly the black community continues to vote for the candidates who are unwilling to resolve the illegal immigrant issue.

The 1890 census recorded a total population of 62.6 million of which 87.8% were white and 11.9% black, the remaining small percent being Native American and other races. The 2010 census recorded a total population of 309 million of which 64% were white, 12% black, 16% Hispanic and the remainder Asian and other races. It is unknown how many people are in the country illegally who were not counted in the census but estimates put this at about 12 million, mostly Hispanic.

The 23rd amendment was ratified during Kennedy's term. This dealt with the District of Columbia to appoint electors authorized to vote in presidential elections. The number was to be calculated according to the population as if DC were a state, but could not exceed the number of electors in the least populous state, which is 3. Since this amendment, DC has always voted Democrat.

Kennedy also initiated the 24th amendment, only ratified in January 1964 after his death. This prohibited the use of a poll tax or any other tax as a requirement for voting in federal elections. The Constitution is clear that voting requirements are the province of each state, a concept the Supreme Court had upheld in 1937 in Breedlove vs Suttles. In fact poll taxes do not infringe on the 14th or 15th amendments as they apply equally to all citizens. Some of the southern states also required literacy tests in order to vote. As long as these were applied equally to everyone there is merit to this. Regrettably they were not. However, Kennedy was not unaware that elimination of all qualifications to vote other than age would inevitably garner more votes for the Democrat party as the less affluent and less educated voters tend to be socialistic. This was important because white southerners were becoming disenchanted with the Democrats' increasingly liberal agenda.

The Kennedy administration, which lasted less than three years, is a good example of public infatuation with an individual. Despite the common knowledge that he was an enthusiastic adulterer, women of all ages swooned at the sight of him and marveled at the charm and grace of his pretty wife. His wealth, youth, charisma and good looks somehow led people to believe that he was akin to a god and could do no wrong. They embraced his dreams without considering the unintended consequences. If he had had the appearance of his Russian counterpart, Nikita Krushchev, it is likely he would never have been elected or if he had, would have raised little excitement.

Vice-president Lyndon Johnson assumed the presidency after Kennedy's assassination in December 1963. By all accounts Johnson was a very savvy politician who understood how to play the system completely. With 34 years in Congress and eventually Democratic leader of the Senate before becoming Vice-president, he had been the master of persuasion. He understood people. Aware of the Kennedy infatuation, he was careful to retain many of Kennedy's cabinet members and continue many of his programs. He was able to advance his own agenda by continuing the techniques of persuasion used in the Senate. When necessary, he met with individual congressmen and senators and worked on them until they submitted. His staff supplied him with extensive information on each reluctant supporter and using this and his uncanny talents of perception he applied carrots or sticks with great success.

As a small-town Texas boy Johnson had had little exposure to other cultures or races and had a magnanimous outlook on society. It seemed that he genuinely believed that everyone in the world could be just like himself if only given the chance. Rather than rely on Congress to initiate legislation, he took it upon himself to work on members to enact laws which, in his opinion, furthered the causes of equal opportunity and racial "equality".

Johnson's administration became known as the Great Society, with the main objectives being the reduction of poverty and racial injustice. The first part of this was enactment of Kennedy's tax cuts which further stimulated an already-booming post-war economy. The other landmark legislation initiated by Kennedy and passed under Johnson was the Civil Rights Act of 1964. Whereas the war years had seen a greater acceptance of blacks in responsible positions in the armed forces and industry, social acceptance was still a problem. The Civil Rights Act sought to force the states to follow social behavior dictated by the Federal government. The authority for this act was derived from broad interpretation of the interstate commerce clause of Article One and the 14th and 15th amendments. It is indeed a very far stretch to interpret the interstate commerce clause to have any bearing on civil rights. Likewise, the 14th and 15th amendments deal with equal application of the laws and there is no mention of discrimination in any other form. The act required fair administration of literacy tests and stipulated that all those with a 6th grade education and above were exempt. It prohibited poll-taxes for voting and any discrimination in education, the workplace and any facility that served the general public, government or private. It did not, however, prohibit most of the voter discrimination practices in southern states. In the final vote on this act it is not surprising that from the eleven states which formed the Confederacy, only seven house members and one senator voted in favor.

The opposition predicted that the bill would lead to forced busing, which they contended would be unconstitutional because it would involve transporting children because of race. By a series a maneuvers the bill by-passed the senate judiciary committee and became law in July 1964. This act is in blatant conflict with the freedom of association enshrined in the Constitution. In a free society citizens have the right to associate with whom they please and if left to themselves without interference, they will associate with those with whom they feel comfortable. This also means that they are free to resist associating with those whose company they do not seek. No government has the right to dictate the terms of association.

Shortly after the violence perpetrated by the police on the Freedom Marchers in Alabama, Johnson signed the Voting Rights Act in August 1965. This act effectively removed all control of voting requirements for federal offices from the states and prohibited any form of qualification to vote for any citizen over the age of 21. This act had a profound effect in the south, where, for the first time since Reconstruction, blacks could freely exercise their voting rights.

As predicted, following strong opposition and massive resistance in some counties, court-ordered busing of students between black and white schools was instituted and enforced in order to achieve "racial equality". After various appeals, in 1971 the Supreme Court finally ruled that it was constitutional. This was a clear case where the democratic principles were abandoned by means of a ruling by nine unelected men. If a referendum had been taken in each state the vast majority of voters would have opposed this ruling.

Indeed it can be argued that the forced "busing" of students to accomplish desegregation did enormous harm to all the children involved, the cities and counties affected and to the education system as a whole. Few whites and not all blacks wanted their children to spend hours in buses going to schools outside their residential districts to sit in classrooms with children who were not their neighbors. All the whites who had the means moved to the suburbs or placed their children in private schools. The inner cities lost their tax base and deteriorated and children remaining in the system wasted endless hours on buses and went to schools far from home and friends. With most of the whites gone, the system ended up busing blacks from one predominantly black school to another. The city of Detroit is a prime example of the devastating effects. American children are now some of the most poorly educated in the civilized world. Many iconic big American cities are now majority non-white.

Education should have remained in the hands of the states. The 10th amendment makes it clear that the Federal government has no jurisdiction regarding education. Logically schools are located to serve communities for many reasons. The parents are on the school PTA's and take an interest in the administration of the school. The children and teachers live in the neighborhood and do not have to travel far. Friends at school are friends at home. Parents and teachers are neighbors. This arrangement results in a cohesive and efficient system. Each community can decide what sort of school they have. Thus the composition of pupils in a particular school should depend simply on where they live. Race should play no part. Each state had the authority to ensure that every school met the same state standards of teaching, had the same level of facilities and the same funding per student. That is what the solution should have been.

The Constitution actually says nothing about segregation in any area. It was not considered the purview of the Federal government. Segregation in one form or another has been a way of life since the beginning of human interaction and will continue to be so. This ruling is a good example of overreach by the Federal government sanctioned by nine men. It is a prime example of taking clear language and attributing to it meanings it does not state. If the majority of the states and Congress feel that changing times justify changing the Constitution there is a well defined process for doing so. Major decisions in a democratic society should not be made by the Supreme Court.

Like the original major question regarding slavery, this is not to say that state or federal statutory segregation is desirable. It is not. Its origins lay in the fact that two very different cultures were obliged to co-exist and since the end of the Civil War, the best solution was thought to be to have each live in its own way. Like slavery, it could and would have ended by common assent when the time was right with encouragement and support from the Federal government, the media and all the decent citizens.

Johnson also signed the Civil Rights Act of 1968 following the assassination of Martin Luther King. This forbade discrimination in selling or renting a property based on race, religion, color or national origin. This is no business of the Federal government. Like all laws intended to protect certain classes, it is a gross infringement upon a fundamental freedom. Who is to judge for what reason an owner of a property refuses to sell or rent to an individual or family? It may or may not be based on the above criteria and the owner should be free to dispose of his property as he pleases. People will live where they feel comfortable if they have the means to do so. This is fundamental. The unintended but predictable consequences of the Civil Rights Acts have simply caused the more affluent people to flee the cities and public schools to the detriment of all and to structure the by-laws of homeowner associations to ensure standards are maintained.

This act spawned the United States Department of Housing and Urban Development (HUD) and its enforcement arm, the Office of Fair Housing and Equal Opportunity, a body which employs 600 people in 54 offices throughout the country. Anyone who feels discriminated against can file a complaint at no charge and the accused must defend himself at his own cost. There is nothing fair about this.

Although the subject is seldom discussed because it arouses strong feelings in both directions, the question must be asked as to why Southerners favored segregation in the first place. At the time of the Civil War, they had lived together with blacks for almost two hundred years. Most Southerners did not own slaves. After many generations in the USA these blacks were fully conversant with American ways and spoke only English. Thomas Jefferson, James Monroe and Woodrow Wilson were just some of the prominent figures who were ardent segregationists. The Southerners generally were not simply mean-spirited although there were certainly those who abused their power over others as humans are wont to do. As the group that understood blacks best, they were unwilling to share power because their experience had led them to conclude that it would not be used wisely. In examining the racial unrest in many big cities in the US today this conclusion is difficult to dispute. The various civil-rights laws had many adverse effects. In general, wherever blacks settled in large numbers, whites moved out. This means that people segregate by nature. Despite all the civil-rights and affirmative action initiatives, voluntary segregation is more prevalent today than it was before these laws were enacted.

Johnson also greatly expanded the Social Security initiative implemented by Roosevelt, creating Medicare, Medicaid, food-stamps, aid to dependent children and various other programs to assist the poor and aged. Although well intended, social programs inevitably involve taking money from some citizens to give to others. Johnson was also not oblivious to the fact the recipients of social services would continue to vote for the party that provided them. Nothing in the Constitution authorizes the Federal government to involve itself in these areas. Furthermore, both poverty and racial injustice are open to interpretation. There will always be those who have less than others and those who believe their treatment is based on their race rather than their behavior. In a fair society there are only three groups that qualify for special treatment: veterans disabled due to their military service and their dependents, dependents of those killed in action and those who are physically or mentally disabled and have no other means of support. Whereas over history family, friends and churches have assisted the needy, as soon as the government assumes this responsibility they curtail or reduce their support. If the government takes money in the form of taxes to be used for charitable purposes why should anybody else contribute privately?

It is inherently wrong to give free to some what others have to work for. The only thing a government should offer to able-bodied adults is meaningful work. Every country needs workers to construct and maintain its infrastructure and those unable or unwilling to find work for themselves can be made useful doing these jobs at wages less than the marketplace. More than any other factors, Johnson's Great Society has led to the cycle of dependency a large segment of society finds itself in today.

The effort to force "racial equality" in the schools has resulted in a decline in the quality of public education. The pressure on employers to hire and promote based on race instead of competency has degraded efficiency. The aid to dependent children program has eroded the family unit and allowed deadbeat fathers to avoid marriage and live off the payments for their children. There are now 47 million people receiving food stamps. This is not the way to raise living standards. The correct approach is to promote strong family units with core values and an understanding that hard work and personal responsibility are the only means to prosperity. Private businesses are what create good jobs and they must be permitted to conduct their affairs without unnecessary and burdensome government regulation. Education must be competitive and focus on needed and useful subjects at a high standard.

In retrospect it can be argued that the effects of the Great Society have been devastating rather than beneficial, especially to blacks and Hispanics. Once a cycle of dependency evolves, it is very difficult to contain. The family unit has been decimated with predictable rises in crime and unemployment. Affirmative Action has disadvantaged competent blacks and Hispanics with the implication that they owe their positions to quota requirements instead of their own talents. Universities are pressured into manipulating standards so that more members of these groups can gain admission. All these actions indeed imply that the average members of these groups cannot make it on a level playing field, which is a cruel insult that they should strongly object to.

Giving special treatment to particular groups amounts to an admission of inferiority and incompetence and every self-respecting member of these groups should strongly oppose it. No Olympic athlete could be proud of his medal if he was allowed to start fifty yards ahead of his competitors. No qualification can be respected if it is conferred using lower standards.

The respectful and considerate treatment of all citizens by other citizens is a noble and important goal and the intent to reach this point was understandable and commendable. Great progress has been made in this area. Unfortunately in other areas the consequences have been disastrous. Many sections of the nation's large cities, once vibrant and attractive, are now virtual slums. Black and Hispanic unemployment, crime and drug usage is endemic in these areas. Inner city schools are more dangerous than the battlefield. This is because the whites moved out and the cities are run by councils who do not make good decisions. Twenty two large cities have black populations of over 50%. White police trying to maintain order are at risk and if they over-react trying to subdue a suspect who resists they are subject to prosecution or attack. Many have been killed. Several cities have seen rioting, looting and arson on a major scale when a black criminal is injured or killed by the police. Nobody suggests that the blacks in these areas should not commit crimes and should obey the police. Nobody suggests that as a group, these people should get married and stay married before having children, instill in their children proper values, get jobs and arrive on time every day. Only they can solve their problems. Governments cannot.

Johnson's presidency saw further increases in the power of the office. An admirer of Franklin Roosevelt, Johnson had been in Congress when the Reorganization Act of 1939 was passed. He took this to new levels, micromanaging his cabinet members and prohibiting them from talking to the press or divulging any information without his prior approval. He managed the press according to his agenda. He wanted to run the show completely and in fact did so.

CHAPTER 14: THE NIXON AND FORD YEARS

Towards the end of Johnson's elected term he realized that the Vietnam war had evolved into an embarrassing disaster. Huge urban unrest as a result of the war and the civil-rights movement had disrupted law and order. Probably also concerned about his health, after poor showing in the first primaries he made the famous proclamation: "Accordingly I shall not seek, and I will not accept, the nomination of my party for another term as your President." No-one was disappointed. Although a cunning and experienced politician, Johnson was lacking in social graces and childlike in certain respects. After the assassination of Robert Kennedy following the California primary, the presidential race in 1968 was between Nixon, Hubert Humphrey and George Wallace. Johnson had alienated many Southerners with the Civil Rights Act and those who did not vote for George Wallace gave support to Nixon, resulting in a very narrow victory for him.

The Second World War, the Korean and Vietnam wars had another important effect in the USA. Many politicians and citizens believed that if a person were old enough to be drafted into the armed forces to fight a war, he or she was old enough to vote. The debate raged on without action until 1971. With the public strongly opposed to the Vietnam war, President Nixon finally signed the 26th amendment to the Constitution, lowering the Federal and State voting age from 21 to 18. It took this long because the Constitution expressly empowered the States to decide voting issues and the Supreme Court had to get involved to find a way around this and authorize Congress to set both Federal and State qualifications.

The wisdom of this amendment can be questioned. The real question should have been the minimum age to be drafted into the armed forces. Is the average 18 year old mature enough to make life and death decisions in the field? Should these youngsters, most of whom have never lived outside their homes, be put at risk at such a young age before they have had any adult lives? Most 18-year-olds have little knowledge of or interest in politics. Sadly many of every age do not. At the onset of the 26th amendment voter turnout on Federal elections by the new 18-20 group was low and had little effect. It took Barack Obama's election campaign to fire them up and an unprecedented 49% of them voted, mostly for him. Most young people tend to be liberal and this philosophy is strongly promoted in the colleges and universities. It is indeed a failure of high schools to educate their pupils in the realities of politics and finance. Most 18-year-olds leave school with very little idea on how to manage their money or their votes.

The Nixon era focused heavily on foreign affairs but several domestic initiatives affected Americans directly. The Korean and Vietnam wars had driven the deficit to worrisome levels and inflation and interest rates were increasing. Nixon authorized unpopular wage and price controls, allowed the dollar to float freely and ended the convertibility of dollars for gold at the historical rate of $35/ounce. These actions had some effect on inflation but caused predictable devaluation of the dollar. One of the most immediate effects of this was the quadrupling of oil prices caused by the devaluation of the dollar and the US support for Israel in the Yom Kippur war. OPEC declared an embargo on the US which caused a shortage of gasoline, added to inflation and had a ripple effect throughout the world as an economic recession. Americans moved to smaller cars with lower profit margins and wasted countless man-hours with the highway speed limit reduced to 55mph.

Ted Kennedy and Nixon also sought to expand the public healthcare system with the federalization of Medicaid and the creation of Health Maintenance Organizations. Nixon believed in returning certain powers to the states and reducing government departments to eight but the Democratic congress did not support him and little progress was made.

Although not an ardent environmentalist, Nixon supported the formation of the Environmental Protection Agency and Occupational Safety and Health Administration and signed the National Environmental Policy Act and the Clean Air Act. He vetoed the proposed Clean Water Act on the grounds that its implementation would be too costly but the veto was overridden by Congress. Nixon subsequently impounded the funds necessary to enact this.

Nixon wisely ended the futile war in Vietnam with the signing of the Paris Peace Accords in 1973. After the loss of almost 60,000 American lives and 140 billion dollars (direct costs at that time) the result was the same or worse than if the US had never involved itself. George Bush repeated the mistake in 2003 in Iraq and Afghanistan. Nixon also presided over the efforts to desegregate schools and forced busing of schoolchildren to achieve this. During his 67 months in office he was able to appoint four Supreme Court judges which probably had the greatest lasting effect. These were Burger, Powell, Blackmun and Rehnquist. The revelations publicized on the Nixon tapes during the Watergate crisis clearly demonstrated the degree of autocracy a president may feel himself entitled to. Rather than face certain impeachment, Nixon resigned the presidency in 1974.

Vice President Gerald Ford assumed the presidency. High inflation continued as an aftermath of the war and the budget was in deficit for the entire Ford presidency. Ford appointed John Paul Stevens to the Supreme Court, who became one of the most liberal judges. Under Ford, negotiations began to cede the Panama Canal to Panama. Like the US pressure for Britain to give up the Suez Canal, this was a foolish abandonment of a highly valuable strategic asset. The taint of Nixon's dishonesty and lackluster performance of Ford led to the election of Jimmy Carter in 1976 with 50.1% of the popular vote.

CHAPTER 15: JIMMY CARTER

Like a young girl dating on the rebound, Carter's election was the public's reaction to a flawed Republican administration. By all accounts Carter was a good and honest man who genuinely strove to do his best for the country. Unfortunately he was naive in the ways of Washington and believed that honesty and integrity could prevail. The media had a bonanza lampooning his country ways and simple beliefs and it was not long before he lost all respect. He inherited the financial woes caused by the Vietnam war and turbulence of the Nixon and Ford eras and inflation and interest rates hit all-time highs.

The signing of the Panama Canal Treaty in 1977 was strongly opposed by most of the public and the Republican Party. The rational was that the canal was in foreign territory and the land should be returned to its rightful owners. This was a spurious argument. The isthmus of Panama was originally part of Colombia and the French negotiated with Columbia to start building the canal in 1881. By 1889 the French company was bankrupt and work stopped. In 1894 a second French company took over the assets with a view to preparing them for sale. In 1903 the US assisted Panamanian rebels in separating from Colombia and creating the new country of Panama. In 1904 the US bought the French equipment for $40m, paid Panama $10m and $250,000 per year for the right-of-way and also paid Colombia the same in return for its recognition of the new country. The US spent a further $375m to complete the project in 1914. There was absolutely no moral or financial incentive to give this valuable asset away to a corrupt Panamanian government whose leader had to removed by military force under George H. W. Bush.

The government continued to run deficits and under Carter the National Debt rose from $620b to $900b, or 45%. Carter created the Department of Energy to oversee conservation and plan for the future. Another energy blow was struck in 1979 as the Shah of Iran fled the country and control fell into the hands of the radical Muslim Ayatollah Khomeini. This created a second panic which caused oil prices to almost quadruple again and led to a repeat of the 73 crisis with long lines at gas stations and inflation rising to over 13%. Mortgage rates rose to all-time highs and with the taking of American hostages by Iran in 1979, public moral took another blow. These problems were not of Carter's making but he failed to motivate the public and restore confidence. The aborted hostage rescue mission was the final nail in his coffin.

In response to lobbying against any discrimination in the mortgage business, in 1977 Carter signed the Community Reinvestment Act. This sought to pressure banks and other lending institutions to relax normal qualification criteria when considering loan applications from persons in low-income neighborhoods. These loans were designated sub-prime and carried higher risk. The high inflation rates caused by the oil crisis had the effect of causing corresponding high interest rates. This put a severe damper on housing construction and this, combined with regulations limiting interest rates the savings and loan institutions could pay depositors, placed these S & L's in a financial crisis. They could not attract investments at the below-market rates they were allowed to pay and could not make loans outside the housing industry which would render higher rates. To make the crisis worse, the Federal Savings and Loan Insurance Corporation was low on funds to bail out troubled units. This was a major crisis involving about 4000 S & L's with assets of $600b, most of it in low-interest mortgages from prior years. To resolve this problem, in 1980 Congress passed and Carter signed the Depository Institutions Deregulation and Monetary Control Act. This effectively reduced oversight, allowed S & L's to offer adjustable-rate mortgages and expand their lending authority into other areas. The 1980 Act was followed by the 1982 Garn-St. Germain Depository Institutions Act. The result was a move by S & L's into high-risk investments and shoddy accounting which played a part in their ultimate failure and was a contributing cause of the 2007 housing bust.

CHAPTER 16: REAGAN AND BUSH

In 1980 Ronald Reagan won the presidential election with 50.7% of the popular vote and 489 electoral votes, winning all but six states. Reagan was a very different type of man from Carter. As a former movie star and TV personality for General Electric he was polished and at ease in public. He radiated a quiet confidence and projected optimism. As governor of California for two terms he had been popular and gained valuable management experience.

The cornerstone of Reagan's philosophy was the value of the freedoms granted by the Constitution. He favored returning to the states powers which had been hijacked by the Federal government. Having started his political life as Democrat, he voted for Eisenhower in 1952, Nixon in 1960 and formally switched to Republican in 1962, declaring that the Democratic party had left him. His views were probably influenced by the management at GE and his relationship with Nancy Davis, his future wife. He strongly opposed the government's involvement in areas outside the authority granted by the Constitution.

He opposed certain parts of the civil rights legislation, believing that individuals and private businesses had the rights to sell property to whom they pleased. Once in the White House he proposed a constitutional amendment to eliminate the misinterpretation of the establishment clause of the first amendment. It stated

"Nothing in this Constitution shall be construed to prohibit individual or group prayer in public schools or other public institutions. No person shall be required by the United States or by any state to participate in prayer."

This was in reaction to the Supreme Court ruling in 1962 banning prayer in public schools, in his opinion a serious infringement of constitutional freedom. However, with the House controlled by Democrats throughout his administration he was unable to get the necessary support.

Having inherited a financial mess, Reagan sought to stimulate the economy by lowering marginal tax rates and controlling the money supply to tame inflation. The loss in revenue was made up from other tax increases and the expanded tax base resulting from an improved economy. In fact this was the case, the GDP grew at an average annual rate of almost 8% and revenues increased from $300b to $550b from 1981 to 1989. He favored a return to some form of the gold standard but was unsuccessful in accomplishing this. Despite the thriving economy and increased revenues, Congress could not restrain its appetite for spending and borrowing and during the Reagan years the national debt ballooned from $900b to $2.85t or 216%, the highest percentage in modern history. This was one of Reagan's greatest regrets. Part of this was Reagan's own military build up which played a part in ending the

Cold War and part was also the high inflation rates inherited. Alarmed at the burgeoning deficits and public debt, in 1985 Congress passed and Reagan signed the Gramm-Rudman-Hollings Balanced Budget and Emergency Deficit Control Act. This sought to limit discretionary spending to eventually eliminate the deficit. It had little effect.

Reagan signed the Tax Reform Act of 1986 which had a major effect on speculative investments by limiting the deductions that could be taken for business losses. Much of the institutional investment in housing and real estate was affected. This, together with rising interest rates to tame inflation and outright fraud by a number of Savings & Loan executives signed the death knell for these lending houses. The loss of these was a severe blow to prospective homeowners and was one of the factors leading to the 2007 housing bust. The 1986 Act eliminated interest deductions for personal returns except for the home mortgage and home equity loans. As stated previously, this deduction encourages people to borrow money for this purpose while other taxpayers are obliged to finance a portion of their interest costs. This is not correct and this deduction should be eliminated when the entire tax code is rewritten.

Largely by his charisma and simple but logical appeals to the electorate, Reagan succeeded in restoring moral, taming inflation and getting everyone back to work. However, the ballooning debt in the absence of any major war or other catastrophe was a high price to pay.

Reagan believed in free markets and ended price controls and regulations. He made it clear that unlike his predecessor, he would fight for his beliefs as demonstrated by his firing of striking air-traffic controllers, actively confronting the Soviet Union and supporting opponents of communism in various countries. Together with Margaret Thatcher he advocated demolition of the Berlin Wall and reunification of Germany. He projected strength.

Reagan attempted to resolve the illegal immigration issue by signing the Immigration Control and Reform Act in 1986. This act was presented by a bipartisan committee on immigration reform in order to curb the influx of illegal immigrants and to deal with those already in the country, estimated at about 4m. Its basis was to impose harsh penalties on anyone hiring a person without verifying legal status, to adopt a guest-worker program to provide temporary labor for agricultural needs each year and to allow those already in the country to obtain legal status by meeting certain conditions. Unfortunately it had quite the opposite effect. The hiring restrictions were not enforced and the granting of legal status provided incentive for millions more to enter the country illegally, to the point that this group is now estimated to be over 20 million. Part of the 1986 act involved the allocation of permanent visas on a first-come, first served basis. This was modified and eventually ended up as the Immigration Act of 1990 under Bush. This established a lottery system for the awards of 55,000 residence visas per year. The principle aim of this program was to enhance "diversity" in the US population. These visas were granted with no regard to qualifications of any kind and once in the country, these recipients could bring in an unlimited number of their relatives, which they did.

No amendments to the Constitution were passed during the Reagan years but he did appoint two new justices to the Supreme Court, Sandra Day O'Connor and Antonin Scalia and promoted William Rehnquist to Chief Justice. Aside from the huge debt incurred, it can be said that Reagan left the country and the world in much better shape than he found it. Had he had a Republican congress he may have been able to accomplish more.

In 1988 vice president George H. W. Bush won the presidency with just over 50% of the popular vote. He was perhaps the most qualified of all presidents, being the son of senator Prescott Bush, a naval aviator in WW2, a Yale graduate in economics, a self-made successful businessman, congressman, ambassador to the UN, chairman of the Republican National Committee, envoy to China, Director of Central Intelligence and Vice-president. By all accounts he was a smart and principled man who, like Reagan, was independently wealthy and ardently patriotic.

Bush realized that the large deficits incurred during the Reagan years needed to be addressed and it was his desire to accomplish this by reducing spending. A Democratic-controlled Congress refused to accept this, forcing Bush to propose a compromise of spending cuts and tax increases. Republicans refused to support this with the end result that both taxes and spending were raised, exacerbating the problem. This alienated many conservatives and this, together with the third-party candidacy of Ross Perot, led to Bush's defeat in the 1992 election.

Bush was pragmatic but not a president who could fire up the public like Reagan. He presided during the breakup of the Soviet Union and subsequent fall of the Berlin Wall. Faced with increasing problems in Panama, where the US had been instrumental in bringing the corrupt Manuel Noriega to power, he sent in US troops to remove Noriega and restore the newly elected president Endara. When Iraq invaded Kuwait Bush conducted a brief war to remove Iraqi troops but did not occupy Iraq.

Bush appointed David Souter and Clarence Thomas to the Supreme Court. He also advanced the North American Free Trade Agreement (NAFTA) between the USA, Canada and Mexico but this was only ratified under his successor, Bill Clinton. Under Bush the economy did well after an initial short recession but the national debt increased from $2.6t for fiscal 1988 to $4t for fiscal 1992, or 54%.

CHAPTER 17: THE CLINTON YEARS

Bill Clinton was the unlikely winner of the 1992 Democratic primary and was successful in defeating incumbent Bush for reasons stated above. A graduate of Yale and a Rhodes Scholar, he emulated his hero John Kennedy in projecting a young, vigorous candidate with lofty dreams. Like Kennedy and Franklin Roosevelt, his appetite for the company of attractive women seemed to be greater than his wife could satisfy. After taking office, both spouses came under severe scrutiny for various actions considered immoral if not illegal and the President was impeached by the House for perjury in the Monica Lewinsky affair in 1998 but the following year he was acquitted by the Senate.   It is rather disappointing that a man in the highest office of the land, entrusted with the welfare of the country, was acquitted after literally being caught with his pants down in the Oval Office and then lying under oath. It is a sad example of the low standard public figures are held to. If any CEO of a large corporation had been found guilty of using his position to take advantage of a young female employee he would have been fired immediately and sued for millions..

One of the first items on Clinton's agenda was reform of the healthcare system. Costs were rising exponentially and many could not afford the insurance premiums. There is no question that the system needed reform but Clinton made a fundamental mistake in involving his wife Hillary as leader of the task force charged with designing the new system. The basic concept was mandatory insurance coverage for all inhabitants with caps on premiums and services. Not surprisingly, this was strongly opposed by conservatives and libertarians as being outside the authority of the Federal government. On the commercial side it was opposed by pharmaceutical and insurance companies and healthcare providers. After much acrimonious interaction between competing forces, the initiative was finally declared dead in 1994 by senate majority leader George Mitchell.

Except for the first two years, Clinton had a Republican-controlled congress with which he wisely sought to find common ground. The impetus for economic recovery begun during the Reagan years continued during the Clinton administration and the country enjoyed healthy growth, low unemployment and low inflation. During the run-up to the 1994 mid-term election, Republican congressmen Newt Gingrich and Richard Armey presented the Contract with America program which sought to reduce debt by reducing the size of the Federal government and overhauling the welfare system. This gave the party its first majority in the House in 40 years and during Clinton's second term the budget showed a theoretical surplus. In fact this was simply accounting manipulation, the national debt increased every year, growing from $4.3 to $5.6 trillion (30%) during his administration including an increase of $0.2 trillion during the years of "surplus".

The Contract with America contained eight operational reforms to the procedures in Congress and ten bills considered necessary to address issues deemed important. Among these bills was a proposed constitutional amendment to require a balanced budget each year unless overruled by a three fifths majority. This amendment passed the house with the necessary two-thirds majority but failed in the senate by one vote. This was a tragic lost opportunity.

Part of the strategy to rein in the runaway spending was to give the President the authority to veto parts of bills which came to his desk. Congressmen had discovered that the way to get money for their pet projects was to combine these with important bills. Senators Bob Dole and John McCain introduced the Line Item Veto Act in 1995 and it was signed by Clinton in 1996. Unfortunately the Supreme Court ruled it unconstitutional in 1998. Clinton signed the Balanced Budget Act and Taxpayer Relief Act in 1997, designed to balance the budget by 2002. The Balanced Budget Act required savings from Medicare and payments to medical providers but these never occurred and deficits continued.

Another important initiative of the Contract with America was the Common Sense Legal Reform Act. This sought to curtail frivolous litigation and excessive awards by changing to a "loser pays all" system as practiced in other civilized countries. This passed in

Congress but was vetoed by Clinton. This was a great tragedy. The US tort system is the underlying cause of many of the nation's problems and increases the cost of everything from healthcare to ski-lift tickets. Many major vital businesses have been bankrupted by excessive litigation and for this reason many locate their headquarters outside the US. An extension of this, the Private Securities Litigation Reform Act was also vetoed by Clinton but this was overridden and the act became law in 1995.

Clinton signed various bills which had lasting effects, the major one being Personal Responsibility and Work Opportunity Act which reformed the welfare system. He also repealed the Glass-Steagall Act and signed the Commodity Futures Modernization Act, thereby undoing the safeguards put in place after the Great Depression and contributing to the 2008 depression. Clinton signed the Defense of Marriage Act which effectively defined marriage for Federal purposes as heterosexual. In 2013 section 3 of this act was deemed unconstitutional by the Supreme Court, opening the door for federal judges to overturn state constitutional definitions of marriage. In 2015 the Supreme Court gave final ruling, declaring that no state could ban same-sex marriage regardless of voter preferences. Another case of five judges subverting the principles of democracy. Clinton appointed two Supreme Court justices, Ruth Bader Ginsburg and Stephen Breyer. Both have tended to favor the liberal philosophy when interpreting the Constitution.

In 1993 the escalating radical Muslim terror attacks came to the US mainland with an attempt to blow up the World Trade center. It caused considerable damage but failed to topple the tower. Clinton failed to take advantage of an opportunity to capture or kill Osama Bin Laden but did bomb a pharmaceutical plant suspected of terrorist ties in Sudan. In 1999 Clinton involved US forces briefly in a NATO bombing campaign in the former Yugoslavia to restore relative peace after nasty clashes between Christians and Muslims. Ironically, Clinton is remembered by many as a great president. Notwithstanding his flexible principles, infidelities and lies, he presided over a period of prosperity not really of his making. He did have the good sense not to spoil a good thing and for this he deserves credit.

CHAPTER 18: GEORGE W. BUSH

The 2000 presidential election was undoubtedly one of the most contentious in the history of the country. There were only two serious contenders. Vice-president Al Gore had all the advantages of incumbency and legacy of a popular Clinton administration but lacked charisma and came across as a man of limited intellectual resources. George W. Bush was the oldest son of former president George H. W. Bush and had the experience of two terms as governor of Texas. Neither was a star performer on the campaign trail. When the election was over the results in Florida were so close that the count came under scrutiny. The card-punch system employed there was subject to mechanical flaws and Gore insisted on multiple recounts by hand in certain counties. After mandatory deadlines for this were not met, the Florida secretary of state declared the original counts valid and the election over. Gore appealed this decision to the US Supreme Court but it elected not to intervene. The final result gave Gore 48.38% and Bush 47.87% of the popular vote but because of the Electoral College votes, Bush won with 271 to Gore's 266. As in many elections in recent years, a map of the country colored by states' electoral votes majorities showed 30 of the fifty states red (Republican), which by land-area constitutes about 75% of the country. The Democrats normally carry states with very high urban concentrations and strong unions.

From the moment he entered the White House, Bush had contingency plans drawn up to intervene in Iraq. Although Iraq had nothing to do with the 2001 attacks on the World Trade Centers and Pentagon, Bush used the tragedy and some flawed intelligence regarding Iraq's possession of weapons of mass destruction to convince Congress that Saddam Hussein must be removed. Disregarding the advice of former chief military commander Colin Powell, then Secretary of State, the US occupied Iraq and deposed Hussein. It appears that nobody except Powell had considered the long-term consequences of intervening in a foreign country with complicated religious and ethnic divisions. Hussein came to full power in 1979 and shortly thereafter attacked Iran in an effort to topple Khomeni's new Shiite regime. This evolved into an eight year war of attrition, killing hundreds of thousands and accomplishing nothing. In deals with the devil, Iraq received West German and US assistance in materials and intelligence. Chemical weapons were used against Iranian forces and the Kurds. It can be argued that out of necessity Hussein had ruled with an iron fist but had kept the peace. Trying to introduce conventional democracy to a nation of divided fanatics was a fool's errand and the Iraq war was an unnecessary and catastrophic disaster for Iraq, the USA and the entire Middle East. At a cost of over five thousand US lives, thirty thousand US wounded, massive Iraqi loss in lives and infrastructure and over $2T cost to the US taxpayer Iraq is an ongoing disaster with no relief in sight. The billions spent on training and equipping the Iraqi military were for nothing, at the first sign of conflict with the new terrorist group ISIS, they abandoned their US weapons and fled. The renegade ISIS movement became well equipped with US weaponry and emerged as growing threat to the stability of the entire region.

The Bush policy in Afghanistan at least had some justification as this country was a major training ground for Al Qaeda terrorists. After nineteen years of US intervention however, the situation is little better than Iraq. It seems that despite centuries of information on war and conquest the US has not learned that occupying other countries with a view to converting them to stable democracies is a lost cause. No country wants foreign occupation. Many are totally unsuited to democracy. These two wars have been a major blow to the US economy, have incensed the Arab world against the western democracies and given the terrorist organizations an incalculable boost in recruitment. The entire middle-east is now in conflict and rampant terror attacks occur are a constant threat.

On the economic front Bush initiated the Economic Growth and Tax Relief Reconciliation Act of 2001. This sought to rework certain provisions of the tax code to both put more money in citizens' pockets and reduce the national debt. This seems, and was, an impossible result unless accompanied by massive spending cuts. The program was to be phased in and would automatically expire in 2010, theoretically after elimination of the national debt. Not surprisingly, the

251

provision took effect much faster than planned and almost the entire plan was extended after the "sunset" date. As no cuts occurred and two wars were started and continued, the debt under Bush's two terms grew from $5.63T to $9.65T or 71%.

Tinkering with the tax code has tempted many presidents and is part of the reason it has evolved into such a complicated mess. The obvious solution is to scrap it altogether and start from zero, using solid logic and making sure it is fair and simple. Ideally no taxes should be levied on incomes at the federal level. The only way to restrain the excesses of the federal government is to starve the beast. The simplest and fairest means of taxation is a federal sales tax on all goods and services except basic food and clothing and medical expenses. This requires no IRS and no effort on the parts of citizens. People can choose what they purchase and thereby control their finances.

After spectacular failures of large publicly-held companies Enron, Worldcom and others, revisions to the regulations covering public businesses accounting practices were proposed by senator Paul Sarbanes and representative Michael Oxley. The Sarbanes-Oxley Act was enacted in July of 2002. Whereas these additional requirements sought to prevent future manipulation of accounting information, for most honest businesses they simply amounted to a huge complication and additional cost of doing business. They did not prevent the abuse in the mortgage and derivatives markets which caused the housing crash of 2007 and the resulting spectacular failure of Lehman Brothers and other brokerage houses.

Bush instituted a federal program to eliminate AIDS throughout the world. While this was a commendable humanitarian initiative there is nothing in the Constitution authorizing presidents or Congress to use taxpayer money for such purposes. Whereas the media portrayed this program as a wonderful example of a humanitarian accomplishment by the US president, it must be understood that this was done with other people's money, not his own or voluntary contributors'. Worse still, the US already had a huge national debt and had to add to its borrowing to finance this program. It was not a huge sum ($15b) as a percentage of the budget, but serves as an example of unauthorized use of taxpayer funds. As any accountant knows, many small outlays soon add up to large sums.

In 2005 Bush had to deal with another crisis. The hurricane Katrina slammed into the gulf coast causing tremendous damage from Florida to Texas and flooding 80% of the city of New Orleans. It was the costliest hurricane in US history. The handling of this event was severely criticized, resulting in the resignations of the heads of the Federal Emergency Management Agency and the New Orleans Police. Bush, as ultimate authority, took a lot of heat for his failure to oversee both the preparation for and aftermath of the disaster. The catastrophe demonstrated several major problems inherent in the country. Firstly, the utter lack of initiative on the parts of many of the residents of New Orleans. They simply sat by as the water rose and waited for someone else to save them. As a nasty adjunct, many took the opportunity to loot and wreak havoc. The most disappointing aspect was the gross mismanagement of relief funds from both government and private sources. Billions of dollars were dispersed without any constraints and happy recipients bought new televisions etc. with money intended for emergency food and shelter. Much of the money went directly into the pockets of officials, including the mayor. Thousands of trailers bought for temporary housing were rendered uninhabitable because of toxic chemicals in their insulation and were scrapped. It is estimated that Katrina cost taxpayers over $100b. In contrast, when the city of Galveston was struck in 1900 and more than five times the number of lives were lost, no federal funds were used for relief or rebuilding.

Katrina highlighted another gross inequity in the federal system. In order to encourage development in high-risk coastal areas, the Federal government subsidizes the insurance on homes and businesses deemed at risk from weather-related causes. If it were left to commercial insurance companies alone to insure these structures the premiums would be such that few would build there. This use of taxpayer money must be questioned. Nothing in the Constitution mentions it and it is therefore outside the purview of the Federal government. In areas that have been struck by hurricanes multiple times, home and business owners have had their structures rebuilt multiple times at the expense of the taxpayer.

The subsidization of insurance for flood-prone areas originated with the National Flood Insurance Program of 1968 after hurricane Betsy caused severe losses in 1965. The program was enhanced by the Flood Disaster Protection Act of 1973 which made purchase of insurance in designated high-risk areas mandatory. The system was further modified in 1982, 1994 and 2004.

In 2006 the bubble in housing prices peaked and 2007 saw rapid declines, creating another crisis for Bush to deal with. The housing crash is a good example of good intentions overriding good policy. Politicians like to enact laws which please their constituents and the "American Dream" required home ownership to be fully realized. Of course relatively few families own their homes outright, most are mortgaged to a greater or lesser extent. Notwithstanding this, politicians encouraged home "ownership" and enacted policies that facilitated this. The banks and mortgage houses over the years had arrived at a formula which qualified home-buyers for mortgages. This was based on statistics and found to be sound. Applying this formula inevitably disqualified certain applicants whom the lenders deemed incapable of servicing the loans they sought. These people were better off renting their accommodations. The government pressure to allow these people to buy homes, the wide use of adjustable-rate mortgages, the securitization of sub-prime mortgages and rising interest rates caused major disruptions in the financial systems throughout the world. Thousands of foreclosures occurred as sub-prime borrowers could not meet their mortgage payments and housing prices plummeted. This put many of the loans "underwater" in that the outstanding balance on the mortgage was greater than the market value of the house. In these cases the borrower was better off simply abandoning the house, further exacerbating the problem. The Dow Jones Index dropped from 13000 to 6000 and aside from the spectacular Wall Street failures, many other large institutions were put at risk of failure.

The error of repealing the Glass-Steagall Act and other deregulation of financial institutions now became obvious. Banks and investment houses had ventured into various complex instruments which were not part of the required reporting system. These had imaginative names such as Credit Default Swaps, Mortgage Backed Securities, Collateralized Debt Obligations and other derivatives. Large flows of cash into the US made for easy credit. Predatory lenders had enticed many unqualified borrowers into debts beyond their means. The perfect storm had hit. It was a case of having to learn the hard lessons of 1929 for a second time.

The stock-market has always been a high-risk investment and has seen many spectacular crashes over the centuries. In its simple form, an investor pools his money with other investors to finance a business venture in return for shares of that company. The price of the shares theoretically reflects the future value of the company and the returns it may pay out in the form of dividends. Today, however, the investment business has evolved into a complete casino whereby "bets" are placed on every kind of scenario which have no bearing on the underlying commodity or equity. Derivatives are extensions of risk based purely on chance with odds far higher than the spin of the roulette wheel. Risk is sold and hedged multiple times and automated computer trading manipulates prices in milliseconds based purely on the parameters programmed. Perhaps this is "freedom" but as occurred in 2007-8 it can wreak havoc.

Interest rates play a major role for investors. Those in their senior years and others reluctant to take high risk prefer to invest their money in safer instruments which include bonds, certificates of deposit and money-market accounts. Until the 70's, the prime rate stayed in the 2-6% window. With the two oil crises and resulting inflation, it peaked at 20% in April 1980, returning to 6% in 1992 at the end of the senior Bush administration. After the 2007 crisis the Federal Reserve reduced its rate to almost zero in order to stimulate the economy, resulting in a prime rate of 3.25% since December 2008. This meant that bonds paid little more than this and CD's and money-market paid less than 1%. The result was that the only investments which could keep up with inflation were equities and other high-risk instruments, so even those averse to risk were obliged to get into the stock market or fall behind. Inevitably this has led to an abnormal percentage of investments in equities which, when interest rates rise again as they must, will lead to some degree of correction.

It was left to the Bush administration to find a way out of this mess before it escalated further. The first attempt was the Economic Stimulus Act, signed in February 2008. This authorized rebates of up to $600 for single and $1200 for married taxpayers whose tax liability or income fell below prescribed thresholds. It also imposed stricter requirements on mortgages qualifying for purchase by Fannie Mae and Freddie Mac. The program was calculated to cost $152b for 2008. All this money added to the deficit. In addition to this, in October 2008 Bush signed the Troubled Asset Relief Program (TARP), which originally authorized the Federal Government Treasury to purchase or insure up to $700 billion in "toxic assets". The Dodd-Frank Wall Street Reform and Consumer Protection Act subsequently reduced this to $475 billion. The money was disbursed to large banks, brokerage houses, insurance companies, General Motors and Chrysler in return for "equity warrants" (the option to purchase non-voting shares at an agreed price). Although controversial, by December 2012 the government had recovered $442b on outlays of $426. This was somewhat effective in preventing further chaos but the economy was still reeling in shock and further intervention was implemented by Obama.

Bush appointed two Supreme Court justices, John Roberts and Samuel Alito. John Roberts replaced William Rehnquist as Chief Justice. Both men were considered to be conservative but once in office, Roberts has ruled with liberal justices on several important issues.

CHAPTER 19: BARRACK HUSSEIN OBAMA

National disaster can happen when otherwise decent people become too enchanted with a single person or party who promises them the world or a philosophy which is idealistic. The absurd and outrageous are accepted as normal. Rational thinking is abandoned. It is a sad example of the total failure of democracy. The election of Barack Obama as president of the United States is a strong signal that the country has reached this point. Here is a man who has minimal qualifications to serve as leader of the largest economy on earth. His career prior to entering state politics was primarily devoted to promoting socialism both in his capacity as community organizer and while lecturing at the University of Chicago Law School. His association with radicals clearly demonstrated his philosophy. He lived and worked in the most corrupt city in the USA where he lent his support to former congressman and governor Rod Blagojevich, who was given a 14 year jail sentence for corruption. His record as a senator was unimpressive. He was able to run as a candidate for president apparently without even presenting his birth certificate to verify his eligibility. How on earth did this man get the majority vote of the American people not once, but twice? Many educated and intelligent people voted for him.

The answers are lamentable. George Bush, his predecessor, made the tragic mistake of involving the USA in two foolish wars. These left the country with a huge increase in the national debt and no-win military or political conclusions. Bush also presided over the excesses of Wall Street and the manipulation of the mortgage system which led to a financial crisis. The 2008 Republican candidate, John McCain, came across as a whining reactionary and the Republican Party should never have supported his candidacy.

Having endured several major crises, two ongoing wars, high unemployment and a stagnant economy during the Bush years, the public was ready for a new agenda. The Clinton years were remembered favorably, so when Hillary Clinton presented herself as a presidential candidate it was commonly believed that she would win. It was assumed that her husband would help to steer the ship of state. The Democratic Party, however, was not so sure. The Clintons were cunning, experienced and ambitious and therefore could not be easily controlled. The party calculated that if it could find an attractive black candidate it could fire up the black vote as never before and swing the election. The party knew it could count on the die-hard democrats, the unions, the liberals, the academics, all those receiving public assistance and a high percentage of the Latino and women's votes. If they could get blacks to turn out in large numbers victory was assured.

They were quite correct. A first-term senator from Illinois was exactly what they were seeking. With an engaging smile, a quick wit and polished oratory. Barrack Obama was their man. He was good on the stump and preached what the Democrats and many independents wanted to hear. There were also those who simply wanted to vote for the first black president regardless of his competence for the job. Few of these supporters bothered to examine his credentials.

The Obama campaign did an outstanding job of fund-raising and motivating the electorate. It was assisted by the Republicans' incredibly poor choice of McCain and Palin as opponents. To Hillary Clinton's dismay, Obama won the Democratic primary. Because of the powerful propaganda of the mainstream media known as "political correctness" no-one wanted to criticize Obama in any way for fear of being branded a racist.

The strategy worked perfectly, the blacks gave Obama over 95% of their votes and turned out in unprecedented numbers. It mattered little that Obama was born to a white mother and largely brought up by his white grandparents. They saw in him a savior who would promote their causes. The mainstream media, like Goebbels' Nazi propaganda machine, swooned over "the first black president" and reported only those news items which reflected favorably upon him

In the 2008 presidential election, Obama won decisively with 365 electoral votes to McCain's 173. Obama won 53% of the popular vote. The total votes cast were 131 million or 43% of the total population, the highest share in US history.

To further promote this departure from reality, the trustees of the Nobel awards bestowed the Peace prize upon him before he had been in office a month. He is undoubtedly the least deserving of all recipients of this largely symbolic award which is now a mockery of its original intent.

Many romantic and idealistic citizens were captivated by the concept of voting for "the first black president". This was sheer lunacy, no different than voting for the first red-headed president or a person with any other distinguishing feature. There is only one reason to vote for a candidate and that is that he or she is the most competent amongst the contenders. The blacks believed that Obama would further their causes. In fact his blatant racism, incompetence and underhand tactics have harmed all blacks. He could have done tremendous good if he had given candid advice to blacks in order to encourage the restoration of family and personal responsibility. Instead, he and his attorney general, Eric Holder, fanned the flames of racism by jumping to conclusions before the facts were known and failing to condemn riotous behavior. The US congress, like the German Reichstag in 1933, appeared to be unwilling or unable to hold the President to the constitutional constraints of his office.

Obama's slogan was "Hope and Change". This was a familiar cry, also employed to elect Jimmy Carter, the naive electorate feeling that anything would be better than the previous administration. This is a dangerous and disingenuous philosophy as the Germans discovered when they abandoned the Weimar Republic in favor of the Hitler dictatorship. "Change" can be good or bad. Those who took the trouble to read Obama's first book, Dreams of My Father, should have understood where Obama stood on the basic issues. He made his philosophy abundantly clear. However, his campaign message was fairness, transparency and honesty in government, three attributes hitherto unknown in politics which remained unknown under his administration.

The most pressing problem as Obama entered office was the economy. The housing crisis and its collateral effects had scared the world and the credit markets dried up as banks tightened their lending practices. The Fed had already reduced interest rates to almost zero but the fear remained and businesses were reluctant to invest or expand, resulting in high unemployment. In February 2009 Congress enacted the American Recovery and Reinvestment Act of 2009 which was signed into law by Obama. This act sought to stimulate the economy and create jobs by a second direct infusion of (printed) cash into various areas of the economy including direct cash payment to citizens and investments in infrastructure, healthcare, education, energy, homeland security and law enforcement. Its projected cost was $787b (later revised to $831b). There was considerable controversy regarding the merits of the "stimulus" strategy. When the government simply prints money to disburse in various areas without the underlying goods or services being present, at some point in the future the value of the currency must be diminished. On the other hand, in a crisis situation it is somewhat effective and perhaps justifiable. Nobody knows what the result would have been if the Bush and Obama stimuli had not occurred and the marketplace had been left to correct itself.

Obama lost no time in reveling in the power of his office and set about creating a common enemy, the "rich." He is not the first politician to do so. Going back to the English hero Robin Hood and throughout the ages the have-nots have sought to share in the assets of the haves. However, in the Robin Hood philosophy it is the people taking back from corrupt and abusive rulers. Obama seeks to have the government take away from productive people to give to less productive people. He surrounded himself with political cronies rather than competent ministers. In his first two years in office when Democrats controlled both houses of Congress, his charm changed to arrogance and he pushed hard for universal healthcare

Obama's principle theme was to reduce "income inequality." This is a vague objective which appeals to a large segment of the population who are understandably enthusiastic about getting more of someone else's money via government sponsored redistribution of wealth. In reality it is not very different from those countries where the rule of law is non-existent and the have-nots simply assault others in their houses and on the streets and steal their money and other possessions. Whereas previous presidents have made some attempt to conceal their activities which may be considered unethical or unpopular, Obama and his ministers have blatantly played politics. Obama's Attorney General has been unashamedly partisan and indeed openly supportive of black causes before any facts were available and encouraged disregard for certain federal laws. The explanation is that Obama is half black and no-one is prepared to call him to account for fear of being branded as racist. Far from bringing a breath of honest air to politics, the Obama administration had the least qualified ministers chosen with blatant patronage and ran the most deceptive and opaque administration in the history of the country. Elected because some believed he would improve racial harmony, race relations in his administration reached a low not seen since the civil-rights era.

The first two years of his administration were facilitated by a Senate and House controlled by the Democratic party. Its respective leaders, Harry Reid and Nancy Pelosi were unabashedly partisan and notable only for their complete lack of personal appeal. This congress passed and Obama signed the Patient Protection and Affordable Care Act in March 2010. This was the culmination of the Kennedy dream of universal healthcare. Far from being transparent and fair, it was concocted by a small group and passed late one Sunday night without a single Republican vote and worse still, without anyone having read the monstrous bill. As

Nancy Pelosi famously remarked "you have to pass it before you can see what's in it".

There was a lot in it, much of it unrelated to healthcare. Obama knew that had it been implemented as soon as possible he could never get re-elected, so the terms were cunningly arranged so that it would only come into force in 2013. There is nothing in the Constitution authorizing Congress to involve itself in healthcare and indeed a challenge was mounted concerning the penalty that would be levied upon citizens if they elected not to enroll. The eminently valid argument was that citizens cannot be forced to purchase anything. This came before the Supreme Court in June 2012 in National Federation of Independent Businesses vs Sebelius. Most surprisingly, Chief Justice John Roberts sided with the liberal members of the court by claiming that the penalty was in fact a tax and therefore fell under the taxing authority of the government. However, some leeway was granted to the states in their obligation to expand Medicaid.

Regardless of the merits of or objections to this act, its passage was a clear example of the government ramming a bill which few understood and fewer agreed with through the legislative process to become law. Obama and its supporters had expressly denied that the penalty was a tax. Furthermore, the bill in fact did contain a number of taxes which were only revealed after it had passed. Obviously subsidizing healthcare for millions of uninsured people required major funding. As the public discovered in 2013, their Medicare contributions were now indexed to income, those above an income threshold saw their capital gains tax rate increase by 3.4% and a new tax was levied on "medical devices" which would seem counterproductive. This law did nothing to rein in the excessive costs of healthcare, which should have been its primary objective.

The law highlights a number of serious problems. Firstly, in a democracy, the government should not be capable of enacting legislation which the majority opposes. Secondly, Congress should not vote on any legislation it has not read or understood. Thirdly, again and again in many countries it has been shown that the government is the least efficient administrator of any system involving money. Already the fraud in welfare programs, Medicare and Medicaid is horrendous. If any tinkering with healthcare is needed, and it is, the major focus needs to be on reducing costs and getting the government out.

After the 2010 election deprived Obama of the majority in the House, little of any significance was accomplished. The country became bitterly divided as never before and Obama used the vague term of "executive authority" to use presidential executive orders to manipulate and override legitimate laws passed by Congress. An unprecedented number of Americans received some form of government handout, many received multiple handouts. These exclude Social

Security and Medicare payments, which are earned via the Payroll Taxes levied on every working American. The USA registered the lowest percentage of workforce participation in recent history. After first hitting $1T in 1988, the National Debt rose to a formidable $19T, more than doubling. .

The use of "executive authority" is not new, it has been used many times by many presidents. It was originally accepted so that in cases where rapid response is absolutely necessary the president can make a decision without the cumbersome procedures of Congress. However, once the crisis has been addressed, the matter should revert to Congress for constitutional regularity. The Constitution clearly states that only Congress can make or revoke laws.

Obama took the privilege to new levels. He amended the terms of Obamacare 30 times without the consent of Congress. He and/or his administration involved itself in circumventing clear legislation and manipulating government agencies to their party's advantage. He blatantly disregarded federal immigration law and gave unauthorized status to a large segment of illegal aliens. Had Congress not objected, he would have entered into a treaty with Iran regarding the development of nuclear weapons without the consent of the Senate. Again, referring to the powers granted to the president the Constitution is clear in Article II, section 2.

"He shall have Power, **by and with the Advice and Consent of the Senate**, *to make Treaties, provided two thirds of the Senators present concur…… "*.

Why can a president not be stopped from exceeding his authority? Surely it is the major duty of the Supreme Court to monitor all legislation and executive orders to ensure they meet the terms of the Constitution. This should be automatic. Apparently it is not. Anyone bringing a case to the court must have "standing". This is to say that he or she must be personally adversely affected by the said legislation. This is simply ridiculous. The court on its own initiative should examine every piece of legislation and it should not become law until the court has approved it. What would happen if a modern day Caligula were elected to the presidency? How would he be prevented from tyranny? The Roman Senate assassinated Julius Caesar when he attempted to exceed his authority. Napoleon and Hitler became tyrants simply because nobody stopped them at the onset. It is ludicrous that any US president is permitted to exceed his authority when 535 congressmen and senators and the Supreme Court have clear authority to stop him.

There are, as always in politics, conflicting opinions on the Obama administration. The facts are that it has been the least transparent, the most conniving and the most divisive in recent years. Race-relations reached a low not seen since the 60's. The economy recovered but only grew at an anemic rate. Official unemployment declined but the percentage of the population employed did too. Real income for the middle class declined. The foreign policy was a disaster and the world sunk into conflict not seen since the Second World War, with daily atrocities committed by renegade groups. Most alarming of all, the national debt increased exponentially with no plan to address it.

Obama has squandered a unique opportunity to use his position to provide good leadership to blacks. There are millions of hard-working and responsible blacks who are exemplary citizens. As president, Obama could have applauded these good people and thoroughly debunked the cries of victimization as preached by the likes of Al Sharpton, Charlie Wrangle et al. He could have emphasized the importance of family, marriage, parental guidance and personal responsibility for all citizens. Instead he fanned the flames of racism and implied that blacks are victims of white exploitation.

Obama appointed two Supreme Court justices, Sonia Sotomayor and Elena Kagan. Both these women tend to interpret the Constitution with liberal opinions which gave the court a distinct liberal bias. From what we now know, it appears that during this administration the organs of government were used for political purposes. The justice department, the FBI and the intelligence agencies and even the IRS were all subverted at the top to serve the agenda of the Democrat party. Americans have now lost all confidence in these departments, whose sole purpose is to ensure the equal application of the law and keep Americans safe. The impact of this failure should not be underestimated. A country in which the custodians of the law subvert the law is on the road to anarchy.

The Obama years can be summed up as the beginning of a toxic divide between parties and philosophies not seen since the civil war. The concept of Congress working together for the good of the country was replaced by rigid party politics whereby the party in power called the shots and refused to pass any bill which would give the other party credit. The general population became equally divided and instead of rational debate, predetermined opposing philosophies were propagated by each side and defended acrimoniously. Race and "identity politics" became the focus of every initiative. The concept of "white privilege" was invented despite the fact that blacks have been given numerous advantages in hiring, promoting, college acceptance and other areas. These are not accorded to any other race and were all bestowed by predominantly white legislatures.

CHAPTER 20: DONALD TRUMP

Leading up to the 2016 election, Hillary Clinton was commonly believed to be the predetermined winner after having Obama outflank her in 2008. Since they entered politics in Arkansas the Clintons have pushed the limits of ethical behavior. There has been the perception of sleaze throughout their political careers. From the moment they entered the White House in 1993 there were accusations of abuse of office and questionable activity. They have brushed them all off and survived. The Clinton Foundation has provided a means of controlling a large fund of money contributed by others. There is considerable evidence suggesting Hillary used her position as Secretary of State to influence decisions regarding business and politics between the USA and other nations in return for generous contributions to the Foundation and outrageous speaking fees for Bill. Large corporations and foreign governments are unlikely to contribute large sums simply out of charity. There is always a quid pro quo. Most corporations contribute to both parties to ensure that whoever gets elected is beholden to them. These same donors do not contribute to their foundation or pay the Clintons huge speaking fees out of philanthropic zeal or to hear their speeches. They were buying access to people who could arrange favorable legislation or approvals. They were hedging their bets on Hillary Clinton gaining the Presidency, in which case they would call in their markers. This is no different than the transaction between a john and a prostitute. The john pays money for an expected favor. The prostitute makes it obvious that the favor will be granted. No responsible citizen should vote for a candidate with this history.

The constitution is clear on these points. Article I, section 9 reads in part:

"And no Person holding any Office of Profit or Trust under them, shall, without the Consent of the Congress, accept of any present, Emolument, Office, or Title, of any kind whatsoever, from any King, Prince or foreign state".

This should include domestic and foreign businesses. A person in office who accepts any money or other favor in return for special treatment from that office is guilty of bribery.

After never-ending and exhaustive investigations by both parties and a multitude of investigative reporters, we now can conclude that Hillary Clinton is guilty of numerous offenses.

As Secretary of State she broke with departmental policy and established communications via her own personal server located in the basement of her house. Why would she do this and how did she persuade State Department officials to permit it? The obvious answer is that she did not want any public record of her transactions. The only reason for this would be that her actions would not bear scrutiny. The Benghazi disaster has never been fully explained nor have the huge and numerous contributions made by foreign governments and businesses to the Clinton Foundation. When faced with investigation, Clinton destroyed countless e-mails, acid-washed the hard drive on her server and demolished her mobile devices. These are not the actions of an innocent person. Had Richard Nixon destroyed all his tapes there would have been no evidence to impeach him.

As if this were not enough, it seems she instigated the Democratic National Committee to engage the research group Fusion GPS to conduct opposition research on the Trump campaign. Fusion in turn hired a former British intelligence agent to work with Russian sources, resulting in a fabricated dossier detailing numerous offenses and indiscretions committed by candidate Donald Trump. This dossier has since been found to be largely false and the Russian source has in fact disassociated himself from the published version.

Although the DOJ, FBI and US intelligence agencies knew this dossier was unsubstantiated, they took the unusual step of pursuing the charges and appointing a Special Counsel to thoroughly investigate them. This counsel ran through the 2018 election and the cloud of suspicion it created regarding Trump most likely caused the loss of the House by the Republicans.

This is no small matter. Opposition research is fine and normal. Fabrication of lies to influence an election is criminal, especially when these involve foreign governments hostile to the USA. Democracy in civilized countries relies on a fair fight between candidates. This subterfuge by Clinton and most likely heads of agencies who supported it must be most severely punished so that it never occurs again. It is a very big deal. Not only was the entire Trump administration adversely affected and distracted but the loss of the House resulted in complete gridlock and ongoing investigations by the Democrats based on very scanty evidence. Urgent legislation on immigration, trade and other matters was blocked simply because the Democratic party did not want Trump to have any success. This policy was totally corrupt and unpatriotic. All these actions by Clinton and others are criminal offenses and yet until today, no effort has been made by either party or the Department of Justice to prosecute her or any collaborators.

On the Republican side the entry of three non-establishment candidates to the presidential race stirred up the field considerably. The front-runner, entrepreneur and billionaire Donald Trump, had distinct advantages. He could self-fund and therefore theoretically was beholden to no-one. He was not afraid to speak his mind and totally rejected political correctness. He was experienced at management of a huge multinational corporation and had proved himself a skilled negotiator. He understood the problems facing the country and was prepared to confront them. Although a ruthless negotiator, by all accounts he has operated within the law and has raised his children to be cultured and productive. The fear was that he was a loose-cannon and would act impulsively. Trump in reality is an independent, like many citizens he has no use for either party. He ran as a Republican because he was more aligned with republican principles but many republican congressmen and senators were not on board. They wished to retain the status quo and perpetuate the corrupt system.

To the surprise and chagrin of many, Donald Trump won the primaries decisively. Presidential elections have become prolonged and expensive circuses, largely due to the media which reap billions of dollars in direct campaign advertising and increased commercial revenues because of greater viewer participation. Trump broke all the rules of tradition and spoke his mind, often saying or tweeting things that appeared to be inappropriate. He continues to do so. We do not know whether he does this purposely or simply cannot control himself but the net effect was that he received a record amount of free television exposure simply because ratings soared when he was on. Perhaps he was crazy like a fox, spending less than half of what the Clinton campaign spent and winning.

Donald Trump was the first president in a century who was not a puppet controlled by his campaign donors and special interests. His simple objective was to save the country. The Trump campaign abandoned Political Correctness and unequivocally focused on topics many Americans believed were vital to the preservation of their culture and jobs and long-term fiscal stability. To the left this was anathema which they believed rendered him ineligible for the presidency but to the other side it was a return to reality after many years of fiction. Trump was not reticent in highlighting the many absurd and corrupt practices employed by both political parties and the blatant left bias of the mainstream media. Despite his complete lack of experience in public office, seen as an advantage by many, and every effort by the media to destroy him, he won the presidency. The concept that because a person has not had long experience in public office he is automatically unqualified to hold the presidency is spurious. The presidency is an executive position which requires the talents of integrity, strong leadership, wise decision-making and the humility to seek the best advice from the best people in the various fields involved. It is not very different from the position of Chief Executive in any large corporation, as Trump was. It also requires clear understanding of finance and fiscal responsibility, areas where predecessors have failed miserably. Conversely, it can be claimed that a disappointing number of previous presidents, including Obama, had no experience of leading or managing anything prior to their elections and have increased the national debt exponentially.

The election also highlighted the blatant partisanship and deception by both national committees during the primaries. It was clear that the two parties wanted Jeb Bush and Hillary Clinton as candidates for president. Although it can be argued that Bush is a decent man, he could not compete with Trump in areas of charisma and leadership. He was the quintessential politician, born and bred in the system. As previously mentioned, Clinton was perhaps the most flawed candidate ever to run for this office. It is astounding and disturbing that the FBI, after laying out a cast-iron case for her misconduct in handling classified information, numerous counts of perjury and abuse of office, came to the conclusion that no charges should be brought. This result in a large part contributed to the firing of James Comey, head of the FBI, in May 2017.

Primaries and caucuses form part of the election circus. A very low percentage of the electorate participates and in most cases the candidate the party wants wins. In many cases, as with Trump, only 45%% of primary voters favored him which means 55% wanted another contender. Furthermore, in the case of Clinton, before voting even begun the party had lined up a group of "super-delegates" for her who were not bound by the majority vote and made a mockery of the whole process.

Both parties have unpledged delegates who may vote as they please during the nomination process at the party convention. These are known as superdelegates. The difference is that Republicans only have three per state, usually members of Congress, and Democrats had seven hundred and twelve, 570 of whom voted for Hillary Clinton in the 2016 primary election. Superdelegates made up about 15% of the 4763 votes cast at the Democratic convention. The Democrat formula was arrived at after much soul-searching caused by the losses of Hubert Humphrey in 1968 and Carter in 1980. It was felt by the party that the existing selection process was delivering unelectable candidates. After Carter's loss, the Hunt Commission put forward a formula for up to 30% of delegates to be unpledged and comprised of loyal party public officeholders and members. Obviously this formula can reverse the results of the primary votes at the convention and circumvents the democratic process. In contrast, Republicans have a maximum of 150 unpledged delegates in a total vote of 2472. In the 2016 election there were 104 total, 95 of whom voted for Trump.

The whole concept of primaries and delegates needs to be examined. Without any pre-selection process a multitude of candidates could run, splitting the votes so that no-one may get a majority, resulting in one or more run-off votes which would be expensive and time-consuming. The alternative is for each candidate to collect written pledges from eligible voters over a prescribed period whereby the person who wins the most states becomes the candidate. The current system of debates is self-destructive, comparable to a football team facing a strong opponent with every player wanting to be the captain and thereby doing everything to make his team- mates look incompetent. To compound the problem, once a president has been elected, the opposition party does everything possible to thwart his initiatives and destroy him. This is a foolish policy which serves as a major distraction and impedes the president from doing the job for which he was duly elected.

Very few in the media expected Trump to win the election. The bookmakers gave Clinton a 90% advantage. They completely missed the mood of mainstream America who were sick and tired of Washington and corruption. Trump worked harder than any previous candidate, holding rallies all over the country until the night before the election. He spoke to the people personally and did not rely on surrogates to deliver his message. His rallies were packed. He used internet media like Twitter and Facebook to circumvent the mainstream media. His son-in-law, Jared Kushner, brought in a team of highly skilled geeks to collect and analyze data so that Trump could campaign with high efficiency. Once it was clear that he was going to win, the entrenched establishment went wild, trying to find every excuse to discredit him and imply the election had been unfair. They claimed the Russian government had been responsible for hacking DMC computers and revealing information detrimental to Clinton.

To become indignant that a foreign government attempted to influence an American election is the height of hypocrisy. The USA has interfered in more foreign countries than any other nation, funding dissidents, sending arms, training subversives and even supporting the assassination of the newly elected president of the Congo in 1960. Furthermore, there is no claim that the information revealed in hacked e-mails was untrue, in which case whoever revealed it did the American voter a favor, just as any investigative reporter does routinely. The hack was very crude and only worked because the victims were conned into revealing their passwords. Although there seems to be evidence that the hackers were Russian, it is difficult to prove that the Russian government directed the revelation. On the surface the logic would suggest that Putin would far rather have a weak and pliable US president Clinton than a savvy and tough Donald Trump.

Democrats howl that Clinton won the popular vote by about three million. This is irrelevant. Presidents are not elected by popular vote and do not campaign to win the popular vote. It is all about the electoral vote. Trump did not waste any time campaigning in the west coast because these states are dyed-in-the wool

Democrat and a lost cause for Republicans. If California is removed from the count, Trump won the popular vote in the other 49 states by 1.4 million. It is ironic that many states are predetermined and the election actually hinges on a small number of "swing "states. As discussed in a previous chapter, the Electoral College system is flawed but as long as it remains the law candidates must campaign accordingly. Both Bill Clinton and Lincoln won the presidency with about 40% of the popular vote.

Once in office, Trump wasted no time in moving along with executive orders to make good on his campaign promises, a very rare occurrence for any politician. Not surprisingly the media and left howled and screamed, refusing to accept a president elected by wide margin who made his platform clear from day one. There are obviously very powerful forces against Trump because he is the first president in modern times who is not beholden to anyone and threatens the cozy and corrupt Washington establishment.

Trump's agenda was long overdue and very necessary. His primary goals were to:

Nominate supreme court justices who would uphold the precise terms of the Constitution.

Put a stop to uncontrolled illegal immigration by means of litigation, southern wall and control of visa abuse.

Abandon the current lottery and chain legal immigration systems in favor of a strict merit-based system based on need. Clarify the anchor baby interpretation of the Constitution.

Put America first in foreign policy.

Rebuild the US military and overhaul the veterans' administration system

Develop a viable and effective health care policy.

Punish countries which finance and support terrorism.

Adopt a true free-trade agenda on a reciprocal basis.

Persuade rogue nations to abandon their nuclear aspirations by means of carrot or stick.

Get US troops out of endless wars which have no hope of success or benefit to the US.

Persuade NATO nations to pay their agreed percentages of GDP to fund NATO.

Promote self-sufficiency, family, principles and hard work.

Abolish political correctness and return to free speech, especially on college campuses.

Support all law-enforcement arms of the government, states and cities.

All these are logical and necessary and few fair-minded voters should disagree.   Missing are:

Reducing the national debt.

Reforming the tort system to a loser pays all system.

Delivering on one of his first campaign promises, Trump issued an executive order temporarily restricting travel to the USA by citizens of seven countries identified as supporting terrorism or harboring terrorists. This made complete sense, no amount of vetting can guarantee a person does not have terrorist intentions or will not be recruited to them in the future. As always, there are good people affected but this is the price each country must pay, just as in any war. Not all Muslims are terrorists but most terrorists in recent years are Muslim. The Muslim worldwide community must stamp this out or suffer the consequences.

Despite the clear intent of this Executive Order, its execution was bungled in that immigration officials were not given sufficient notice and explanation and when it went into effect it created chaos at the nation's airports. The order implied that any person from these seven countries including legal US residents with "green" cards were affected. In fact no person who is not a US citizen has automatic right of entry and visas and green card can be revoked if there is sufficient cause. There is no guarantee that US citizens are not or will not become radicalized but they have equal protection under the law whereas non-citizens who are not in US territory do not enjoy the same protection. Despite all this, liberals took full advantage of the chaos and within a few hours an army of lawyers had seized the opportunity to challenge the order, resulting in an immediate stay of execution filed by one judge in Washington state. The fact that one unelected man can overrule an elected president is deeply worrisome. The Constitution and various subsequent laws passed by Congress give the President very clear authority regarding matters of immigration and national security.

The matter of legal immigration and admittance of refugees needs to be clarified. There is no sense in any prosperous nation which already supports a large segment of its population via various social programs to import more poverty, ignorance and disease. No homeowner hangs a sign outside his house proclaiming that all-comers are welcome to live there. The definitions of "refugee" and asylum must be refined. If a country such as the case of Syria embarks upon a civil war then its own citizens must decide whether to sacrifice their lives in its pursuit. Only when a government embarks upon the merciless slaughter of innocent unarmed citizens as in Germany, Russia and Africa in the last century should other countries intervene jointly to put a stop to it and punish the perpetrators. Trump was correct in punishing Assad for the continued use of chemical weapons. Furthermore, in such cases where genocide occurs, the refugee option should be temporary until the problem has been resolved, after which the refugees should be repatriated. Preferably refugees should be protected in neighboring countries having the same or similar cultures. There are probably billions of people in the world living in danger and misery for various reasons. Civilized countries cannot change this unless they assume control of those countries and this is not a good option.

It is impossible for any country to absorb hordes of other cultures on a permanent basis without diluting or even sacrificing their own culture and, eventually, standard of living. It is a sure thing and largely irreversible. In Europe, where the indigenous population is in decline, the claim is that immigrants are necessary to provide labor to maintain living standards. The obvious solution is for ethnic citizens to produce more children and to do for themselves the work that the immigrants would do. Importing vastly different cultures who multiply exponentially is a temporary expedient with disastrous long-term effects. Eventually control will cede to the migrants and standards will drop to those the migrants sought to escape from in their home countries. It is a fact that many residents of those countries which were colonized and then were given independence to rule themselves seek refugee status to migrate to the countries of their former colonizers.

There are those who believe the preservation of ethnic culture is undesirable and indeed offensive. They believe a complete mixture of cultures will result in a country with the benefits of each. Unfortunately this is only a dream, and a very dangerous one. As with any mixing of ingredients, the average will be lower than the best ingredient. If sufficient numbers of cultures of failing and chaotic countries are introduced to orderly and successful countries these countries will eventually revert to poverty and chaos. This is already evident in the US in the big cities. It is a sure thing and irreversible.

The vote in the United Kingdom to secede from the European Union is a belated signal that the majority of English citizens are alarmed at the transformation of their country due to an uncontrolled influx of other cultures. The younger (and less savvy) segment of the population opposed this initiative, worrying that it would have a negative economic impact. Perhaps in the short term it will. However, the English must decide which is more important: preservation of their culture and way of life or prosperity via cheap immigrant labor. In the long term, if they choose short-term prosperity, they will lose both. It is the culture which makes a country prosperous or chaotic. The European Union was an idealistic dream which is bound to fail eventually. The citizens of the more prosperous members will not accept degradation of their lifestyles in order to subsidize less prosperous members indefinitely. Most people want to live in their own countries.

To many good-hearted and well-intentioned people it is a civic duty to help those in need. This is commendable but must be done with discretion, taking into account the long term consequences. If, in the USA, in order for a refugee to enter the country he would need a commitment of complete support by private individuals or organizations, relatively few would get this sponsorship. All the zealots who believe in open borders would change their stances if they personally had to support an immigrant family until it could support itself completely. It is just too easy to claim compassion using taxpayer or borrowed money. Just as a father helps his own children first, so a country should help its own citizens first when taxpayer money is involved. With a $28 trillion national debt the USA is in fact in no position to help anyone. It would mean saddling future generations with an incredible burden and potential financial ruin.

Perhaps human life is taken too seriously in today's western culture. Every living thing on earth will die. It is simply a question of when and how. Left to itself, nature balances populations of every species for their long-term survival. In the last few centuries mankind has upset this balance and, as previously mentioned, burgeoning human population has destroyed the habitat of many other species. If left uncontrolled, it will eventually render the entire world's population a squabbling mass striving for basic survival. As can be seen today in parts of the world such as Sudan, the populations have increased to the point that their habitats can no longer support them. Other nations can send food but this is a slippery slope leading to permanent and ever-increasing dependence. Once land is depleted to desert status it is almost impossible to recover. There is no simple solution. China has made some progress with the very controversial "one child" policy but even this has had unintended consequences, upsetting the ratio of men to women. It appears that the more civilized countries are self-controlling but the very populations that are least able to fend for themselves are multiplying exponentially.

The answer is not to speculate about occupying Mars. Responsible nations must arrive at a formula for reducing human population to numbers that our beautiful Earth can support comfortably. Then everyone can enjoy a decent quality of life and the planet can recover.

Trump vowed to "even the playing field" regarding trade and tariffs. Free trade is desirable as long as it works equally in both directions. Over the years, in its efforts to score political favor and short-term advantage for Americans, the US has favored other countries with little or no duty on their goods and services entering the USA. The reverse has not applied however, many countries levy huge duties on American imports or prohibit them altogether. The result has been cheap foreign goods for Americans and a huge loss of the

American manufacturing base with its accompanying jobs. The goods may be cheaper, but the cost of supporting millions of unemployed or under-employed citizens is high. Furthermore, loss of strategic manufacturing capability is dangerous to the security of the country. Tariffs will not only cause other counties to reconsider their trade policies but will restore lost American jobs and bring in considerable revenues, as they did at the founding of the country. This should result in lower tax rates. Citizens will probably pay more for certain products but this will be offset by lower taxes, greater prosperity and lower unemployment. Manufacturing jobs also pay more than the bottom-level service jobs many are now reduced to taking. Exporters to the US must decide whether to lower their prices further to offset tariffs and remain competitive and/or open up their markets to US goods by removing tariffs and other restrictions.

Trump pursued his promise to rework healthcare and cajoled Congress to pass a bill to accomplish this. It is indicative of the ineptness of most of the Republican congress that seven years after the unilateral passage of Obamacare they have not come up with a decent solution of their own. The bills presented to date, the last of which passed narrowly in the house, do little to bring down costs and improve access. One man in the senate, republican John McCain, thwarted the effort to repeal Obamacare. Trump has been silent on one of the fundamental cost-drivers to many aspects of American life which is the convoluted tort system. This and other requirements for decent health care have been discussed in a previous chapter. It seems that the trial-lawyer lobby is too powerful for even Trump to attack, which is a sad reality.

The appointment of justices Neil Gorsuch, Bret Kavenaugh and Amy Barrett to the Supreme Court mark the fulfillment of one of Trump's most important campaign promises. All are constitutionalists similar to Scalia who believe that the words of the Constitution mean exactly what they say and are not open to "interpretation". Scalia was noted for being a "textologist" and "originalist" in the same vein. It is no credit to the Democratic party that they chose to oppose these appointments not on ideological grounds but in childish retaliation for the Senate majority leader's refusal to bring Obama's last nominee to a vote. The Senate's recourse to change the rules of approval to a simple majority should not have been necessary and will backfire if the Democrats regain the majority in the Senate as one day they must do.

Trump has been accused of being a reactionary who refuses to acknowledge the changing world and is intent on turning back the clock. There is a difference between turning back the clock and returning to principle, logic and common sense. Furthermore, it is not Trump who is driving this policy, it is the American voters. They voted for an end to political correctness, hypocrisy and self-destructive policies and Trump is bound to act on their behalves.

The enormous national debt continues to climb exponentially and Trump counted on increased prosperity and reduced federal spending to create budget surpluses. History shows that more revenues have not generated surpluses which could be used to pay down the debt. On the contrary, Congress has simply found ways to spend more money. This irresponsible behavior will be difficult to stop. Sadly the Chinese virus decimated all the world's economies and massive bailouts have increased the deficit tremendously.

On the world stage Trump inherited a huge mess. He is quite correct in acknowledging that Russia and China hold the keys to cleaning this up. The NATO group in combination with these two powerful countries can collectively put enough financial, logistical and political pressure on those countries which promote terrorism and threaten the world with nuclear weapons to force them into compliance with the civilized world. Without Russia and China on board any military solutions may lead to disastrous escalation. There were some very tough decisions to be made.

Since he presented himself as a candidate the democrats have vowed to impeach Trump and to employ any other means possible to destroy him. Instead of attending to the nation's business, members of congress swear an oath to perform, the democrats continued their relentless quest to prove Trump colluded with the

Russian government and obstructed justice during the Mueller investigation. Since then no meaningful business has been done, the House was in gridlock and committees spent all their time looking for evidence to impeach Trump. Evidence now available to the public suggests that the Special Council should never have been convened as the charges were unsubstantiated, but after two years and $35m of taxpayer money, Robert Mueller finally completed his report. Mueller did not deliver a clean report, but instead chose to exonerate Trump on the collusion issue but not on the obstruction of justice. The attorney general made clear that there was insufficient evidence to prosecute an obstruction of justice claim and furthermore, it is not unreasonable for a man to vigorously defend himself against a crime he did not commit. Despite this, the democrats continued to pursue the issue.

The evidence now available via Inspector General Horowitz report, Judicial Watch and the freedom of information act confirms that the entire collusion accusation was a bogus affair initiated by Hillary Clinton and the Democratic National Committee to firstly tarnish Trump before the election and if he won, create a case to remove him from office. All the facts are not yet out, but if this conspiracy proves to be true, the real criminals are the Clintons, the DMC, the heads of the FBI, the CIA, the Justice Dept. and it is difficult to conclude the White House was not aware of the scheme. In this case it will go down as the most treasonous affair in American history and all those involved should be held fully accountable under the treason laws. Amazingly, despite all this, there has been no effort to bring all the collaborators to justice. This is very troubling in a country where the rule of law must be applied to everyone equally.

Having been thwarted by the Mueller report, the Democratic leadership relentlessly pursued any and every possible means to destroy Trump. The move for impeachment was based on his requiring Ukraine to clamp down on corruption and investigate suspicious behavior by the DNC and the Bidens is ill-founded. The President has every right to set conditions for US foreign aid and indeed no aid should be remitted to corrupt regimes anywhere. Dictators around the world have become billionaires on US taxpayer foreign aid. The entire impeachment process was no more than a clown show and will go down in history as a disgraceful abuse of congressional majority power. Those who voted for it will not be remembered for any good they may have done, but for puppets dancing blindly to the tune of the party leaders. The 116th Congress will go down in history as the most corrupt, partisan and unaccomplished. All their time was taken up trying to discredit Trump and little was done to further the urgent business of the country. The 2020 slate of Democrat presidential contenders was the most bizarre in history, most promoting radical socialistic agendas and none with any record of personal accomplishment in leadership or management. It is astounding that any have been taken seriously and this is evidence of an electorate far removed from reality.

Since he became a candidate, Trump has been criticized because his company has vast real-estate holdings and franchises in many countries and this situation would tempt him to pursue an agenda favorable to his personal interests. It is impractical to believe that any candidate for public office should divest himself of all his worldly assets. Entering into politics is intended to be a temporary public service, not the priesthood. George Washington and Thomas Jefferson were not required to sell their farms when they became presidents. Certainly, every action taken by every politician should be scrutinized to assess its value to the country as a whole and it is indeed a fact of life that certain legislation will benefit certain politicians as a side-effect. If legislation is good for citizens in general, public officials should not be required to forego these benefits.

In January 2020 the Chinese virus named Covid 19 started appearing in the USA and despite a ban on flights from affected countries ordered by Trump, it spread rapidly throughout the heavily populated areas. Like any good leader, Trump assembled a team of the most highly regarded virologists to advise him on how to proceed. Despite all their experience and knowledge it appears in retrospect that this virus is unique in many respects and the experts changed their advice as more was learned. This changing scenario created confusion and unnecessary reactions and resulted in a total shutdown of the country. As with Herbert Hoover and the Great Depression, the virus was not of Trump's making and he reacted to it as any responsible leader would. He mobilized the full might of the Federal government to provide needed beds, military doctors and nurses, equipment and logistics. He pre-ordered vaccines and streamlined the regulatory process to get them to the public in record time. Notwithstanding this, the media and the Democrat party accused him of mismanagement and gave him no credit for his rapid responses. This, and the unorthodox election caused by the virus cost Trump an election which otherwise he would have easily won.

At this time there is still no clear consensus as to the origin of this virus. The evidence available leads to the conclusion that it came from the virology lab in Wuhan, China. Whether by accident or design is unknown. What is true is that China benefitted from the epidemic, removing Trump from office and weakening the western economies. Incredibly it was the USA, France and Canada who collaborated with the Chinese in setting up and funding this laboratory. It is likely we will never know the true origins of the virus.

It remains to bee seen how history will treat the Trump presidency. In evaluating his performance it is undeniable that he has delivered on most of his campaign promises despite Democrat roadblocks, unlike the vast majority of politicians. The economy flourished, ISIS was decimated, the illegal immigration disaster was slowly improving and unemployment reached record lows. Foreign policy initiatives and trade were making progress and prescription drug prices came down. It is not what a politician says that is important, it is what he does. The forces trying to destroy Trump literally and figuratively were formidable from both parties and from other entities within and outside the US. It is lamentable that the Democrats in Congress support only their own party's interests with no apparent regard for the good of the country. Many Republicans are guilty of the same. Trump's only recourse was to communicate directly with the American public and convince them to use their power of the vote to promote his agenda. He made mistakes and was forced to compromise on certain issues but as long as his key initiatives have been accomplished he will have benefited the US. The 2020 election was the first time in the history of the country when the choice was not between two slightly diverging paths. It was a Tee junction in which the choices were straight or left. The straight would be continuation of the centuries old policies and adherence to the Constitution. The left would be socialism and a vastly increased role of government in everyone's lives. This will involve higher taxes, more regulation, loss of liberties and a decline in lifestyle for all but a very few.

After his loss in the 2020 election Trump and millions of Americans could not be criticized for questioning the validity of the election. Who, in his right mind, would reject a strong, accomplished leader who put America first and delivered on all his promises and elect a 78 year old professional politician with no record of accomplishment and questionable cognitive abilities? The unorthodox form of this election, massive numbers of unsolicited mail-in ballots and last minute rule changes cast serious doubt upon the results. In addition to this, it appears that the voting machines were connected to the internet at least for the periods of data transmission and this opened them up to hacking by domestic and foreign entities. Since 1980 the percentage of votes compared to eligible voters has only exceeded 60% once when Obama was elected. The turnout was 61.6% largely because blacks came out in unprecedented numbers. In 2016 the turnout was 59.2% and then suddenly in 2020 it jumped to 66.7%. Was this because of unprecedented voter enthusiasm, mail in ballots and the long period of early voting or fraud? Sadly the media and the courts had no interest in investigating irregularities and Trump and concerned Republicans were vilified for even suggesting fraud. We will probably never know the truth.

The storming of the Capitol by zealots and extremist groups from both sides was blamed on Trump notwithstanding the fact that his speech before this clearly ordered his supporters to protest peacefully. Trump has condemned any type of violence throughout his tenure. A spiteful congress rushed through a second impeachment without any due process or evidence. During the subsequent senate trial it was revealed that the case against Trump contained manipulated twitter messages and edited videos. There is serious disagreement whether the senate has any jurisdiction over a private citizen, the Constitution is somewhat ambiguous on this matter. Trump's defense team highlighted the extreme hypocrisy of the case and scolded the house for initiating a spurious impeachment driven only by hatred, without any evidence. The facts show that the riot at the capitol was pre-planned by extremists from left and right and Trump played no part. He was entirely within his rights to question the validity of the election and call for a thorough audit, supported by a number of Republican senators. Of those who died on January 6th at the Capitol, three died of natural causes outside the building, one was shot by capitol police and a police officer died the following day from causes not yet established. It is now established that a member of Antifa donned a MAGA cap and encouraged rioters to "burn the building down". He subsequently sold his video footage to CNN and MSNBC for $70,000. It is not clear if this transaction was pre-arranged. Compared to the summer rioting which lasted months and caused hundreds of millions of dollars of damage the Capitol riot was short lived and caused minimal damage. The shooting death of an unarmed white woman by Capitol police caused no outrage. The hypocrisy of the Left has no limits.

Despite a robust case presented by the defense for acquittal, 57 senators voted to convict Trump without any evidence of guilt. A disgusting partisan kangaroo court. In fact the stage was set for rioting all through the 2020 summer when Democrats refused to condemn the rioting, burning, looting and murder by BLM and Antifa in a number of big cities controlled by Democrats. Furthermore, the police were vilified and city mayors refused Trump's offers of National Guardsmen to quell the riots. The rioters at the Capitol believed they would never be held accountable and the Capitol police were reluctant to use force for fear of being prosecuted. No president has ever accomplished so much good for the American people and the free world in a single term. No president has ever been opposed so viciously by the media in all its forms, Silicon Valley and sadly, behind the scenes, many Republicans in Congress and White House employees.

Like many charismatic leaders Trump is guilty of self-promotion, exaggeration, ill-considered outbursts and harsh criticism of those who opposed him. He expected loyalty and results and does not suffer fools gladly. These traits undoubtedly cost him support from some of those who agreed with his policies. On the other hand he is a man with an impressive physical presence who towered over most of his opponents throughout the world and drove a hard bargain in the interests of the American people. He is like no other president and it is a great tragedy for the USA and the world that he will not be able to continue to work for the good of all Americans. Despite continuous baseless accusations and investigations and obstruction by the Democrats in Congress he has left the country in the best shape it has ever been in economically and strategically. No doubt Biden will claim credit for much of this as it rolls over into his term, as Clinton did after Reagan's terms.

If the facts are ever established and recorded accurately the eight years of Obama will go down as the most corrupt and damaging period in US history. The Democrat party and the media will be reviled as plotting and conspiring to destroy a duly elected administration without any regard for ethics, the rule of law and the good of the American people. They have shamelessly lied, fabricated and distorted to achieve their own party's control. They have been guilty of brazen hypocrisy. They subverted and politicized the very organs of government which are charged with protecting citizens from rogue administrations and used these organs to fabricate distortions and spy on Americans. They have refused to pass any legislation which gave Trump credit and have incited racial hatred, riots and condemnation of law enforcement. It is the Democrats and media which have divided the country, making race and "diversity" the focus of every initiative. All this was in plain sight and yet we are asked to believe that Biden and Harris won the 2020 election in a fair and normal election. Imagine what could have been accomplished had the media and Democrats put country before party.

In the current toxic environment in Congress there is really no need for it to assemble at all. The senators and congressmen are no longer civic-minded patriots voting their well-considered policies as individuals. They are two groups of sheep being told how to vote by their leaders. The leader with the most sheep can push through any legislation he or she desires. This is a far cry from representative government. Joe Biden has spent his first days in office signing executive orders prepared by party zealots with the express purpose of undoing all the good achieved by the previous administration. The country has reached the point the Founders most feared, the President behaving like a king with no opposition from Congress or the courts.

CHAPTER 21: THE FUTURE

The time has come for a major re-evaluation of the Federal government. It has reached the point very similar to the oppression of the Monarchy of George III which the country went to war to escape from. The major difference is that England took 500 years to subvert the Magna Carta to almost irrelevance whereas the USA has reached the same point in half the time in eviscerating the Constitution. Whether it can be done without another war or major revolution remains to be seen. In fact the problems created by the government facing all citizens can be identified quite simply and can be corrected by minor amendments to what started out as a good Constitution.

The following is a list of these problems and possible solutions in order of priority. There are undoubtedly other problems and other solutions but these are some to consider.

1. The composition and power of the Supreme Court. This body, comprised of nine judges appointed by the President to lifelong service, has far too much power and has the means to thwart the decisions of the two other elected branches of government and the will of the people. The Supremacy clause of Article VI of the constitution has given rise to Federal courts over-ruling state courts on issues outside of those defined by the Constitution to be under

their jurisdiction. It has been remiss in not holding Congress or the President to account when it should have. The court has evolved into a de facto supreme unelected body having the means to effectively amend the Constitution unilaterally. It does this by assigning its own expanded version of what clear and simple language means.

There appears to be insufficient clarity in the Constitution regarding the powers granted to the Supreme Court. The Court's main function is to ensure the government adheres to the Constitution as written. It is not unreasonable to conclude that the Framers wished the Federal government to be small and have powers limited to those issues affecting all the states jointly. They certainly did not contemplate a federal court which could overrule any decision by state courts, as has occurred many times. As described in CHAPTER 3, the Supremacy Clause came into question as early as 1797 by Jefferson and Madison and it is regrettable that their correct interpretation was overruled. Amendments IX and X seek to make it clear that if there is any doubt regarding allocation of powers then it is the people and the states that must be favored, but this has not occurred.

The Constitution was worded carefully and the actual words must be respected. It does not need interpretation, it is written in plain and simple English. The Supreme Court has made a practice of assigning broader meaning to words which has resulted in departure from the good intent the Framers sought to preserve. In order to eliminate these distortions, the 28th amendment should be to the effect:

No branch of the Federal government may assign any other meaning to any word in the Constitution than that defined by common use at its time of writing. Furthermore, Congress may make no law and the Supreme Court shall have no jurisdiction regarding any issue other than those within the defined powers of the Federal government specified in the Constitution.

Free speech means exactly that. Speech can have a profound effect on the minds of humans but it cannot inflict bodily harm, physically obstruct free movement nor destroy property. The courts have repeatedly interpreted speech to encompass any type of demonstration of discontent, insisting this is valid as freedom of "expression". This has included burning of the flag, rampant vandalism and if taken to the extreme, could then include burning of the White House. There is nothing in the Constitution implying this interpretation and any reasonable person would agree that it is counterproductive. The Constitution guarantees the rights to free speech, freedom of the press and peaceful freedom of assembly and these three rights are all that are necessary for citizens to express their views.

The 14th amendment has been used by the courts to sanction a multitude of activities which go far beyond the equal protection clause used to justify them. In part:

"No State shall make or enforce any law which shall abridge the privileges or immunities of citizens of the United States; nor shall ant State deprive any person of life, liberty, or prosperity, without due process of the law; nor deny to any person within its jurisdiction the equal protection of the laws."

The country has reached the point where everyone believes he or she is entitled to "happiness" via interpretation of laws and words. In the professions, certain criteria must be met to practice. Everyone is free to meet these criteria if they work hard and meet the requirements. This should apply to all definitions involving inclusion. To allow some who clearly do not meet requirements to claim inclusion because they would otherwise be deprived of happiness is absurd.

The composition of the Supreme Court has proved to be problematic for a number of reasons. Firstly, as attempted by Franklin Roosevelt, there is a risk that a president can stack the court with justices who support his agenda. Although these must be ratified by the Senate, if the President's party happens to be in the majority, there is a high likelihood that impartiality will be sacrificed. By definition, judges should interpret the law without any regard for their personal preferences. There should be no such thing as a liberal or conservative judge. In reality judges are certainly influenced by their personal feelings and this is human nature and cannot be eliminated. Secondly, the requirement of a simple majority between only nine justices is too volatile. If the court is close to evenly divided on an issue it is because the issue is not clearly defined and then one justice has the power to swing the ruling either way. Lastly, the appointment for life may have made sense when life expectancy was 50 but with today's longevity it is absurd.

It was a combination of men from each state which wrote the Constitution. It should therefore be a combination of judges from each state which forms the Supreme Court and renders rulings. Ideally each state legislature should appoint one judge, giving 50 in all. The US Senate should be responsible for confirmation as has been the case since inception. Judges should sit for ten years and every two years 20% should be replaced. Every ruling should require a 2/3 majority. If this is not forthcoming, it would be signal that the clarity of the Constitution is insufficient and it needs to be amended by the prescribed process. It can be argued that this system would be cumbersome, partisan and state legislatures could elect judges sympathetic to their causes. This is true, but it is infinitely preferable to the current system whereby the President nominates the judges and one judge can swing an otherwise evenly divided ruling.

These judges should not even sit in Washington. They should remain in their home states and consider cases on their own, rendering their opinions to a central tabulator in DC who simply reports the count, like the court bailiff.

The 29th amendment should be along the following lines:

The Supreme Court shall consist of 50 well-qualified and experienced judges, each appointed by a 2/3 majority in each state legislature. Each nominee must be approved by 2/3 of the US senate. Each judge shall sit for a maximum of one 10 year term, with ten states electing justices every two years in rotation. Every ruling handed down by this court shall require the support of at least 33 judges. If this is not forthcoming, the issue shall be referred to Congress and the states to amend the language in the Constitution related to the case in question so that there is complete clarity. After this the case will be re-tried if necessary. Every piece of new legislation passed by Congress shall be subject to timely approval by the Supreme Court before being submitted to the President for signature. Every executive order signed by the president shall be approved by the Supreme Court before taking effect. In the case of impeachment of the President, the court shall rule on the constitutionality of the articles before the impeachment can proceed.

2. The ability of the Federal Government to tax income. The 16th amendment has given the government access to the fruits of individual labor on a progressive basis and in doing so, has confiscated far too high a proportion of the GDP to spend as it pleases. It has given the Federal government access to far too much revenue and thereby usurped the taxing powers of the states.

To promote a healthy economy and limit the size of the Federal government, it is necessary to eliminate the power of the Federal government to tax income or to directly tax individuals in any way. If the revenues are limited the size is limited. The Founders knew very well that it would be a major error to give the Federal government access to too much of the nation's wealth. They therefore wisely prohibited the taxation of income. It was intended that the Federal government get its funding from tariffs and general fees which would affect everyone equally. Each state was free to tax its citizens as it pleased to fund those activities each considered necessary to accommodate the needs of its own people. These taxes would be the majority of public revenues and the Federal revenues would be a smaller portion. From its inception until 1913, except for a period during the Civil War, the Federal Government did just fine without income taxes.

The 30thth amend should simply read:

The 16th amendment is hereby repealed. The Federal government shall have no authority to tax the incomes or assets of individuals or businesses, this power shall be reserved for each state if so desired.

For this to be viable it is necessary for the Federal government to restrict its activities to those defined in the Constitution and to reassign all others back to the states where they belong. This should be accomplished by the abovementioned suggested 30th amendment and it should eliminate about 80% of the Federal government. Each state should have the liberty for its citizens to determine the extent to which they desire government to get involved in their lives and how best to pay for it. The state of Texas has eliminated income tax, instituted tort reform and various other beneficial initiatives. It is solvent and attracts new citizens and businesses. The danger in one state managing itself extremely well is that people from mismanaged states will move to that state and perhaps eventually vote in the same type of incompetent legislature they voted for in their own states. California is in this position.

The questions then arise as to how much money the Federal government needs to pay for common interests and how to collect this money. There are basically three areas the Federal government is responsible for which involve considerable cost: defense, infrastructure and protection of the environment and natural resources. A realistic budget covering these needs must to be established on a conservative, programmed basis. This figure must then be considered as a percentage of GDP. Except in cases of war, this percentage cannot be exceeded. The government must then live within this budget and prioritize expenditures like any other business.

Revenues need to be derived from sources which are simple to administer, unavoidable and fair. These should be a combination of tariffs, excise taxes and sales taxes. The IRS can then be drastically reduced and no individual or business would need to spend valuable time and money preparing tax declarations. The taxes would be effectively progressive, as those making more money tend to spend more money. No individual or business could evade these taxes. This would result in every inhabitant contributing something for the welfare of the country.

3. The election of senators. The 17th amendment has rendered the Senate prone to same corruptive temptations as congressmen which has effectively destroyed the separate status intended for it.

The Senate was intended to be a separate body within Congress which had the power to approve or veto bills passed by the House and appointments made by the President. It also gave each state equal representation in these duties. To avoid the temptations of bribery and corruption which members of the house were subject to, the Constitution required that the election of senators be decided by state legislatures. This way no campaign is involved and no money is involved unless members of the legislature accept bribes. The 17th amendment changing the election to direct by the people was a big mistake. The justification for this amendment was the corruption in state legislatures leading to the election of senators sympathetic to the agendas of labor bosses and business tycoons. The correct solution is to eliminate the corruption. The 31st amendment should simply read:

The 17th amendment is hereby repealed.

4. The General Welfare clause of Article I, section 8 of the Constitution. This is too broad and has given rise to many of the excesses of the Federal government. The Confederate constitution, written almost a century after the original, wisely omitted this clause based on experience.

The General Welfare clause needs to be removed. The 32nd amendment should read:

Taxes collected by the Federal Government shall be used only for those purposes specified in Article I, section 8 of the Constitution and for no other. The term general Welfare in section 8 shall be eliminated.

5. Qualifications for public office. It is absurd that whereas every other responsible job requires candidates to possess appropriate qualifications

to perform satisfactorily, none is required of candidates for public office. This means that the semi-literate, ignorant, ill-informed and immoral can and do sit in Congress and state legislatures.

Certain qualifications must be required of candidates for high public office. These should include providing a valid birth or naturalization certificate and a background check. If any subversive behavior, association with radicals or criminal activity are revealed this will disqualify the candidate. Candidates must also demonstrate proficiency in the English language and have a record of at least 4 years in a successful career in a responsible management position in the private sector. This is no different than those seeking to enter the legal, medical, engineering and various other professions which affect the safety and wellbeing of others. All these professionals are required to get licenses to practice, demonstrating competency in their specific fields.

In the case of the President, it is not enough that he meet these requirements in order to be effective. He must have the presence and charisma of a born leader who can motivate the electorate to do the right thing. The problem is that often the most charismatic people are also the most immoral. Many smart, honest, successful people never run for office because in order to win they must sacrifice their principles. This means that the majority of the electorate do not consider honesty and integrity important, which is a cultural problem in itself and one of the reasons for regression.

The presidency is vastly different from the other two branches of government in that it places all the formidable power of this co-equal branch in the hands of one individual. It is therefore logical that any candidate for this office must be very thoroughly vetted both for competency and integrity. Supreme court judges must endure this process, conducted by the senate, and rightly so. The question then arises by whom and how should presidential candidates be vetted? The senate is partisan and cannot be trusted with this task. There is no obvious answer, but certainly a clear and explicit set of conditions should be developed which every prospective candidate must meet before being cleared to run. A small panel of federal judges is perhaps the best body to verify and evaluate candidates' credentials.

Notwithstanding the above, a first step as a partial solution is covered in the suggested 33rd amendment described below under (6).

6. The unlimited terms that elected officials may serve. This has led to professional politicians whose main interest has been preserving their own positions. It is equivalent to hereditary power. Sadly it is the least competent who cling to their offices, preferring the considerable perks

and zero responsibility to earning their livings in the open market. Congress has degenerated into a veritable house of prostitution where most members are willing to sell their honor to the highest bidder.

It is time to place term limits on all members of Congress. Serving in Congress was never intended to be a lifelong career. This will also eliminate the advantage incumbents have in elections and preclude their wasting taxpayer money campaigning for the next election while in office. The 33rd amendment should be as follows:

No member of the House of Representatives shall serve more than two four-year terms and no member of the Senate shall serve more than two six-year terms. No president or vice-president shall serve more than two six-year terms. However, these terms cannot be served consecutively. Spouses may not serve additional terms once two terms have been served by either spouse and one spouses may not succeed the other consecutively. No member of Congress, the President or Vice President may run for any other Federal office while serving their terms. Terms for congressmen and senators shall be staggered such that every two years one half of congressmen and one third of senators shall be replaced. No member of Congress, President or Vice-president shall be entitled to any special privileges involving healthcare, retirement, life insurance or legal representation not available to the general population.

While in Congress or the White House, members and the President shall only be entitled to the same medical insurance provided to rank and file federal employees. Those over 65 shall enroll in Medicare. All candidates for Congress, President and Vice-president shall submit to background checks and if any criminal or subversive activity is discovered, their candidacy shall be permanently barred. If any of these transgressions are committed while in office, the individual shall be immediately dismissed. Candidates for President and Vice-president shall present their birth certificates to prove eligibility for the offices. Candidates for Congress shall present birth or naturalization certificates to prove citizenship. All candidates must have at least 4 years' experience in a responsible position of management in the private sector. All members of C ongress shall be subject to recall procedures if their constituents perceive that they are not upholding their campaign promises.

7. The ability of the Federal government to run budget deficits at will and to borrow without restriction in times of peace. The country now has a $28 trillion national debt with escalating interest costs and no reduction in sight.

Governments in most countries spend more than their revenues provide and rely heavily on borrowing. Businesses also need to borrow money. The difference is that businesses borrow to make more money whereas governments borrow to spend more. If an analyst were to investigate the habits of the Federal government and recommend a solution to return to solvency as he would for a troubled business, the solutions would be fairly obvious. Lay off all non-essential employees, eliminate all departments which do not pertain to federal duties laid out in the Constitution, eliminate all loans and grants to other countries, and restrict borrowing to emergencies in time of war or to projects which yield a fiscal return. A good start would be to reduce the allowances for members of Congress to only cover the salaries of one staff member each and place each on a modest per-diem payment for time spent in Washington while Congress is in session.

The 34th amendment is required to solve the crippling debt problem:

Congress shall not spend more money in any year than revenues collected during that year. Furthermore, Congress shall allocate specific funds from each budget to eliminate the national debt within 20 years and thereafter maintain a positive balance sufficient to cover unforeseen expenses. In the case of war or other unusual calamity Congress shall immediately temporarily raise taxes, tariffs and fees sufficiently to pay for additional expenses. These shall terminate no more than five years following the end of the crisis. Every appropriation bill shall include funding for a single purpose and each shall be voted upon separately. No "earmarks" shall be attached to any spending bill.

Single item budget approvals will eliminate the need for the President to have line-item veto power.

8. The tort system. This has given rise to excessive litigation whereby companies and individuals can be destroyed and a small number of plaintiffs and lawyers reap outrageous awards far out of proportion to the perceived harm. It has raised the cost of everything and encouraged businesses to move their headquarters to other countries.

The entire system of justice needs to be overhauled. It is a racket. In theory citizens are entitled to speedy trials and consistent justice. In practice, trials can run for years at outrageous cost and the end result may depend more on funds expended than on the fair prosecution of the law. The solution does not involve an amendment to the Constitution. The primary problem is the tort system whereby zealous trial lawyers can encourage and indeed solicit lawsuits on a contingency basis involving no expense to the plaintiff. In the first place, frivolous suits should not even make it to trial, a judge or panel of judges should reject them after review and impose a stiff fine upon the lawyer presenting them. The second requirement should be that the loser of any litigation should be obligated to pay all the legal expenses incurred by the winner. In major cases, each side should be required to post a bond covering these anticipated expenses before trial to ensure that payment will be rapid and complete.

In legitimate cases of willful malfeasance involving punitive damages, these damages should revert to the treasury of the state involved and no part should accrue to the lawyers or plaintiffs. The plaintiff has no right to these damages, he or she has already received compensatory payment for the perceived harm done. In these cases where there is incontrovertible evidence that corporate individuals knowingly concealed relevant information or proceeded with actions they knew to be unlawful and potentially harmful, these individuals should be prosecuted and held liable for damages.

The current system has led to incredible abuse which has had the serious effects of bankrupting large and viable companies, increasing costs for healthcare astronomically, reducing the freedom of all citizens and driving a great deal of US manufacturing and technology to other countries. Many useful drugs and medical devices are not available in the USA because their suppliers fear that lawsuits will cripple or destroy them.

Over the years, lawyers have become a special class according themselves a lofty status and high fees. Under the current tort system, citizens and businesses are at risk from frivolous lawsuits which can bankrupt them and they are therefore are intimidated. Often, even when innocent, it is cheaper to settle than go to trial. The lawyers know this. There is no logic in requiring lawyers to get undergraduate degrees before entering law school. Like doctors, this raises the cost and deprives others who wished to qualify for these undergraduate degrees. The bar exam can easily be taken and passed after the three or four year undergraduate law school. Those who wish to specialize may enroll in a two year masters program. This and tort reform would reduce litigation costs enormously while sacrificing nothing in terms of quality.

9. The unions. The need for them has long passed. The labor laws are now well established and these are sufficient to protect employees from abuse. Unions served a purpose but they now are equivalent to monopolies which can dictate terms in the marketplace. They also contribute large sums to influence politicians in return for legislation favorable to their agendas.

Unions were necessary to protect workers before there were any state or national laws protecting them. The country now has very strict labor laws dealing with safety, work hours, overtime, workers' compensation for job-related injury and discrimination. All states have established a minimum hourly wage. The unions have played a major role in driving up costs, reducing efficiency and affecting the outcomes of state and federal elections. We cannot have the tail wagging the dog. It is absurd that the biggest unions are now those involving government employees. They should be subject to the same antitrust laws as corporations.

Collective bargaining should be restricted to each site so that no enormous groups can disrupt the efficient conduct of business. Each state should make its own laws regarding unions and no government employee should be eligible. The Federal government should have no jurisdiction regarding unions except in nationwide antitrust cases.

10. Campaign financing. For democracy to work as intended there can be no financial or patronage incentives. Candidates must have only one incentive, to promote the good of the entire country. Elections have become auctions far removed from the democratic process. The sums involved have become astronomical. Lobbying is just another name for bribery. Posturing begins eighteen months before an election, saturating the public with misleading propaganda and for those seeking re-election, detracting from the duties they are elected and paid to perform. In most cases the candidate who raises the most money wins. This is not because more average citizens contribute, most of the money comes from businesses and groups who seek favors. They want candidates who will deliver these favors and not feel constrained by honesty, integrity and statesmanship.

Since the early days of the Republic, democracy has been an illusion. Powerful men behind the scenes and the media owners have selected the candidates and promoted them for office. The general population is faced with choices of candidates that nobody wants and for this reason voter turnout is usually low. It is very difficult for a well-intentioned good individual to enter politics on his own. The time and cost of running for federal office has reached the point where the democratic process has been effectively abandoned. It is accepted that candidates need financing but this should be uniform and limited. This is a difficult issue because individuals must be free to support the candidate of their choice in primaries and elections but no individual should be able to have more influence than another. To accomplish this, the maximum donation by any person to any given candidate should be limited to a sum every person can reasonably afford. Furthermore, each person needs to be restricted to contribute only once to one candidate in both the primary and in the election. Contributions may not be accepted from any source other than registered voters. The 35th amendment should be something like:

Only registered voters may contribute to political candidates' campaigns and no contribution may exceed the sum of $1.00. Each voter may contribute to one candidate one time in each of the primary and general elections for any Federal office. Contributors must register each contribution with the local elections office in their precincts. Candidates must provide accounting records for all funds used in campaigns. Candidates and their parties may not offer anything of value to citizens to entice them to vote. This includes food, *drink, clothing, transportation or any other tangible item. Candidates may contribute no more than $1.00 to their own campaigns. Once in office, no contributions in cash or kind may be accepted. No campaigns may begin sooner than 6 weeks before election date.*

This does not preclude individuals, corporations and even foreign governments from airing their views in the media or via other publications, according to the first amendment protection of free speech and freedom of the press. There is no way to curtail this and it is not unreasonable to assume that this type of publicity will be used by both sides and indeed serve to educate the public. However, no funds from these sources may go directly to parties' or candidates' campaigns and every form of this propaganda must clearly and publicly identify all the major donors at every airing.

These changes cannot solve the problem entirely. The free press and other media play a major role in promoting or destroying candidates and it would be dangerous to restrict them. It is therefore up to the voters to educate themselves sufficiently to make reasoned choices. The franchise changes outlined in point 15 will assist in this.

11. The executive power of the President. This has been gradually expanded by successive presidents to the point that these powers have been used to circumvent and manipulate laws

passed by Congress. The Obama administration
blatantly disregarded the immigration laws.

The Constitution makes it very clear that Congress is
the only branch of government that can make laws and
appropriate the funds to enforce them. The President
has absolutely no authority to make, modify or
disregard all or parts of laws passed by Congress. He is
charged with executing laws faithfully as written. The
36th amendment should read:

*The President is specifically prohibited from modifying
or nullifying the terms of any bill passed by Congress
once it has been signed into law. He is responsible for
faithfully executing the laws as passed for which he has
taken an oath of office. He shall do this in a timely
manner with full support. The practice of Executive
Orders shall be eliminated except in cases of national
emergency. In these cases the order must be approved
by the Supreme Court and ratified by Congress within
60 days or be revoked.*

12. Illegal and legal immigration. It is absurd that
    thousands of people can enter and leave the
    country every day and live and work in the US
    without having gone through any of the required
    legal formalities. They include criminals,
    terrorists and those carrying infectious diseases
    and drugs. Open borders are very similar to
    military conquest. Over a period of time control
    of the country will pass to a different culture. In

the USA this is predicted to occur within 20 years unless corrected. This situation makes a mockery of the legal immigration system. Today most of the jobs in lawn care, house-cleaning, construction and agriculture are filled with Hispanics, both legal and illegal. These jobs were traditionally filled by native-born Americans, many of whom now survive on unemployment and welfare money. In reality we do not know how many people cross the border illegally, we only know how many were caught.

We are told by the media and naive politicians that the solution is sending more taxpayer money to the countries from which these illegals come. This is a foolish strategy and complete waste of money. These countries are impoverished because their citizens are incapable of governing themselves efficiently and because of their cultures. These are not going to change.

There is a great deal of sympathy for people entering the country illegally or simply overstaying the terms of their entry visas. We are told they are only seeking a better life for themselves and their families. This argument can be applied to every criminal, it is no different than the case of the bank robber. People have always sought to go where the grass is greenest, just like in the various gold-rushes. They are prepared to endure great hardship and risk if they believe the future rewards justify the sacrifice. It is naive to believe that the problem can be solved by securing thousands of miles of land and sea border or tracking down those who overstay visas. There is need for a wall on the southern border simply because it is too easy for people and drugs to cross between border posts and certainly people who overstay their visas should be tracked down and deported permanently. However, the root cause is the current immigration laws and their application. People come illegally not because they are being persecuted or are poor, but because they can. The word is out that anyone who can set foot on American soil can stay, work and receive benefits.

The laws must be changed such that asylum is granted only for very specific cases of persecution and this must be applied for at the US embassy in the country of origin or the closest embassy. In cases of war refugees must take refuge in the neighboring countries or stay home and support the efforts of whichever side they choose. Asylum must also be temporary. However, there is only one real solution, which is establishing a national identity system which makes it impossible for persons in the country illegally to earn money, drive, bank, travel by interstate bus, train or air or conduct any business. This should take the form of a tamper-proof card with biometric information stored on an embedded chip. This must be presented and verified electronically for every major transaction. This will also serve to eliminate the ridiculous problem of identity theft. Legal visitors should be required to present their passports when conducting business and if the visa has expired they will be reported to the INS and be required to leave the country at their own expense. Anyone employing a person without verifying legal status should be subjected to a significant fine.

The "natural born" clause of the fourteenth amendment needs to be clarified to preclude abuse.

Automatic eligibility for US citizenship shall be restricted to those born in the USA who have at least one parent who is a US citizen at the time of birth. For those born outside the USA, citizenship may be granted if at least one parent or grandparent is/was an American citizen. This right shall not extend to more than two generations.

This will eliminate the problem of "anchor babies" which attracts more illegal immigrants.

There is wide disagreement on how to handle the estimated 12-20 million people in the country illegally now. There is no good solution to this problem and the Federal government has been derelict in its duty by not enforcing existing laws and permitting the problem to reach this scale. Any grant of amnesty or path to citizenship will be grossly unfair to all those who have applied legally for residence and will serve as a continuing incentive to more illegal entries. The first edict must be a clear understanding that because of breaking the law, no person entering the country illegally or overstaying the terms of his visa will ever be eligible for citizenship or permanent residence. If the 35th amendment above is enacted then children of these people will need to apply for citizenship through the normal channels.

The only reasonable solution to those already in the country is for them to be processed by a special department set up for this purpose. Those who can prove that they have been employed full-time for at least two years in legal activities with an income sufficient to support themselves and families and have no criminal record can be given special ID cards permitting them and their immediate families to remain as long as they are employed and remain crime-free. They will need to pay taxes and purchase medical insurance. They will not be eligible for any government assistance programs. Their children must pay out-of-state tuition at public universities. The card will need to be renewed annually. There will be a one-year window for them to obtain these cards initially. Any of these people may apply for legal residence and a path to citizenship by leaving the country during the one year window and applying at their local US embassy like every other prospective immigrant. After that, any person without a valid ID or visa will be deported and never be permitted to enter again. The national ID card will solve the problem for any new illegal entries without any government intervention, if illegals cannot earn money or receive benefits they will self-deport. Once the word gets out that they cannot earn money, they will not come. Aside from these measures, the southern border must be made secure, it is just too convenient a means for criminals, drugs and terrorists to enter the country clandestinely.

13. Racial and other group preferences. A fair and just society cannot give advantages to any group of people except those certifiably physically or mentally disabled.

The western world needs to get back to reality regarding race. Society seems to be obsessed with color. Color is merely one of many features which places a person within a certain group. Perception is all about behavior and competence. Giving special benefits to any defined race or "minority" is contrary to the principles of fair treatment and simply creates resentment and greater divisions. The current generation had nothing to do with slavery, the Holocaust or any other gross mistreatment of certain groups. No group can use history as justification for special benefits. If certain groups under perform then it is their own fault, not the fault of society in general. The USA prides itself on being "The land of the free." Let it be so then. Let every individual and business decide for themselves who they associate with, who they serve, who they hire and who they fire. Let compensation and promotion be purely on merit. Remove the word "race" from every government document. Eliminate special treatment for "minorities." Every citizen is entitled to judge others as he or she sees fit and it is not the business of the government to get involved. Every decent person should treat others with respect and consideration unless provoked to do otherwise. Every individual is entitled to like, dislike or feel neutral to others. Left to themselves, they will associate with whom they please. This is normal and good. Forced association is simply hypocrisy and counterproductive.

14. Education. The public schools and universities have become houses of indoctrination instead of institutions of learning. The attempt to foster the illusion that all children are equally gifted is a dismal failure. Children require discipline by their parents and at school. Under the current system, schools cannot instill discipline for fear of lawsuits. Teachers' unions protect incompetent teachers. Healthcare and litigation costs are the highest in the world also because the medical and legal professions require their members to get undergraduate degrees in often unrelated fields before entering medical or law schools, raising costs and denying undergraduate positions to those who wish to pursue those fields. College admission requirements are influenced by race and standards have been lowered to prevent high drop-out rates. Private universities admit a high percentage of foreign students, thus denying these places to equally competent Americans and exporting valuable technology to hostile states. It is crazy to admit

students from nations which are adversaries of the US and compete militarily and economically. Universities in particular have degenerated into political institutions in which students are brainwashed to promote a political ideal, normally socialistic.

Every civilized country educates its children to some degree. Whereas there is nothing in the Constitution authorizing the Federal government to undertake this service, it is clearly a need that communities should provide to all children. Initially basic education was provided by local schoolhouses and churches and it should have evolved simply to a state responsibility. Instead, the Federal government has inserted itself to create a behemoth at great cost and with poor results. The root problem, however, lies with the current culture, parents and the teachers' unions. Current culture tries to persuade everyone that all students are equally talented. To foster this illusion classes are not streamed according to performance and competition is discouraged. Even sports have been degraded and winning is not championed as the primary objective. The predictable result is that standards drop to the lowest common denominator. The first step that needs to be taken is to dispel this foolish myth and reinstate streaming.

More insidious is the fact that many schools and universities have now become unwitting puppets for the socialist agenda and engage in brainwashing as much as education. Education involves imparting true and useful information for the benefit of the individual and society. Philosophy involves presenting different viewpoints on various subjects and allowing the student to decide which makes the most sense. Brainwashing amounts to preaching incorrect or distorted information with the object of promoting a political or social agenda. We have seen over the centuries that even otherwise intelligent students are very susceptible to brainwashing with disastrous results. Governments enact laws that are intended to ensure a safe and prosperous society. These laws can control what citizens can and cannot legally do. They cannot control what people think. Skillful brainwashing via education, the media and Hollywood can and do.

This hijacking of the American education system and bogus reporting by the media must be stamped out.

Equally important is to foster the traditional family whereby most children are born to married couples who remain together and provide a father and mother. Nothing motivates a child better than strong family values and personal pride. Lastly, public school teachers should be prohibited from unionizing and should be paid very well to attract the best. Discipline must return to the classroom and any misbehavior should be harshly punished. Parents of unruly children also need to be held responsible. Curricula need to be tailored to necessities and include strong language, mathematics, science, finance and civics courses. Children do not go to school to satisfy their desires, they are there to learn skills which enable them to support themselves. For those clearly not blessed in academics, courses in hands-on careers should be offered. The Federal government must restrict its involvement to simply establishing national standards agreed upon by a 2/3 majority of the states. Everything else should be left to the states.

Almost daily statistics are published decrying the poor academic performance of black and Hispanic students. Every excuse is offered except reality. No-one is prepared to accept the fact that when taken collectively, different groups have different talents and cultures. No amount of money poured into education can change this. Indeed it can be argued that more money should be spent on talented students than poor students. It is the talented that will supply the scientists and engineers which give the country its competitive edge. Furthermore, the practice of giving certain groups preferential treatment when grading or considering admission to higher education is morally wrong and practically harmful. In a fair society public institutions must hold everyone to the same standards. Liberals argue that eliminating preferences will deprive certain groups of their God-given rights to the "pursuit of happiness." The truth is that these preferences are depriving everyone else of opportunities they should have been entitled to.

Part of the argument in favor of preferential treatment is to create "diversity" in schools and universities. There is no evidence that this diversity is desirable or beneficial. Although perhaps some weak students benefit from association with smart ones, inevitably the smart ones are compromised by lower standards and slower pace required to accommodate the weak ones. It is not the business of government to decide what percentages of various groups should make up the student body at any public institution. School precincts and merit should be the only defining factors. Neighborhoods are far more cohesive when the children attend the same schools and have their neighbors as playmates.

Higher education is not for everybody. The present culture implies that it is and that 100% of students are entitled to university degrees. Many graduates now leave expensive colleges with useless degrees in vague fields and end up taking menial jobs to pay off their huge loans. Higher education is best suited for the top students who have the talent, perseverance and desire to pursue a valid profession in a useful field. Whereas private universities are free to operate as they please as lon g as they do not accept any taxpayer funds via any programs, public universities involving taxpayer subsidies should admit students solely on merit. The number of foreign students admitted should be limited to a very low percentage and only those exceptionally talented as measured by US standards. No taxpayer funds should be allocated to foreign students, they should self-fund at full out-of-state rates. Large corporations desirous of attracting good talent should select candidates from high schools and sponsor their educations in return for an equal number of years service. This is a win-win strategy employed successfully in many countries. In addition, apprenticeship programs need to be reinstated to allow those who wish to enter the trades to learn the required skills without expensive loans and while earning wages.

Many believe that if only the general population were better educated they would vote more responsibly and the country would be governed better. In fact it is the academics in higher education who are the most out of touch and vote their unrealistic dreams to elect totally incompetent representatives. They do their best to impart this culture to their students with surprising success. It is those who understand real life and its hardships who are most likely to vote responsibly. All they need for this purpose are basic reading and writing skills.

A major cultural shift regarding personal responsibility has taken place over the last 50 years. This starts in the schools where discipline has been replaced with various drugs and psychological counseling and it is taboo to suggest that the child shapes up and takes responsibility for himself. The culture of dependency continues into adulthood resulting in a nation which expects the government to come to its rescue in all circumstances and no personal blame is ever contemplated for any misfortune.

It is time to re-institute the military draft for every citizen and resident regardless of sex. It will serve to teach all young people that reality is not what is preached by schools and the media. They will be forced to associate with others from every race, every social background and every religion. They will see the good, the bad and the ugly sides of humanity. They will see that nobody is "equal." A period of harsh discipline, heavy exercise and contribution to the defense and well-being of the country will benefit all. Those with religious objections to the military can be put to good use building infrastructure and learning useful skills. The draft would begin on July 1st for all those who have finished high school and anyone else who had turned 18. It would last for 12 months. Unless essential, none of these first year draftees would be assigned to combat. At the end of the 12 months draftees who met military standards could elect to remain in the military for a further three years, after which they could attend a state college and have tuition paid by the US treasury.

15. The franchise and voting . The current system is wide open to manipulation. No proof of citizenship is required and many voters are poorly informed regarding the important issues. Many states do not update voter rolls and do not require photo ID at polling stations. When a person moves from one state to another there is no automatic removal of his/her name from the

voter roll of the state he/she left. This is left to the individual. Absentee/mail-in ballots have no unique identification. There is nothing to stop each state from printing excess ballots which dishonest precinct pollsters can use to substitute for valid ballots. Ballot harvesting is legal so that party representatives can entice mail-in ballot recipients to vote for their party. In short, the entire system is ripe for fraud and there is no means to verify this. Re-counts simply re count the fraudulent ballots in the first count. Nobody knows the precise number of registered legal voters in each election. States do not update voter rolls efficiently and North Dakota does not even require voter registration. For this reason there is no way to verify if there are more votes than legal voters in each precinct.

Voting should be a privilege which must be earned. Regrettably, unless there is a major crisis, the majority of the population has little interest in politics. Others believe that the system is so corrupt that the outcome is predetermined and their votes cannot make a difference. For this reason voter turnout is usually less than 50%. In primaries it is often less than 10%. Often, those who do vote base their selections on completely unimportant criteria such as a candidate's smile or the subject of abortion. Few voters really study the candidate's biography, experience, philosophy or qualifications to serve. Perhaps a low turnout is a good thing. In countries like Brazil, voting is mandatory and its governments over the years have been far from efficient and corruption is endemic.

The Founders understood the situation and wisely instituted an aristocratic system for election of federal representatives. This has been gradually changed to a democratic system with predictable results. Notwithstanding voter apathy in general, any attempt to impose standards for voting will undoubtedly be met with strong resistance, aided and abetted by current officeholders. For this reason it will be almost impossible to institute a system which is both fair and efficient. The obvious solution is a voter qualification requirement as explained earlier whereby citizens must show proof of citizenship and pass a voter test to demonstrate that they understand the workings of government. If a citizen does not value his privilege to vote sufficiently to make the effort to qualify himself then he has no business voting.

The intent of the Founders regarding the election of presidents has been circumvented. One option is to restore it according to the Constitution whereby state legislators appoint one set of electors and each of these is free to vote has he or she sees fit. State legislatures are notoriously corrupt so there is risk to this. The other is to eliminate the Electoral College and elect the president by popular vote. There is risk to this too because voters cannot be trusted to make wise decisions and the system is prone to massive fraud.

The actual mechanisms for voting must be scrutinized carefully. In this age of sophisticated electronics and rampant hacking the current voting machines cannot be trusted. Sadly, humans cannot be trusted either in manual systems. Perhaps the only reasonably practical solution is to have two independent systems, one administered by the Democrat party and the other by the Republican party. The voting machines must generate prints for each voter which he/she must check before delivering to the counting machines. Each party should have its own counting machine and each ballot fed sequentially through both machines by party representatives. At the end the two counts must match. All the prints must be secured after scanning and placed in a tamperproof container with two locks, one for each party.

Mail in ballots must be kept to a minimum and only sent to persons who have valid reasons to use them and apply for them. Each ballot must have a unique barcode recorded at time of mailing and only ballots with these codes can be counted. Ballot harvesting must be outlawed in every state and signature check required.

16. The poor. The welfare system has created a cycle of dependency and has exacerbated the problem.

Every country will have its poor, the only question being the definition of poor. Historically the old, disabled and helpless had been taken care of by relatives, churches and charities. The lazy and incompetent had elicited little sympathy. The original solution for these people was workhouses whereby able-bodied adults unable to find work on their own were gainfully employed by state or local institutions in return for board and lodging. In President Johnson's Great Society politicians sought to expand the social programs instituted during Roosevelt's administration, disregarding Roosevelt's own prediction that this would inevitably lead to a culture of dependency. As part of the Civil Rights movement, the Federal government got involved in medical programs for those under 65 who were unable to afford their own insurance, financial aid to mothers with dependent children, food stamps and unemployment benefits for those who had lost their jobs. These are not programs specially funded by payroll taxes like Social Security and Medicare, they are funded from the treasury general account. Nothing in the Constitution authorizes Federal funds to be used for these purposes. Each state could and should have addressed the issues in their own ways using their own revenues.

These programs have indeed created a culture of dependency for a segment of the population and this has passed from generation to generation. A major part of the problem is children born out of wedlock and absentee fathers who are not held responsible for their own children. Despite all the assistance programs, a large percentage of the poor is made up of unwed mothers and their children. The cultural revolution of the 60's and the easy access to contraception and abortion have removed the historical stigma attached to children born out of wedlock. Today over 40% of American children are born out of wedlock, a record in the developed world.

The USA has one of the highest percentages of incarceration in the world. This is is due in no small way to children born to unwed mothers who grow up in ghettos and poverty and have resorted to crime to support themselves. Sadly, according to a number of studies by researchers Donohue and Levitt, Roe vs Wade vastly increased the number of abortions and eighteen years later this resulted in a dramatic decrease in crime. Many inmates are repeat offenders. Inmates should be trained in useful professions and put to work while incarcerated so that when they are liberated they can earn a living.

The best thing a government can do for the poor and unemployed is end the handouts and give them meaningful jobs. Society as a whole should discourage out of wedlock births and divorce.

17. The breakdown of the family. The USA now has the lowest percentage in its history of children raised in families with a mother and father present. This not only plays a part in poverty but it also influences the characters of the children involved.

There is nothing a government can do in terms of legislation to restore the concept of family. This is a cultural issue. Government and society can and should promote and encourage resurgence of the traditional family. The tax system is structured such that two high-earning productive people pay more taxes when married than when single. Married couples in all income ranges should get substantial tax advantages both to encourage traditional marriage and because a family living together is more efficient than individuals living apart. Hollywood and all the media should extol the virtues of traditional marriage.

18. Minority rights. These continue to be a major issue which is showing no signs of improvement. Minorities now override the rights of the majority.

The 14th amendment needs to be amended to include the following language at the end of Section 1:

No law or regulation shall be enacted by Congress or the President which gives special treatment to any group or individual based on race, sexual preferences, religion or ethnic origin. No public institution wholly or partially funded by the federal taxpayer shall give special treatment to any group or individual based on these same criteria.

19. Foreign policy. US interference in the internal affairs of other countries has been a disaster for those countries and the US. The Constitution does not empower the government to expend treasury funds to disperse to other nations for any purpose whatsoever.

From the time of it's founding until World War 1 the USA stayed out of wars which did not directly threaten it or its interests. As previously described, Woodrow Wilson made the mistake of deviating from this policy and involving the US in a European war which posed no military threat to the USA. Wilson began a trend which most subsequent presidents have followed to the detriment of the US taxpayer and the world in general. Regardless of their problems, other countries do not appreciate foreign interference. They happily accept donations of cash and goods but they reject attempts to control their affairs. The interference of the USA in Europe, Russia, the Middle East, South America, Asia and Africa has been a disaster. It has cost taxpayers trillions and killed and wounded hundreds of thousands of young men while creating chaos in the countries involved. It is not in taxpayers' interests to supply foreign aid and there is nothing in the Constitution which authorizes this. Most of the aid ends up in dictators' bank accounts or building infrastructure outside the USA when it is needed at home and no political advantage is gained. It is time for the US to stay completely out of other countries' affairs unless they pose an imminent threat to the security of the country.

Whereas great effort and expense are devoted to saving lives in the normal course of events, it makes no sense to then send healthy and productive young men and women to foreign countries to be slaughtered and maimed. The 9/11 attacks killed over 3000 civilians and to avenge these the USA engaged in two foolish wars which then killed over 5000 US soldiers and maimed 30,000 more. All for nothing, both Iraq and Afghanistan are in more turmoil today than they were before 9/11.

20. The Electoral College system for election of presidents. The case for it has long passed. The Constitution never intended voters to get involved in presidential elections other than to elect their state legislatures. The Framers did not want or predict a two-party system.

With universal franchise throughout the country today, the need for the Electoral College has long gone. Indeed the elections of Lincoln, Wilson, George Bush and Trump clearly demonstrate the flaws of this system, all were elected by a minority of the popular vote, meaning the majority of the population favored another candidate. It can be argued that having Congress elect the president has the advantage of precluding gridlock but the drawback is that the president is then beholden to Congress. A simple popular vote, though not perfect, is therefore the best option, with a run-off if the first ballot does not render a clear majority if there are more than two contenders. In a run-off, voters have a chance to re-evaluate their choices so that the winner is always the person who wins more than 50% of the popular vote.

21. The cost of healthcare. Healthcare has become a major racket with outrageous   costs and massive fraud.

There is no justification for healthcare to cost multiple times the cost of any other professional service. The current situation is bankrupting the Federal government, state governments, businesses and individuals. There are several root causes for this.

Firstly, any time a service is funded by insurance there is abuse. Healthcare abuse is far worse because there is no competition across state lines and the average individual has little understanding of medicine. If every individual had to pay his medical bills from his own pocket costs would drop dramatically. The insurance companies are public, for-profit businesses and their duty is to deliver maximum returns to their shareholders. There is no perfect solution to this but a lesser evil would be mutual-assurance systems whereby the participants are owners and there is no incentive for profit. They would need to be regulated by the state insurance commissions to ensure they operated legally under accepted accounting practices.

The second major contributor to cost is the tort system as explained in point 8 above.

Thirdly, the education of doctors must be examined. There is no reason those wishing to enter the profession should not begin their college education in medical school and thereby graduate in fewer years at lesser cost. Far more people would be likely to enter the profession, they would begin earning sooner and more doctors would allow better access for the patients and lesser stress to the doctors. This would lower costs dramatically and reduce the lost time spent in waiting rooms.

22. The rackets. A great many commercial enterprises are rackets which have   evolved to restrict competition and benefit the owners at the expense of the public.

The USA promotes the free-enterprise system with good reason. This encourages innovation and competition. The unions are largely to blame for the corruption and regulation in certain fields which result in abuse. The taxi industry is a good example. It is claimed that a taxi medallion in New York City costs $1m. This is outrageous. The rapid growth of the internet drivers such as Uber demonstrate the failings of the traditional taxi system. Not surprisingly, officials in New York do everything possible to prevent Uber from operating there.   Real estate commissions are another rip-off. In 1960 the average house cost around $20,000. A 6% commission of $1200 was not unreasonable. Today when the average cost is $330,000 a $20,000 commission is excessive. On a sale of $1m the realtors split a $60,000 commission. They may have devoted many hours or very few to the transaction. They take no responsibility and a real estate license requires no expensive or prolonged study. Unions and cartels should have absolutely no influence on business practices. Entrepreneurs should be free to innovate as they please as long as they obey basic laws which make sense. Teachers' and police unions serve largely as a protection for the incompetent which has had very serious effects for our children and our safety.

23. Legal immigration. This must be re-evaluated.

As discussed, the country does not need more people in general. It cannot open its doors to every individual in the world who wishes to live in the USA. The traditional formula involving preferences for family members amounts to a geometric progression which also cannot be sustained. Until the illegal immigration problem has been completely solved there needs to be a moratorium on all immigration except for exceptionally talented and qualified individuals and their immediate families from countries which embrace American culture. A maximum percentage should be agreed upon. Even so, it must be well proven in each case that equally talented Americans are not available to provide the required service and each must be sponsored by a viable American company which guarantees employment for a period of at least five years.

CHAPTER 22: WORLD PROBLEMS

No country is a political island. In the case of the USA, decisions and actions made by the Federal government have a ripple effect throughout the world. There are a number of problems affecting the world in which the USA can play a major role. With communications throughout the world in milliseconds the world needs a strong leader. The USA is the most logical choice and it needs to assume this position in sincerity without regard for petty party politics. Whereas thousands of individual Americans travel the world doing good on their own initiatives, the US government has been a poor steward for mankind.

1. Global warming. There is considerable disagreement regarding this subject, both whether indeed it is true and also on the causes. A great deal of misinformation is driven by politics. The facts point to the conclusions that temperatures are rising in a pattern beyond normal cyclical fluctuations and that humans contribute at least in part to this. No-one is focusing on the primary cause, which is population increase over the last century at a rate never before seen. According to available information, world population first reached 1B in 1804 and 2B in 1927. Since then it has risen exponentially to a projected 8B in 2027. By 2048 it will reach 9B. Since the discovery of fire for domestic use, man has used fuel for various purposes. Today fuel is vital to the lifestyles of most of the world and it is being consumed in quantities never before seen. Except for

hydro, nuclear and in very minor quantities wind and solar power generation, energy is supplied by combustion. Any combustion involves both heat and carbon dioxide emissions. Whereas the caveman had one small fire to cook and warm himself, the average American uses some kind of energy for almost everything he does. A great deal of energy is used in vehicles where 65% of it is simply wasted as heat. Thus not only does the average human today use ten times the energy of a century ago, but there are four times as many humans. In addition, manufacturing has also increased exponentially, pumping huge amounts of heat and CO_2 into the atmosphere. In civilized countries, the hotter and colder extremes mean greater use of air-conditioning and heating, compounding the problem. In the case of air-conditioning, aside from the electric energy required, huge amounts of heat are emitted to the atmosphere by the condenser units.

High populations have had another equally devastating effect in clearing forest and pasture for residential, fuel and farming purposes. Huge areas that used to be green are now paved or parched. It is plants that convert CO_2 to oxygen and there are far fewer of them. Creating far more direct heat and CO_2 and converting less and less CO_2 to oxygen must inevitably have an effect. Paved and constructed areas cannot absorb water and therefore rainfall is diverted by means of drains to rivers and canals, causing flooding. The world can either adapt to a very different climate or take steps to reverse the damage already done. For all reasons, reducing world population is the most effective and sensible first step. Despite its inherent risks, careful use of nuclear power is the best hope for basic future energy supplies. Electric vehicles have a huge advantage not only because they emit no harmful gases but because they are 90% efficient.

The US government must take a stand on this substantiated by credible facts and research and unaffected by any financial, political or strategic considerations.

2. Terrorism. It is preposterous that a very small number of fanatics can hold the entire world population hostage to their acts of terror and cost untold sums in wasted time, inconvenience, destruction and lives. It is high time for governments of all countries to act harshly to totally stamp out this practice. The only solution is for responsible governments to totally isolate countries whose governments do not fully co-operate.   The world needs to form a "Gentlemen's Club" of responsible governments which refuses any interaction with rogue governments and their citizens. This will make life so uncomfortable for the host countries that they clamp down on the terrorists and disavow their causes. We are told that "it is only a small group of fanatics" but these fanatics are getting financing, shelter and co-operation from much larger groups sympathetic to their causes. Those countries which sponsor or condone terrorism have no place in the civilized world and their citizens need to be barred from travelling to the civilized world

or doing business there. Terrorism, as in any attack on unarmed civilians or destruction of property, should be a capital offense with mandatory death sentence worldwide. No time or money should be wasted on trials when reliable video and multiple witnesses are available.

Historically the US and other western democracies have been complicit in promoting terrorism, aiding and supporting groups that they believe further their causes in other countries. They called these groups "freedom fighters." Any group that attacks innocent civilians in any way is a terrorist group and there can be no condoning of this practice regardless of any cause. Of course there will always be deranged individuals looking for attention who murder innocent people. The media should deny them any coverage other than to acknowledge the crime. No photos, no names.

The problem in getting together a world coalition is Russia. As long as Russia defies the western democracies by supplying rogue states with arms and other products and as long as these states can find markets for their products they can continue to function. The first step must therefore be to convince Russia to cease and desist or face isolation and isolate any other state which buys rogue products.

Any country which openly declares itself an enemy of the civilized world and trains operatives to send out to wreak havoc against innocent people without any formal declaration of war needs to be treated as a military foe. In wartime there is no distinction between "good" and "bad" sections of the community of an enemy state, the entire population is regarded as enemies and treated accordingly. If the "good" people of that state do not agree with this then it up to them weed out the "bad" or impose a different government by one means or another.

The fact that many of the countries supporting terrorism have substantial supplies of oil should not be a factor in determining their status. The world has many alternatives sources and in fact it would not be a bad thing if total world consumption were reduced for two reasons. Firstly, oil is invaluable as a lubricant and source of many essential chemicals for the production of plastics and other materials. It is wasteful to simply burn it. Secondly, as noted in (1) above, world combustion of hydrocarbons needs to be reduced. Rogue countries need the cash from oil sales to function and to fund terrorism. Isolating them will hurt them far more than the rest of the world.

The USA can lead the way by simply identifying those countries which support terrorism in any way and cutting off all trade, banking, telecommunications, service by US airlines and landing rights for their airlines. In addition, curtail all travel to the US by citizens of these countries. There may be a price to pay in lost revenues but this is minor in comparison to the harm done by terrorism. In order to be readmitted to the civilized world, these countries must demonstrate vigorous prosecution of rogue groups within their borders and publicly disavow any sympathy with their causes on all their forms of media.

3. Finance. The world economies are now so intertwined that a crisis anywhere can affect everywhere. In macro terms there are the haves and have-nots in the national sense. The have-nots naturally want to share in the treasure of the haves. They accomplish this by demanding and receiving huge handouts from other governments and by immigrating to prosperous countries by legal and illegal means. The logical solution to this is for the successful countries to manage the unsuccessful ones, increasing efficiency and reducing corruption. The old system of colonization by the large European monarchies in fact did bring prosperity, law and order to formerly primitive areas. Again, the aftermath of the Second World War created a new school of thought which naively believed that these countries would be better off ruling themselves. The entire African continent has regressed and shows little sign of ever returning to civilized control. It is being exploited by the Chinese in a different form of colonization which is probably not beneficial to the inhabitants or to the rest of the world.

In order to bring some semblance of order back to global finance, some constant must be reinstated. A floating US dollar has not taken the place of gold and currencies are now in a constant state of flux, creating havoc for most and fortunes for few. Whereas paper money is almost obsolete, it is vital that some solid reserve currency is adopted which cannot be multiplied at will. Gold is probably still the best medium.

4. War. Before the Industrial Revolution war was waged with primitive weapons on a man-to-man basis primarily to acquire treasure and land. The costs in casualties and destruction of property were low compared to modern wars. From the time of the Civil War however the causes were weak and the destruction immense. It is absurd for countries to send millions of their prime young people to be slaughtered and maimed and to destroy trillions of dollars worth of property and infrastructure based on disagreements between a few politicians. No modern war has accomplished anything positive for any combatant. On the contrary, each has been disastrous and financially ruinous. This is a guaranteed outcome which all prospective belligerents need to understand.

The United Nations was formed to create a rational body of civilized countries which could jointly dissuade any potential belligerent from embarking on a course of hostilities. In fact it has been completely ineffective in this and serves mainly as a platform for minor players to rant in public. There are only two cases when this body should involve itself in the affairs of other countries: mass slaughter of any group without provocation and massive damage to the world's environment. Many countries are difficult to rule and democracy is not possible. Other forms of government are not necessarily evil and may be the best solution for certain peoples. It is not the business of the USA or the United Nations to force their ideas of government on these nations nor give financial or military aid to dissident groups intent on overthrowing the governments.

If any nation contemplating aggression realizes that it faces the might of the rest of the world it is unlikely to embark on this course. If it does, it will be swiftly defeated.